William James and *The Varieties of Religious Experience*

William James's *The Varieties of Religious Experience* was an intellectual landmark, paving the way for current study of psychology, philosophy and religious studies. In this new companion to the *Varieties*, key international experts provide contemporary responses to James's book, exploring its seminal historical importance and its modern significance. Locating the *Varieties* within the context of James's other works and exploring James's views on psychology, mysticism, religious experience, emotion and truth, the sixteen articles offer new analyses of the *Varieties* from the perspectives of postcolonial theory, history, social theory and philosophy. As the only critical work dedicated to the cross-disciplinary influence of *The Varieties of Religious Experience*, this book testifies to William James's genius and ongoing legacy.

Contributors: Jeremy Carrette, Eugene Taylor, Sonu Shamdasani, David M. Wulff, Jacob A. Belzen, Grace M. Jantzen, Richard King, Robert A. Segal, G. William Barnard, Ruth Anna Putnam, Richard M. Gale, Hilary W. Putnam, Graham Bird, T. L. S. Sprigge, Michel Weber, David C. Lamberth

Jeremy Carrette is Lecturer in Applied Theology in the School of European Culture and Languages at the University of Kent at Canterbury, England and former Head of Religious Studies at the University of Stirling, Scotland. He co-edited the Routledge Centenary Edition of William James's *The Varieties of Religious Experience* (2002, edited and introduced with Eugene Taylor), and is co-author with Richard King of *Selling Spirituality: The Silent Takeover of Religion* (Routledge, 2005). His other publications include *Foucault and Religion* (Routledge, 1999).

D1694942

William James and *The Varieties of Religious Experience*

A centenary celebration

Edited by Jeremy Carrette

Routledge
Taylor & Francis Group

LONDON AND NEW YORK

First published 2005
by Routledge
2 Park Square, Milton Park, Abingdon, Oxfordshire OX14 4RN

Simultaneously published in the USA and Canada
by Routledge
711 Third Avenue, New York, NY 10017

First issued in paperback 2014

Routledge is an imprint of the Taylor and Francis Group, an informa business

Typeset in Galliard by MHL Production Services Ltd, Coventry

British Library Cataloguing in Publication Data
A catalogue record for this book is available from the British Library

Library of Congress Cataloging in Publication Data
William James and 'The varieties of religious experience': a centenary celebration/
edited by Jeremy Carrette.
  p. cm.
Includes bibliographical references and index.
1. James, William, 1842–1910. Varieties of religious experience. 2. Psychology, Religious.
3. Philosophy and religion. 4. Religion–Philosophy. I. Carrette, Jeremy R.
B945.J24W474 2004
204′.2–dc22

ISBN 13: 978-0-415-33345-0 (hbk)
ISBN 13: 978-0-415-65324-4 (pbk)

In memory of

Robert L. Morris, Koestler Professor of Parapsychology,
Edinburgh University

Contents

Contributors

G. William Barnard is currently a University Distinguished Teaching Professor in the Religious Studies Department at Southern Methodist University, in Dallas, Texas. He is the author of *Exploring Unseen Worlds: William James and the Philosophy of Mysticism* (SUNY Press, 1997), a co-editor of *Crossing Boundaries: Essays on the Ethical Status of Mysticism* (Seven Bridges Press, 2002), and is presently writing a book on the work of Henri Bergson.

Jacob A. Belzen is Professor of Psychology of Religion at the University of Amsterdam, Netherlands. He has published extensively in the disciplines of history and of the psychology of religion. Volumes he has edited in English include: *Hermeneutical Approaches in Psychology of Religion* (1997), *Taking a Step Back: Assessments of the Psychology of Religion* (1997), *Aspects in Contexts: Studies in the History of Psychology of Religion* (2000), *Psychohistory in Psychology of Religion: Interdisciplinary studies* (2001), *Mysticism: A Variety of Psychological Perspectives* (2003). In 2003 he received the William James Award of APA's Division 36 (psychology of religion) for theoretical contributions to the psychology of religion.

Graham Bird held chairs in Philosophy at Stirling University and Manchester University until he retired in 1996. He has written books on *Kant's Theory of Knowledge* (Routledge, 1962) and on *William James* in the Arguments of the Philosophers series (Routledge, 1986) and a number of articles on contemporary philosophy and the history of philosophy. His *Commentary on Kant's Critique of Pure Reason* is due to appear in 2005.

Jeremy Carrette is Lecturer in Applied Theology in the School of European Culture and Languages at the University of Kent at Canterbury, England and former Head of Religious Studies at the University of Stirling, Scotland. He has edited a number of works on Michel Foucault and is the author of *Foucault and Religion* (Routledge, 2000). With Eugene Taylor, he wrote the introduction to the Routledge Centenary Edition of William James's *The Varieties of Religious Experience* (Routledge, 2002). He is also joint author of *Selling Spirituality: The Silent Takeover of Religion* (with Richard King, Routledge, 2004).

Richard M. Gale is Professor of Philosophy and Fellow of the Center for Philosophy of Science. He works in the area of metaphysics, philosophy of religion, and pragmatism. He is the author of *On the Nature and Existence of God* (Cambridge, 1991) and *The Divided Self of William James* (Cambridge, 1999). He is currently finishing a book on John Dewey. He has contributed numerous articles to collections and philosophical journals.

Grace M. Jantzen is Research Professor of Religion, Culture and Gender at the University of Manchester. She is the author of many books and articles, most recently *Becoming Divine: Towards a Feminist Philosophy of Religion* (Manchester University Press, 1998) and *Power and Gender in Christian Mysticism* (Cambridge University Press, 1995). She is currently at work on a multi-volume project entitled *Death and the Displacement of Beauty* (Routledge, forthcoming). She is a Quaker.

Richard King works on Indian philosophical thought, the study of mysticism and postcolonial approaches to the study of religion. His books include: *Early Advaita Vedānta and Buddhism* (State University of New York Press, 1995), *Indian Philosophy* (Edinburgh and Georgetown University Presses, 1999), *Orientalism and Religion, Postcolonial Theory, India and 'the Mystic East'* (1999) and *Selling Spirituality: The Silent Takeover of Religion* (2005, with Jeremy Carrette), both published by Routledge.

David C. Lamberth is Associate Professor of Theology in the Faculty of Divinity at Harvard University. He is the author of *William James and the Metaphysics of Experience* (Cambridge University Press, 1999).

Hilary W. Putnam is Cogan University Professor Emeritus at Harvard University. His books include: *Reason, Truth and History* (Cambridge University Press, 1981), *Pragmatism: An Open Question* (Blackwell, 1994), *The Threefold Cord; Mind, Body and World* (Columbia University, 1999), *Renewing Philosophy* (Harvard University, 1992), *Realism with a Human Face* (Harvard University, 1990), *Words and Life* (Harvard University, 1994), *The Collapse of the Fact/Value Dichotomy* (Harvard University, 2002), and *Ethics Without Ontology* (Harvard University, 2004).

Ruth Anna Putnam is Professor Emerita of Philosophy at Wellesley College. She is the editor of the *Cambridge Companion to William James* (Cambridge University Press, 1997), and the author of numerous articles on James, Dewey, ethics and political philosophy.

Robert A. Segal is Professor of Theories of Religion at the University of Lancaster, UK. He is the author of *The Poimandres as Myth* (Mouton de Gruyter, 1986), *Religion and the Social Sciences* (Scholars Press, 1989), *Explaining and Interpreting Religion* (Lang, 1992), *Joseph Campbell* (rev. edn. Penguin, 1990), *Theorizing About Myth* (University of Massachusetts Press, 1999) and *Myth: A Very Short Introduction* (Oxford, 2004). He is the editor of *The Gnostic Jung* (Princeton and Routledge, 1992), *The Allure of Gnosticism*

(Open Court, 1995), *The Myth and Ritual Theory* (Blackwell, 1998), *Jung on Mythology* (Princeton and Routledge, 1998), and *Hero Myths: A Reader* (Blackwell, 2000). He is also European Editor of *Religion*.

Sonu Shamdasani is a historian of psychology and a Research Associate of the Wellcome Trust Centre for the History of Medicine at University College London. He is the author of a number of works, most recently *Jung and the Making of Modern Psychology: The Dream of a Science* (Cambridge University Press, 2003).

T. L. S. Sprigge was Professor of Logic and Metaphysics at the University of Edinburgh from 1979 to 1989. Previously he was a Reader at the University of Sussex and subsequently he was an Endowment Fellow at Edinburgh until his recent retirement. His several books include *The Vindication of Absolute Idealism* (Edinburgh University Press, 1983) and *James and Bradley: American Truth and British Reality* (Open Court, 1993). Presently he is working on a book on metaphysics and religion.

Eugene Taylor is on the Executive Faculty, Saybrook Graduate School, where he teaches the history of psychology, and he also holds appointments as Lecturer on Psychiatry at Harvard Medical School and Senior Psychologist on the Psychiatry Service at the Massachusetts General Hospital. Working for the past twenty-three years on William James's unpublished manuscript collection at Harvard University, he is the author of numerous articles, book chapters, and reviews on James's life and work. His books on James include: *William James on Exceptional Mental States* (1982), *William James on Consciousness Beyond the Margin* (1996) and, with Robert Wozniak (eds), *Pure Experience: The Response to William James* (1996). With Jeremy Carrette he has also penned an introduction to the official centenary edition of William James's *Varieties of Religious Experience* (Taylor & Francis, 2002). Expected shortly are two new works recently completed: *Radical Empiricism: Essays in the History and Philosophy of Psychology*, and *William James and the Spiritual Roots of American Pragmatism*.

Michel Weber is a research fellow [collaborateur scientifique] at the Institut Supérieur de Philosophie of the Université Catholique de Louvain (Belgium), where he obtained his PhD in Philosophy. His research program mainly consists of developing the activities of three networks he has created with his peers: the 'Chromatiques whiteheadiennes', the 'European William James Project' and the 'Whitehead Psychology Nexus'. He also investigates the facets of Nicholas Rescher and Reiner Wiehl's process thought, edits the 'Chromatiques whiteheadiennes' Series (Ontos Verlag) and co-edits the *European Studies in Process Thought*.

David M. Wulff is Professor of Psychology, Wheaton College, Massachusetts, and is author of numerous works in the psychology of religion, including *Psychology of Religion: Classic and Contemporary* (2nd edn., Wiley, 1997).

Acknowledgements

The papers in this volume were originally presented at an international and interdisciplinary conference in celebration of the 1901–1902 Gifford Lectures, which was held at the University of Edinburgh from 5th to 8th July 2002. They formed the invited papers section of the conference. I am indebted to the late Professor Robert Morris, Professor Timothy Sprigge, Jo Smith and Ian Baker, my co-organisers, for making the conference such a success, particularly Jo for all her organisational skills and sense of humour, which made everything run so smoothly. Those summer days in Edinburgh were memorable, both for the quality of papers and the social happening in, through and beyond the conference. The conference was originally born in discussion with Robert Morris and I am indebted to him for his support and for making it possible. The energy and momentum that followed our initial discussions were a sign of the historical importance of James's work. Robert Morris sadly died before the book was published.

The conference was sponsored by the British Academy (funding the keynote address of Professor Eugene Taylor), the Scots Philosophical Club (funding the keynote address of Ruth Anna Putnam), the Faculty of Arts of the University of Stirling, Routledge (Taylor & Francis), the Institute for the Advanced Study in the Humanities at the University of Edinburgh, the Faculty of Arts of the University of Edinburgh, the Koestler Parapsychology Unit of the Department of Psychology, University of Edinburgh. I wish to thank all the sponsors and all who made the event possible; without this the book would never have appeared in this present form.

I would particularly like to thank Antony Duff, Timothy Fitzgerald, Alistair Kee and Diane Jonte-Pace for their support and all those who attended and offered papers to the conference.

I would like to thank all those who have contributed to the book, particularly Eugene Taylor and Ruth Anna Putnam, for all their time, energy and commitment to the project. In addition, I would like to thank David Lamberth for bringing the work together in his final overview and for his time and patience working with me as I collected the papers and edited the work.

I thank Routledge (Taylor & Francis) for supporting the project, both in publishing the centenary edition of James's *Varieties* and for this publication. I am particularly grateful to Roger Thorp for all his initial support with the project and to Clare Johnson and Lesley Riddle for completing the work and offering extremely useful editorial advice. I particularly thank them for their support in allowing me extra time to edit this volume as I was undertaking my duties as Head of Religious Studies at the University of Stirling. I also thank my colleagues at Stirling for their understanding as I carried out the difficult balancing act between research and management, especially under ever greater pressures on research time.

Finally, I would like to thank Cécile and Célia for their continuing love and *joie de vivre* as I finished the editing.

Jeremy Carrette

Introduction
The centenary and the varieties of interpretation

Jeremy Carrette

Professor James, of the Chair of Philosophy in Harvard University, began the first of two courses of Gifford lectures on natural theology in Edinburgh yesterday. The proceedings took place in the English class-room of the University, where a crowded audience assembled. The general subject of the course is 'The Varieties of Religious Experience'.
The Scotsman, 17 May 1901 (Quoted in the Harvard Edition of *The Varieties of Religious Experience*, Harvard University Press, 1985: 540)

On 16 May 1901 William James began his Gifford Lectures at the University of Edinburgh with 'no small amount of trepidation' and respectfully paid tribute to the richness of European scholarship and the philosophical contributions of Edinburgh in particular. He also offered hope that in the years to come more scholars from the United States of America would lecture and change places with scholars from Scottish universities. James would never have imagined that evidence of such hoped-for exchange would be seen one hundred years after the publication of his very own lectures. It would have been hard to conceive in 1902 that a century later over a hundred scholars would gather in the historic lecture room in Old College, Edinburgh University, to honour his lectures and then meet for three days in the more modern buildings of the Psychology Department, to examine his work from the contemporary perspectives of philosophy, religion and psychology. The centenary of James's *The Varieties of Religious Experience* (hereafter 'the *Varieties*'), originally published in June 1902, saw many conferences and publications honouring this seminal and extremely popular publication. The centenary conference in Edinburgh in July 2002 was part of this set of international events, but it was not only the historical setting and the sense of intellectual pilgrimage that distinguished the conference, and this subsequent volume; it was rather the attempt to acknowledge the multidisciplinary approaches to James's work and the desire to provide a space for such voices to begin some interdisciplinary debate.

This book is a collection of the main papers of the Edinburgh centenary conference, in most cases revised and expanded, and reflects the work of established scholars on James from the respective fields of the history of psychology, the psychology of religion, religious studies and philosophy. Each of the papers reflects the disciplinary priorities in locating and understanding James's engagement with the theme of 'religion', or 'natural theology' as the Gifford lectures prescribed. The central intellectual concerns of this volume are found in the questions of how James's *Varieties* is located within the context of his wider work and to what extent 'religious' experience is of value, both in terms of its 'truth' and its 'cultural' significance. James set up a challenge in his understanding of 'religion' by taking it seriously as a psychological event, recognising its pragmatic value and entertaining its ontological significance, in terms of what he called 'over-beliefs'. These various levels of engagement require different methodological approaches to the work to unpack the lines of argument. By bringing together scholars from a range of different disciplines this collection is able to demonstrate the peculiarity of the *Varieties* and its unique place, not just in the popular imagination, but in the disciplinary frames of intellectual examination. There is no question that James's work on religion had extraordinary popular success, but the full force of its interdisciplinary value had not previously been explored and its place as an intellectual landmark never so poignantly underlined.

The *Varieties* sets up a whole series of problems about the interpretation and definition of 'religion' and 'mysticism', it evokes questions of the cross-cultural significance of religious experience, it raises issues about the importance of pluralism and the tolerance of belief, it opens the problematic of the 'subliminal', raises questions about the nature and practice of psychology, unfolds questions of the 'truth' and the value of religion from a pragmatic and empiricist perspective and offers questions about the nature of consciousness. All of these questions arise in the following set of explorations of James's text. The *Varieties* is, if anything, a text that provokes a multiple array of responses and, as Michel Weber hopes for his own paper, it shows the 'expanded horizon of reading' that the *Varieties* continues to offer. The essays in this volume are also concerned with the limits of the *Varieties*, as well as its richness for new readings. We find here not only the traditional critical concerns about individualism and the neglect of the social dimension of religion, but re-evaluations of those questions and new critical concerns about how the *Varieties* is to be understood in the context of religious violence and contemporary religious manifestations.

The essays in this volume do not simply evaluate the themes of the *Varieties*, they wrestle with the work from the perspective of a number of disciplinary concerns inside the respective fields of the contributors. The key issue marked out in this regard is the question of how the *Varieties* is located within the corpus of James's wider work and this reflects, to some extent, a disciplinary politic. The *Varieties* is both pulled back towards the earlier concerns of psychology in his *Principles of Psychology* (1890) and forward to his work on *Pragmatism* (1907). This is not always simply a matter of the psychologists moving one way and philosophers moving the other, and scholars of religion holding the central ground of the texts' religious thematic, although it does reflect the need to listen across disciplines. The engagements are more complex than any one disciplinary approach and take different strands of analysis in James's wider work to understand the *Varieties*, including concerns with 'truth', 'pure experience', 'subconscious reality', 'feeling' and 'plurality'. The tensions within the *Varieties* both demand and resist easy categorisation inside James's oeuvre. There are fundamental tensions in this collection of papers, and this is the very richness of James and the contributors. This tension is both one inside the *Varieties* as well as the wider positioning of the book. For some the *Varieties* is a 'transitional' book and for others it is the 'central' pivot of his work. What emerges is a creative exploration of the *Varieties* from a whole series of different intellectual agendas and from it we see the fecundity of James himself. What is at stake here is not which discipline is correct in its methods and criteria of selection, but whether James defies the boundaries of modern intellectual concern and how we should read James. David Lamberth is correct in his concluding comments, when he recognises that these papers are not the final word on the subject, but they do open up an extraordinary set of new questions about one book and its place in history. In the end, as Gale recognised in an important footnote to his paper, we must realise the nature of James's thinking before making final assessments. 'James is too profound, subtle, and suggestive a philosopher for any interpretation to lay claim to being *the* correct one. Any account that makes this claim thereby shows itself to be a wrong interpretation.'

The division of the volume into sections of disciplinary concern shapes the location of James, but out of this there are links to be found across disciplines and, as yet unexplored, dimensions bringing these fields of study together. The first section of papers deals with the history of psychology (Taylor and Shamdasani). Taylor, maintaining the style of his original lecture in historical echo of James's original lecture format, calls for a revolution in James studies and seeks to establish a reading of James not through Dewey and Peirce but through Swedenborg, Henry James Sr and Emerson. He seeks to locate the *Varieties* in the context of French experimental psychology and plots the contours of how James's work has developed. Taylor wants to establish an historical corrective and seeks to read James's work, including the *Varieties*, as an integrated whole. Shamdasani opens the discussion further by problematising the category of psychology in terms of the history of science. He locates the *Varieties* inside the problems of the new psychology and the disunity of the field, arguing that the *Varieties* can be seen as a study of 'states of transformation'. Shamdasani's work offers a useful conceptual apparatus for an interdisciplinary approach by offering an epistemological analysis and seeing the inseparability of psychology and philosophy. The very questioning of the unity of knowledge offers us historical ways to rethink the problem and nature of the *Varieties*. Shamdasani's work as an historian of psychology provides a wider context for appreciating James and unsettles the categories of both religion and psychology.

The next section of papers seeks to understand the *Varieties* in the context of the psychology of religion (Wulff, Belzen, Carrette). Wulff and Belzen seek in different ways to re-evaluate the place of the *Varieties* in the history of the field. Wulff recognises the foundational importance of James's work but questions its significance to the field. He identifies the concerns of the psychology of religion and suggests ways James is still useful for the psychology of religion, but also acknowledges the need to examine the neglected 'dark side of religion', particularly in its violent manifestations. Belzen takes a stronger line and suggests that it is not the *Varieties* that is of help to the psychology of religion, but the earlier *Principles of Psychology*. By appealing to 'cultural psychology', Belzen takes the discussion out of the limits of the category of 'religion' and explores the wider location of self. Belzen's critical discussion opens the parameters of James's work by redefining the intellectual scope of psychology. Finally, Carrette examines the *Varieties* from an analysis of James's work on emotion and argues that the *Varieties* has been neglected in such examinations. He seeks to show the developing model of emotion in the *Varieties* and identifies a wider cognitive and social model from that found in James's 1884 work. Where Belzen extends James to cultural psychology, Carrette locates James inside the concerns of a 'social' psychology and highlights the historical importance of Théodule Ribot on the *Varieties*. In effect, Wulff, Belzen and Carrette all seek to read the *Varieties* in the context of the development of psychological theory and look both back towards the history and forward to contemporary debates in psychology and social theory.

The third section focuses on the central theme of mysticism from the perspective of religious studies and the philosophy of religion (Jantzen, King, Segal, Barnard). These essays are concerned with representation, politics and truth within the field of religion and show how James needs to be read in the light of contemporary critical theories of religion, which have developed in the second half of the twentieth century. Grace Jantzen seeks to read James against himself to consider the varieties of religion in a postmodern age. Using Hegel's 'critical sociality', Jantzen calls for a socially engaged political reading, which develops James's 'other orders of truth' in relation to mysticism and his concern for the 'metaphysical monster' of some philosophical work. This analysis enables Jantzen to highlight the omissions within James, not only in terms of sexuality and race, but also in examining the violence of religion, something Wulff and Gale also touch upon. Richard King develops a similar critical reading of James, but from the perspective of colonialism and James's treatment of the Hindu and Buddhist traditions. He shows the problems with the concept of mysticism and the representation of Indian philosophy in the colonized voices of Vivekānanda and Dharmapāla, which James so readily employed. James recognised the importance of scholarship addressing the contemporary world and these critical perspectives reflect the need to position James in the light of ongoing scholarship, as well as appreciating the historical limits and importance of his work. In a different comparative assessment, Robert Segal explores James's and Freud's interpretation of mysticism in terms of their respective truth claims about religion. He argues that, while both relate religion to states of feeling, James makes a 'functional' fallacy in his evaluation by assuming the 'effects' of religion determine its truth and value. By contrasting these two psychologists, Segal seeks to clarify the theoretical basis from which James and Freud explain religion. William Barnard examines James's criteria for making spiritual judgements in terms of immediate luminosity, philosophical reasonableness and moral helpfulness. He argues that together these criteria provide a 'normative assessment of religious phenomena' and show James's concern with the 'truth' of religion and the reality of an unseen world. He argues this takes place in a transition between two different versions of truth, the objective and the pragmatic. To show the value of James's work, Barnard uses his model of spiritual judgements to understand ethnographic work on the Kalahari Kung.

The final section brings together a number of philosophical approaches to the *Varieties* and locates the *Varieties* in the context of James's wider philosophical themes on 'truth' and 'pragmatism' (R.A. Putnam, Gale, H. Putnam, Bird, Sprigge, Weber). These philosophical examinations both respond to the internal 'ambiguities and tensions' within the *Varieties* and seek to position the *Varieties* alongside discussions of truth, pluralism and pragmatism in James's wider writings. Ruth Anna Putnam recognises the complexity of the *Varieties* and identifies four different voices within the text: the experimental psychologist, the pragmatist, the theist or polytheist and the Protestant Christian. Locating the *Varieties* in a transitional space between *Will to Believe* (1897) and *Pragmatism* (1907), she attempts to make sense of the multiplicity of voices through a multiplicity of perspectives and explores the claims of the religious hypothesis in terms of the right to believe, the empirical evidence and James's own theistic 'over-beliefs'. In the context of world conflict, Richard Gale explores the *Varieties* through the idea of ecumenicalism, he argues that this is the basis of James's philosophy and by establishing a set of criteria from a moral democracy to a science of religion, he seeks to show James's 'effective defense of ecumenicalism'. Like Ruth Anna Putnam, Gale importantly draws out the significance of James's category of the 'More', each showing how this concept grounds the discussion of religious truth. Hilary Putnam takes up the question of 'truth' in an illuminating meditation on a single footnote in the *Varieties*. Following on from his previous studies on James and 'truth', Hilary Putnam argues that the footnote is important in showing that the idea of 'truth' as a 'value for life' is 'necessary' but not 'sufficient' for truth. Putnam seeks to show that James is more of a 'realist' and in this regard he responds critically, in an Afterword, to David Lamberth's work. He draws out an important debate on the 'tenseless notion of truth' and shows how he is developing a 'Peircean strain' of James's writing. David Lamberth carefully and systematically responds to these critical comments in his own chapter on the subject. He positions James's notion of 'truth' in terms of radical empiricism and in response to Hilary Putnam opens a number of valuable perspectives on the nature of 'truth' both in the *Varieties* and in James's later work. Here we are witness to how the *Varieties* and the essays in this volume provide an opportunity to extend and develop previous philosophical debates in James scholarship and, as Ruth Anna Putnam is aware, the *Varieties* can also be seen to play an 'indispensable role' in such wider philosophical discussions of James, not least in understanding his notions of pragmatism, experience and truth.

The position of the *Varieties* in discussing questions of truth and pragmatism is taken up by Graham Bird in his epistemological examination of the text. He is aware of the 'ambiguities and tensions' in the *Varieties* and the problems this presents to philosophers. The *Varieties* is an unsettling text in relation to the wider corpus of James's work and Bird seeks to resolve the tensions of the pragmatic and empiricist methods within his approach to the value of religion. Working through these issues, Bird identifies the 'weak' and 'strong' lines of argumentation in the *Varieties* and makes a distinction between 'beliefs' and 'knowledge' in the approach to religion. The multiple levels of discourse in the *Varieties* are also explored by T.L.S. Sprigge. Sprigge exams the tensions between a pragmatism (a truth that helps us live our lives) and a more objective truth (the 'real source' of religious and mystical experience) in James's approach to religion. Like Hilary Putnam, Sprigge argues that inside James's 'muliti-faceted pragmatism' there is a 'realist' view of religious truth, seen particularly in James's ideas of the 'More', 'over-beliefs' and the 'Mother Sea of consciousness'. Sprigge also believes that the importance of James's approach to religion today is to counter the non-realism of such religious thinkers as Don Cupitt and to challenge the mechanistic models of the mind taking root in philosophy and religion. While most of the philosophical discussions of James focused on the *Varieties* in relation to 'truth' and 'pragmatism', Michel Weber extends the discussion to his 1909 work *The Pluralistic Universe* and the concept of 'non-rationality'. After establishing a set of definitions for rationality, non-rationality and irrationality, Weber seeks to show that James's understanding of religion, both in its broad and arbitrary definition, relativize and enrich the concept of non-rationality. He then goes on to show how the idea of 'pure experience' provides an ontological framework for non-rationality and, finally, grounds the discussion of religion in a question of the status of consciousness and in the concept of 'intertrajectorality'. Weber explores a wider reading of the *Varieties* and, like the other essays in this section, opens the text to a range of new questions. In this respect, each of the essays in the philosophical section reinvigorate the philosophical importance of the *Varieties* and re-position the text afresh inside previous philosophical discussions.

The internal complexities and the position of the *Varieties* in relation to James's other works are two of the underlying questions in the philosophical section and it is this that brings James and the *Varieties* into the interdisciplinary problematic of how to locate the work. In his concluding remarks, David Lamberth addresses this question of the location of the *Varieties* as a way of engaging some of the philosophical questions and highlighting themes in the first sections on history, psychology and religion. While not wishing to have the final word on the subject, Lamberth recognises this key problem of location and acknowledges the richness of the *Varieties* in providing such a wealth of responses. He reads the *Varieties* as offering an account of 'experience' and responds to the different disciplinary readings from this analysis.

Historians, psychologists, scholars of religion and philosophers all read the *Varieties* in slightly different ways. The tensions and lively internal debates that fill this volume, both inside and across disciplines, show the continuing importance of James for a whole set of diverse issues in and beyond the theme of religion. The challenging dimension of this centenary volume is the bringing together of different disciplinary voices in order to establish a new set of debates. After listening to the multiple voices – the polyvocality of James – and the complexity of the work, the next step is the much harder task of establishing an interdisciplinary reading of James in the spirit of his work, rather than through a limited disciplinary politic. Like no other text, the *Varieties* offers the possibility of thinking at the crossroads of psychology, philosophy and religion. Written at a period when these disciplines were separating into distinct orders of knowledge, the *Varieties* perhaps now offers ways out of our present limits of disciplinary thinking to find new critical questions to face the new challenges of our times.

The papers in this volume form a unique historical witness to the importance of the *Varieties* to James's wider work and, although each writer will position the text differently, they all show how the wider themes surprisingly interweave inside the *Varieties* and create important contexts for rethinking James and the question of religion. In the end, what the conference and this volume succeed in showing is a renewed vigour and importance to the *Varieties* one hundred years after James stood up 'with no small amount of trepidation' to hope for new intellectual exchanges across the Atlantic. If this volume succeeds in celebrating one hundred years of the *Varieties* it will not simply be the recalling of an historical moment – and seeing the continuing exchange of scholars between different countries – but by establishing an intellectual exchange across disciplines in the spirit of James himself. As James said: 'No one organism can possibly yield to its owner the whole body of truth.' (*Varieties*, Routledge Centenary Edition, 2002: 25).

Part I

James and the history of psychology

Chapter 1

Metaphysics and consciousness in James's *Varieties*

A centenary lecture*

Eugene Taylor

Ladies and gentlemen. Standing here before you now, I feel the weight of history. We have come today to celebrate not only a great work, *The Varieties of Religious Experience*, but also a great man, the American philosopher–psychologist and physician, William James. His readers, his interpreters, and his admirers fill this room in a way that makes his presence palpable. To one degree or another, each one of us holds him in our hearts and our minds, which gives renewed meaning to the apt phrase, 'To live on in the hearts of others is not to die.'

In this regard, I come before you today with what, I hope, will be the promise of a great task; something possibly as significant as the *Varieties* itself; a project larger than one person merely: I wish to invite you to participate with me in launching nothing less than a revolution in James scholarship. I call on you to help me bring the modern world up-to-date on William James, his work, and its implications, and I propose that we take this centenary celebration of the *Varieties* to do it.

We here are, to one degree or another, aware of the range of James's ideas, his international character, and his consummate skill as a writer. Indeed, and I hope you agree, as the psychologist Gordon Allport once said, 'in verve he has no equal.' But, in general, the world at large knows Henry, the novelist, first, and not William. Psychologists tend to ignore William after his *Principles of Psychology* in 1890, while religious scholars stay largely within the framework of his *Varieties* of 1902. Philosophers, meanwhile, cleave to his *Pragmatism* (1907) or his *Will to Believe* (1897), only sometimes considering his *Pluralistic Universe* (1909), *The Meaning of Truth* (1909), or *Some Problems in Philosophy* (1911) and rarely his *Essays in Radical Empiricism* (1912).[1] Indeed, it seems each scholar writes what he believes is the magnum opus on James as if no other such books or articles had been written before.[2]

As a result, the large body of literature by James, as well as on James, is mostly ignored in favor of some new statement of what might actually be an old problem

* Keynote address for 'William James and *The Varieties of Religious Experience*: An International and Interdisciplinary Centenary Conference in Celebration of the 1901–1902 Gifford Lectures' at the University of Edinburgh, Scotland, 5–7 July, 2002.

already dealt with, either by James himself, or by scholars of another generation or different discipline. It is a stark reality that, most often, only a certain point of view is stated because that is the one held by the author and a lineage of colleagues with whom the author most desires to be associated. Or the same old interpretations are recycled because scholars rely too heavily on the more readily available published literature and few rarely go back to check the original sources. And when those few do, there is frequently the question of priority, as well as arguments over interpretation that arise. Meanwhile, exactly the opposite is also the case. Because a significant amount of new information on William James remains to be brought to light, new facts are being presented all the time in various titrations, but they tend to appear in odd places and are neither readily acknowledged nor widely circulated.

All of this I now rather idealistically propose should come to an end. In its place, I propose that we take a great leap forward – here, now – and consolidate what we know from our various points of view. Out of such an endeavor, I hope that a new generation of scholars will emerge who are more familiar with the James corpus than their predecessors, both in-depth and across disciplines. Further, I propose we take as our starting point for this revolution, the text upon which we are now devoting most of our attention today, James's *Varieties of Religious Experience*,[3] largely because I consider it the clearest expression of James's tripartite metaphysics of pragmatism, pluralism, and radical empiricism.

Much has been said about the point of this text, most of which we should consider to be more about the interpreter than the work itself.[4]

My own story begins in graduate school more than thirty years ago in a seminar on the history of psychology. I had elected to present a project on the analytical depth psychology of Carl Jung. The person next to me was doing this psychologist of whom I was only vaguely aware, William James. The quote that caught my attention was a descriptive line from a letter James had written to his wife, Alice, after seeing what was to become their summer home in Chacorua, New Hampshire: 'it had fourteen doors and they all opened outwards.' I took that to mean a statement about expanded consciousness, or at least that was the effect the statement had on me at the moment.

Several years later I was invited by a Yale professor and his student to contribute a chapter in a book entitled *The Stream of Consciousness: Scientific Investigations into the Flow of Human Experience* (1978), the only book written on such a topic since James's coining of that phrase in 1892. I contributed the only non-Western chapter, 'Asian interpretations: Transcending the stream of consciousness,' which later became the most frequently reprinted chapter of the book.[5] The project took me to Harvard to read in the James papers, while at the same time I was applying to graduate school there at the Harvard Divinity School. Graduate students were not allowed to read in the James papers, however, but I had not been admitted yet, so I registered as just a visiting scholar with an MA and a book contract and was immediately granted access.

While reading in the James papers, I discovered 125 pages of handwritten lecture notes for a series of Lowell Lectures that James had delivered in 1896 but never published. The series was called 'Exceptional Mental States.' His individual lecture titles were: 'Dreams and Hypnotism,' 'Automatism,' 'Hysteria,' 'Multiple Personality,' 'Demoniacal Possession,' 'Witchcraft,' 'Degeneration,' and 'Genius.'

At the same time, in a separate part of the reference room at Houghton Library, I found correspondence indicating that 1,000 volumes from James's personal library had been given to Harvard in 1923 on the death of James's wife, Alice. The books were given a special William James bookplate and at the time accessed into the open stacks of Harvard's nine million volume library system by subject. The correspondence I had discovered indicated that many of the books contained James's hand-pencilled annotations, and the general description of their content indicated that many of the volumes were on the subject of the 1896 Lowell Lectures and general topics in abnormal psychology, multiple personality, religious autobiography, and mysticism.

Later, in the Reading Room over in Widener, I was to find the original list of books that made up the gift. The immediate problem when I first discovered the lecture notes in 1977, however, was that, because I was not at first a member of the university, I could not get into the library stacks where these books were all housed. When I was admitted to the university through the Divinity School a few weeks later, to my great delight, I learned that a possible first effect of my presence on campus was to cause to have struck down one of their venerable old institutions – they dropped the graduate student restriction on the James papers. I presumed it was because I was already registered. It was a surprise moment in which one distinctly felt an ever-so-slight trembling of the foundations. Possibly, of course, it may also have had nothing to do with me.

At any rate, once I had found the original list of books given by the James family, a team of Divinity students helped me look up all their call numbers. William Rogers, Parkman Professor in the Divinity School, put me on his faculty library card so I was able to borrow more than 200 of the annotated volumes from the library for a two-year period to study the pattern of James's reading.[6] We also systematically separated out those that contained annotations keyed to the 1896 lecture notes.

Then, I also discovered lists of all the books, called the Library Charging Records, that James checked out of the Harvard College Library during the course of his career as a student and a faculty member up to the late 1890s, when a different manner of recording books taken out of the library was adopted. Many of these latter entries were on the subject of the Exceptional Mental States lectures. The problem was that, while before the 1880s, the author and book title appeared, most of the numbers in the 1880s and 1890s appeared only in two different successive sets of cryptic notation devised by the librarians before the introduction of the Dewey Decimal System. Due to the efforts of Professor Tom Cadwallader, a visiting scholar from the University of Indiana, and two assistants from the Pusey Archives at Harvard, by correlating the accession records – when each book came into the library – with the shelf list – where each book was housed in the library – over a two-year period we were able to reconstruct the history of Harvard's early idiosyncratic library classification systems. We were then able to translate the cryptic notations into the modern shelf numbers, and locate many of these books. Many had been purchased with library funds at James's request. He had kept many of them out for several years at a time, numerous volumes contained his hand-pencilled notations, and many of these were also keyed to the Exceptional Mental States lectures. Also, many of our finds had not been checked out since James returned them.

With these resources, I went on to reconstruct the 1896 Lowell Lectures and to redeliver them at Harvard in 1980. Through the good offices of Professor Jacques Barzun, Emeritus professor and former Dean at Columbia University, who was then an editor for Charles Scribner's Sons, they were published as *William James on Exceptional Mental States* in 1982.[7]

It was widely acknowledged among James scholars that James's 1878 Lowell Lectures on 'The Brain and Mind' had found an important place in his *Principles of Psychology* in 1890, while his 1906 Lowell Lectures had been published as his *Pragmatism* (1907). Why, I asked, would not these 1896 lectures be of similar import? The problem was, it turned out, that they were on heretical topics rejected by psychology as a developing reductionistic science, religion as an exclusively Christian and theistic enterprise, and philosophy as primarily a logical and analytic endeavor. Within the field of James scholarship, it had already been the judgment of early biographers such as Ralph Barton Perry and later interpreters such as Gerald Myers that these lectures were of little consequence.

Nevertheless, my reconstruction of the series in its historical context suggested that the first four lectures appeared to be the outline of a dynamic psychology of the subconscious, such as that found in the modern depth psychologies, while the second four largely demonstrated the pathological working out of the subconscious in the social sphere. Given James's focus on a cognitive psychology of attention in *The Principles* and the primacy of mystical experience in the *Varieties*, and their isolation from each other by psychologists, philosophers, and religious scholars, respectively, it was immediately clear to me that, among other important implications, the 1896 Lowell Lectures represented a transitional text in James's psychology of consciousness between 1890 and 1902. The 1896 Lowell Lectures also coincided with the crystallization of James's philosophical metaphysics of radical empiricism, in what I believe was his search for a new metaphysical foundation underlying experimental science in psychology.[8]

Beyond this single project itself, the archival evidence from the Exceptional Mental States Lectures raised two new questions: first, what were the origins of James's ideas about consciousness leading up to the lectures of 1896? And what were the consequences afterwards on his evolving model of consciousness?

In this regard, reconstruction of the 1896 Lowell lectures served to re-orient my reading of all James's earlier published writings. It also led me to the archives of the former Swedenborg School of Religion in Newton, Massachusetts and the trunk containing Henry James Sr.'s annotated Swedenborg collection. This trunk turned out to be the only permanent piece of furniture the James family hauled around Europe during William's youth. Henry the novelist was to later claim it was so important that the day its contents went up on the mantelpiece they knew that, wherever they were, they were there to stay, and the day the volumes by Swedenborg disappeared back into the trunk, they knew it was time to pack up and move on.

Working in this trunk for the past twenty-three years for me has drawn Emerson into William's orbit in an entirely new way, and also implicated Emerson and Henry James Sr. as a more important influence on Charles Sanders Peirce than contemporary philosophers appear willing or able to admit. Here, I concluded, in the Swedenborgian 'Doctrine of the Rational' and also in Swedenborg's 'Doctrine of Use,' we find an overlooked source for Peirce and James's respective versions of pragmatism.[9] At the same time, as I have indicated elsewhere, the contents of this trunk shed new light on the origins of the *Varieties*, as well as its meaning and significance.[10]

The other wing of my quest was to assess just what impact James's ideas concerning a dynamic psychology of the subconscious had had on subsequent developments in the twentieth century. Pursuing this question, I was led to the scattered archives of James's students, colleagues, and friends, many of whom were pioneers in the development of modern psychotherapeutics, the mind–body problem, and an era of medical psychology that flourished from about 1880 to 1920, before psychoanalysis. It was a period in many ways in advance of medical psychology today. This was the era of the so-called Boston School of Abnormal Psychology, and the larger French–Swiss–English–American psychotherapeutic axis, of which it was a part.[11]

I direct your attention to Figs 1 and 2. Figure 1 depicts the status of scientific psychotherapy throughout Europe in the closing decades of the nineteenth century. The center of the new dynamic psychiatry and psychology is the so-called French Experimental Psychology of the Subconscious. Its influence is depicted as spokes on a wheel – isolated developments in different countries with almost no one communicating with each other across their respective boundaries. Figure 2 shows the same period, over roughly a forty-year span, but revealing a dynamic relationship between researchers in a loose-knit concatenation that I have variously referred to as the so-called French–Swiss–English–American psycho-therapeutic axis.[12]

This psychotherapeutic era continues to be neglected by almost all who write on William James. It influenced James's conception of consciousness in the *Varieties*, at the same time that the *Varieties* had a tremendous impact on the therapeutic conceptualizations of that period. Further, James clearly states in his presidential address to the American Psychological Association in 1894 that scientific evidence coming from this quarter provided the foundation for his soon-to-be formalized conceptualization of radical empiricism as an alternative to reductionistic positivism in psychology, and science generally. Radical empiricism, in turn, became the basis for James's use of the phenomenological method in the *Varieties*.

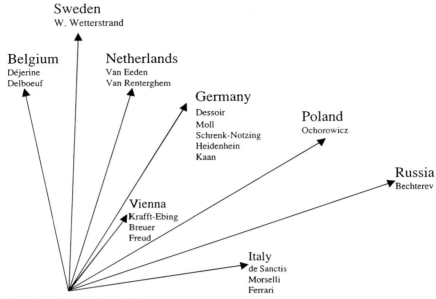

Figure 1   The germ of scientific psychotherapy in Europe (1880–1899).

In brief, the era of the 1890s spawned numerous conceptualizations of a dynamic psychology of the interior life, both before and after the advent of psychoanalysis.[13] Generally, the various theories were dominated by the dissociation model of consciousness. Dissociation, which *The Oxford English Dictionary* credits James with introducing into nineteenth-century psychological medicine, is the concept that the immediate field of waking consciousness could split into two or more states that were discontinuous with each other. The entire field of immediate consciousness could then disintegrate into fractions – compartmentalized states that were not homogeneous, some above and some below the surface. Note that this is a proposition radically different from psychoanalysis.

In this regard, many key adherents of the dissociation model subscribed to the idea that personality is not a forgone unity, but in its natural condition, an ultimate plurality of states, any one of which could take over the field of waking awareness at any time, or influence the waking state through the subliminal region. Further, the nature of these states could be understood as spanning a wide spectrum of possible fields ranging from the psychopathic to the transcendent.

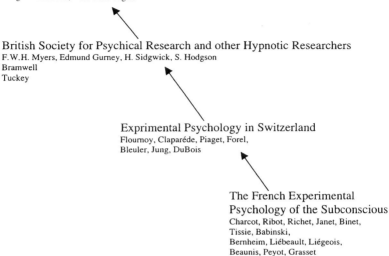

Boston School of Abnormal Psychology
William James, James Jackson Putnam, Henry Pickering Bowditch,
Josiah Royce, Morton Prince, Richard Hodgson, Richard Cabot,
Joseph Pratt, Elwood Worcester, Edward Cowles, A. Meyer,
B. Sidis, L. Eugene Emerson, Wm. McDougall

British Society for Psychical Research and other Hypnotic Researchers
F.W.H. Myers, Edmund Gurney, H. Sidgwick, S. Hodgson
Bramwell
Tuckey

Exprimental Psychology in Switzerland
Flournoy, Claparéde, Piaget, Forel,
Bleuler, Jung, DuBois

The French Experimental
Psychology of the Subconscious
Charcot, Ribot, Richet, Janet, Binet,
Tissie, Babinski,
Bernheim, Liébeault, Liégeois,
Beaunis, Peyot, Grasset

Figure 2 The French–Swiss–English–American psychotherapeutic axis (1882–1920).

In other words, according to this model, in addition to the normal everyday waking state, with its demands of adjustment to the external biological and physical environment, and also the more primitive condition of psychopathic disintegration, there exists within us a growth-oriented dimension of personality; that is, a higher self as opposed to a lower self, a transcendent dimension of consciousness, oriented around ideals and values, to which one may appeal as a standard of health and healing, or as a beacon if committed to the larger, more life-long task of personal development, the building of character, and self-actualization.[14] To describe this dimension as the transformative source of personality and consciousness, understood within the context of cross-cultural comparative science of religions, was the task James set for himself in *The Varieties of Religious Experience* of 1902.

In my own view, the *Varieties* has three important parts: the first is at once a definition and a statement of methodology. At the very outset, James established that religion, by which he means a generic capacity for spiritual experience, lies solely within the individual, rather than in the priesthood, the ecclesiasticisms, the texts, or the monuments usually associated with denominational religion. This means that phenomenology – an examination of the internal world of meanings within the person – constitutes James's method. Second, the *Varieties* not only asserts the validity of non-ordinary states of consciousness, but also locates the core of human spirituality in the mystical experience and claims that the exploration of the individual's own interior subliminal consciousness is the road to the awakening of such profound and ultimately transforming mystical states. Third, the *Varieties* is the key to understanding James's pragmatic maxim; namely, that the truths of these mystical states can only be tested in terms of their fruits for life.

So now, after this long-winded introduction to our subject, let us get down to the heart of the matter. The metaphysics underlying James's *Varieties* seems quite clear to me. As Ann Taves has pointed out, James's work was the first to take an objective view of religious experience, wresting the discussion from fundamentalists arguing for the absolute sanctity of the word of God and the skeptics, particularly in the sciences, who claimed that all religion was superstition.[15] To effect this bridge between 'knowledge about' as opposed to direct 'acquaintance with,' James drew on his developing tripartite metaphysics of pragmatism, pluralism, and radical empiricism.

Radical empiricism, which was actually the centerpiece of his thinking, proposed that in the midst of all the blooming, buzzing confusion of our perceptions, there is a primitive, almost primordial sense of pure consciousness in the immediate moment before the differentiation of subject and object. At once the ground and abyss of our being, as Tillich calls it, there is a significant non-Western literature suggesting that this is what is revealed to one degree or another in our every intuition, and in our every insight, as well as at the peak of the mystic, transcendent experience.[16] Western analytic philosophers remain silent on this subject, however.[17]

Pluralism, or more correctly noetic pluralism, as James called it (noetic meaning visionary knowledge or supra-intuitive understanding), corroborates the possibility of the unitive experience in every person. The problem for James was that he did not believe in airtight systems. Rather, he believed that, as is the case with all such assertions, the 'juices of metaphysical assumptions still leak in at every joint.' Even for the most complete visions of the whole, there were always the few strands left hanging, the desiderata, those inconsequential details that can be conveniently ignored, given the enormity of the big picture. He called these little ubiquitous anomalies the 'ever not quite,' and further proclaimed them as the most important, because they always established the exceptions to the airtight rule. Unitive experiences within the individual life-world can be granted, yes, but, for James, the final conception of ultimate reality might actually be different from person to person. This is why he appended the term 'noetic' to his doctrine of pluralism.

Normally we construct our beliefs on the basis of internalized rules laid down by others. But over the course of a lifetime, out of the depths of our intuitions, insights, and transcendent experiences we both confirm and modify the beliefs upon which we are prepared to act. But the test of a belief, he then said, was its consequences, not its origins. In the case of the transcendent experience, it was the subsequent effect on enhancing the moral and aesthetic quality of our daily lives.

In this way, pragmatism was also a way to compare two radically different sets of beliefs coming from exactly opposite directions. If they led to the same effects, then for all intents and purposes they were equal. This did not mean they were the same, however. James's position was clear on matters of faith. We should all not be required to believe in the same catechism, but rather we should promote a wide individuality in matters of religion, so long as our differing beliefs led to the same consensually validated way of behaving amongst one another. Here, in the *Varieties*, in my opinion, is his clearest statement on pragmatism.

One might also understand James's metaphysics by looking at the evolution of his model of consciousness.[18] James's thinking evolved through successive phases: first, due largely to the influence of Chauncey Wright, James was the only one nearest to Darwin's inner circle in the 1860s to take up the problem of consciousness within the context of the theory of natural selection. Championing a psychology of individual differences, he fought off the Social Darwinists throughout the 1860s and 1870s, a fashionable theory of the times that argued against the individual and for the species and thus seemed to promote implicitly the idea that sexual reproduction only happens between groups. At the same time, James also resisted the reductionists, who maintained that consciousness was merely an epiphenomenon of biological processes. Consciousness was physiological, James said, but that still did not negate our direct experience of it as something more than a mere afterglow of burning energy. Objects, he said, as well as their relations are both equally legitimate parts of experience.

Throughout the 1880s James labored to write his textbook on psychology from a positivistic point of view, meaning truth arrived at by the rational ordering of sense-data alone. What you see is what you get. There is no unseen hand behind the world of appearances. The observable thought alone defines the thinker. Meanwhile, James was becoming increasingly distracted by new and contradictory developments coming from the French Experimental Psychology of the Subconscious and the British and American psychical researchers. Hypnosis, automatic writing, crystal gazing, and other methods seemed to point to alternate states of consciousness quite different from the waking state. Nevertheless, the primary focus of his *Principles of Psychology* in 1890 remained an analysis of the object at the cognitive center of attention, despite the periodic intrusion of a second hypothesis proposing a dynamic psychology of the subliminal and the possibility that the same object could be experienced against the backdrop of more than one state of consciousness.

Thereafter, this second hypothesis quickly developed into his metaphysics of radical empiricism, which permitted him to articulate a dynamic psychology of the subconscious in his Exceptional Mental States Lectures of 1896, to further investigate psychic phenomena, and to collect material that came to constitute the basis of his psychology of religion. He came out with his book of essays on *The Will to Believe* in 1897 and articulated his version of Peirce's pragmatism in 1898. His tripartite metaphysics of pragmatism, pluralism, and radical empiricism was then presented in germinal form in *The Varieties of Religious Experience* in 1902.

Radical empiricism is then more clearly enunciated with his 1904 essays as the name given to the metaphysical assumption underlying experimentation by which the full spectrum of states of consciousness, from the psychopathic, through the normal everyday waking state, to the transcendent, can be studied. But pragmatism, not radical empiricism, was fast becoming an international movement, and so as not to slow down the momentum, James declared that one did not have to know radical empiricism to understand the pragmatic philosophy. His suggestion not only worked, but soon became official dogma. The result has been a monumental distortion of what James meant by pragmatism, and while there has been some acknowledgment of his pluralism, radical empiricism continues to be almost completely ignored.

Further, the origins of these metaphysical principles are not to be found in Kantian or Hegelian philosophy, nor solely within the tradition of the British Empiricists, and they are certainly not echoed in the later interpretation of either the neo-realists of the immediate post-Jamesian era or the contemporary pragmatists of today who continue to insist on interpreting James through both Dewey and Peirce.

Rather, I maintain that their origin can be found in the intuitive psychology of character formation underlying the Swedenborgian and transcendentalist milieu of William's father, Henry James Sr., and William's godfather, Ralph Waldo Emerson. It was this literary and philosophical inheritance that William transmuted within his own more reductionistic and scientific era. The earlier, more literary legacy he turned into a psychology of individual differences, a defense of religious belief, and a far-reaching science of consciousness. With these tools, he meant to overthrow not only materialistic reductionism but also the doctrine of representation by re-establishing experimental psychology as a phenomenologically based enterprise grounded in human experience and foundational to all the basic sciences.

I have detailed elsewhere the influence of James's *Varieties* in a number of fields in the twentieth century, taking a somewhat expanded definition of the term 'influence' by equating the themes in that specific work with James's larger agenda to articulate his metaphysics.[19] My license for doing this, as I have said, is the opinion I fielded earlier that the *Varieties* is the central document in James's work elucidating these ideas all in one place. I wish now only to direct your attention to a preliminary sketch of the fruits of this effort, which I have represented in Figure 3.

The areas in which I have investigated include the philosophy and psychology of religion, anthropology, sociology, depth psychology, clinical pastoral education, classical Eastern psychology, the American self-help movement, parapsychology, humanistic and transpersonal psychology, existential phenomenology, international peace studies, the new physics, mind–body medicine, neuroscience, and now, neurotheology.

If the majority of these fields sound like the alternative reality tradition, they are.[20] Because James's metaphysics launches a major assault on the rationalist

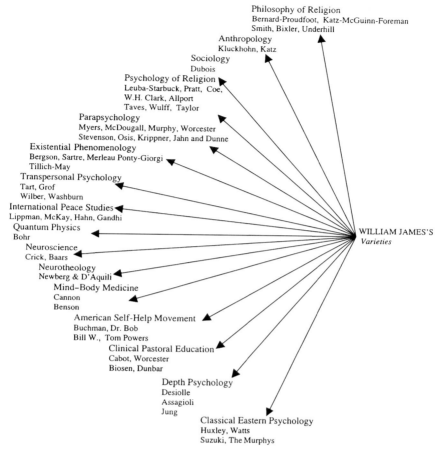

Figure 3 Some influences of James's *Varieties* in the twentieth century.

tradition in Western philosophy, it is only natural that we should have had to endure one hundred years of reinterpretation, misinterpretation, denial, and often outright rejection of James's most controversial ideas by the institution builders of the disciplines such as physiology, psychology, philosophy, and religious studies.

While this attitude of resistance has been sufficient for the past, I propose that it is no longer tenable for the future, given dramatic new developments in the neurosciences, as well as the world-wide events involving the clash of cultures in the immediate present.

In the first instance, since the 1950s, we have been witnessing a major revolution in the way the basic sciences communicate with one another around the biology of consciousness and the mind–brain interface. Whereas before, the disciplines remained relatively isolated in their traditional categories within a relatively fixed hierarchy beginning with physics, geology, mineralogy, chemistry, astronomy, and mathematics, and proceeding to biology, physiology, and so forth, now, the most intense work occurs at the interface between molecular genetics, neurology, endocrinology, immunology, and experimental psychiatry. With this transformation has come renewed interest in philosophical questions generally banned from scientific discussion for most of the twentieth century, but taken seriously by James one hundred years ago. While these questions are directed mainly toward the scientific study of consciousness, their import for re-opening a discussion about the phenomenology of the science-making process itself, as James had tried to do, is obvious.

The important point is that the humanistic implications of advances in the neurosciences have created effects far beyond the control of the reductionistic mentality that spawned them in the first place. The outcome of these changes, while originally controlled by the reductionists, is now unknown. Unlocking the key to the biology of consciousness may, in fact, lead not only to new kinds of knowledge but also to a new kind of science. This is one of the reasons that James's call a century ago for a new epistemology underlying the way basic science is conducted regarding the problem of consciousness appears so new and fresh today. The problem is that scholars in the humanities seem unaware that such a humanistic revolution is going on. One result is that voices trained purely in the epistemology of the Western sciences who have had their most far-reaching philosophical sensibilities winnowed out of them by their training continue to dominate the new philosophical discussions. Further, they persist in recycling the same old categories of intellectual analysis that have in part created this dilemma of consciousness in the first place.

There is also the phenomenon of postmodernism to consider, a form of European social and political criticism that has crept into nearly every liberal enclave in Western culture, especially the soft areas of the humanities and the sciences. The postmodernists believe they have proven once and for all that the scientific world-view is not absolute, because its underlying epistemology is saturated with assumptions and influences that are all extra-scientific. All knowledge is contextual and this context must be taken into account. When it is, science no longer holds the position of absolute authority. However, the postmodernists act as if the relativity of the scientific viewpoint is a major event now behind us, while traditional scientists have yet to notice any big changes in the way science is conducted, and cannot see why these gadflies are still around.[21]

Postmodernism, in my opinion, is thoroughly Jamesian, but does not go far enough, for two reasons. First, it wants to separate the natural from the human sciences but cannot take the next step and acknowledge the fundamental dependence of our definition of the material world on human consciousness in everything that human beings do. Second, while it is an attack against the Western rationalist tradition and has shown itself here and there to be incisive in deconstructing that larger world-view which dominates Western thought, in the end it has nothing to offer as a substitute. At best, it has been a popular intellectual and social movement which at least prepares us for a more important change in world consciousness that you and I may live to see in our lifetime.

That is, with regard to the present cultural scene, as I have predicted elsewhere,[22] I believe that within the next few decades we will experience a cross-cultural exchange of ideas between East and West on a scale unprecedented in the history of Western thought. With this exchange will come not only a flood of new ideas, but an opening to non-Western epistemologies, such that a major re-evaluation of every detail of our own culture will also have to take place.

Such an exchange, in fact, is already under way. It can either be peaceable or violent. We can wait and be reactive at the last minute, armed with outmoded ideas about our superiority, our intelligence, and our wealth, and we can experience extraordinary pain and suffering, even if the old ways of knowing prevail. Or we can attempt to manage the global change that we ourselves are fueling by being proactive and measured, guided by both wisdom and compassion, especially with regard to a more peaceful actualization of our highest values cross-culturally.

We might follow the lead of Eugen Rosenstock Huessy, the German social theorist who was influenced by James to write about the benefits of planetary service;[23] or Gandhi, also influenced by James's ideas, who believed that holding public office was to become a form of spiritual discipline; or the Tibetans, who are possibly the first culture in world history to permanently renounce violence. Or we could possibly learn from aikido, one of the newer martial arts of Japan, the goal of which is to save the attacker from injury because it is based on the higher and more inward aim of universal disarmament and world peace.[24] James himself anticipated such developments in his formulation of the moral equivalent of war, first enunciated in the *Varieties* in 1902.[25]

More prosaically, I only ask among us today for a reassessment of our current reading of James, so that he might at least achieve parity with his more famous brother Henry. To do this:

- It is imperative that we cease interpreting William James primarily through Dewey and Peirce and try to read him in his own right.
- We should read James across his entire corpus, not just parts of him.
- We should acknowledge that James's philosophical roots are primarily Swedenborgian and transcendentalist, not Cartesian, Kantian, Humean, or Hegelian, and take more seriously his true lineage as legitmate philosophy.
- We should understand that James has a tripartite metaphysics of pragmatism, pluralism, and radical empiricism, and that radical empiricism, not pragmatism, lies at the center of his vision.
- We should think more deeply about James's focus on pure experience in the immediate moment, before the differentiation of subject and object, and consider more seriously the consequences of his intent to situate such a phenomenological psychology as foundational to the basic sciences.

- In addition, we should consider more seriously the iconography of the transcendent. As James himself remarked, science cannot possibly be right if it excludes parts of human experience from the total equation. But to acknowledge the transcendent, science as we know it may have to undergo some new phase of development. By so doing, we prepare ourselves to become more sophisticated interpreters of non-Western epistemologies, as James tried to do in the *Varieties* when he embraced the new depth psychologies of his era, and out of that ethos called for the development of a cross-cultural comparative science of religions.
- Finally, we should embark, as James did, upon an unprecedented interdisciplinary dialogue between physiology, psychology, philosophy, and religious studies. There is already such a revolution going on in the neurosciences. Why not extend it to the dialogue between the sciences and humanities?

Although left to go out of print so soon, we now have available, at least in limited quantities, James's collected works through Harvard University Press. The University of Virginia Press is within two volumes of completing William James's collected letters. In addition, we have a half dozen solid biographies, and a steady stream of dissertations and journal articles on James studies, not to mention two dozen editions both in and out of print of the *Varieties* alone. There is then a mass of commentarial literature on James spanning more than one hundred years.

I call upon you to grasp this entire corpus of primary and secondary literature. Not only master it, but keep your understanding of it up to date as well. In particular, study more the history of James scholarship, which is both wide and deep, but still largely neglected. In the words of Professor Robert Rieber, a retired historian in psychology, 'If we would only read more, perhaps we would discover less!' Let us begin an intellectual revolution in James scholarship fit to address the problems of the twenty-first century. Let it begin here and now, in this hall, with this conference. We will need every voice. For as James himself has said, 'Each person being a syllable in human nature's total message, it takes the whole of us to spell the meaning out completely.' Thank you.

Notes

1. See, for instance, Taylor, E.I. and Wozniak, R. (eds) *Pure Experience: The Response to William James*. Bristol: Routledge/Thommes, 1996. This work reprints James's major statement on radical empiricism and follows with twenty-five years of responses by philosophers and psychologists. These documents confirm that most authors had no idea what James was talking about; namely, a new metaphysics beyond logic. Their analyses, meanwhile, can be counted as the origin of the continued misinterpretation today of James, especially by the analytic philosophers, philosophers who cannot transcend the categories of Western philosophy, psychologists who have had their philosophic sensibilities winnowed out of them, and religious scholars who try to make James over into a monistic Christian theist.

2. Prof. Charles Taylor's *Varieties of Religion Today: William James Revisited.* Cambridge: Harvard University Press, 2002, which seems an afterthought, makes a few interesting points about James's *Varieties,* but spends most of its pages talking about something else, and does not mention other work on James.
3. The edition to which I refer throughout is James, W. *The Varieties of Religious Experience: A Study in Human Nature.* With new introductions by Eugene Taylor and Jeremy Carrette. London: Routledge, Taylor & Francis, 2002.
4. See Skrupskelis, Ignas (ed.) *William James: A Reference Guide.* Boston: G.K. Hall, 1977. For a survey of psychologists and philosophers on James, see the annotated bibliography accompanying Taylor, E.I. *William James on Consciousness beyond the Margin.* Princeton, NJ: Princeton Univ. Press, 1996.
5. Taylor, E.I., Asian interpretations: Transcending the stream of consciousness. In K. Pope and J. Singer (eds) *The Stream of Consciousness: Scientific Investigations into the Flow of Human Experience.* New York: Plenum, 1978, 31–54. Reprinted in Pickering, J. & Skinner, M. (eds) *From Sentience to Symbol: Readings on Consciousness.* London: Harvester-Wheatsheaf, and Toronto: Univ. of Toronto Press, 1990, and elsewhere.
6. Richard Wolfe, Joseph Garland, Librarian in the Boston Medical Library and Archivist at Harvard Medical School at the time provided shelf space in the archives of the Countway Library of Medicine for this project.
7. Taylor, E.I. *William James on Exceptional Mental States: Reconstruction of the 1896 unpublished Lowell Lectures.* New York: Scribner's Sons, 1982. Professor Barzun's work on his own chronological manuscript on James had lapsed after he had written his chapter on James's *Principles of Psychology* (1890). After incorporating a chapter on the Exceptional Mental States Lectures of 1896, he went on to finish *A Stroll with William James.*
8. Taylor, E.I. William James and depth psychology. *Journal of Consciousness Studies,* 9:9–10, 11–36.
9. Trammel, Varila, Krolikowski and Appel are among the Peirce scholars cited in Taylor, E.I., Peirce and Swedenborg, *Studia Swedenborgiana,* 1986, 6:1, 25–51.
10. Taylor, E.I. William James and the Spiritual Currents of American Pragmatism. Based on lectures commemorating the centenary of James's *Varieties of Religious Experience.* Delivered before The Swedenborg Society at Harvard University during the academic year 2001–2002. In preparation.
11. Taylor, E.I., *The Boston School of Psychotherapy: Science, Healing, and Consciousness in 19th Century New England.* The 1982 Lowell Lectures for the Massachusetts Medical Society and the Boston Medical Library. In preparation. Sonu Shamdasani (ed.) *From India to the Planet Mars: A Case of Multiple Personality with Imaginary Languages* by Theodore Flournoy, Princeton Univ. Press, 1994. Also, Shamdasani's *C. G. Jung and the Making of Modern Psychology,* in preparation.
12. Taylor, E.I. 'The future of psychology belongs to your work': William James and Sigmund Freud. *Psychological Science* (Journal of the American Psychological Society). 10:6, Nov. 1999, 465–469; Also, Taylor, E.I., Was There a Boston 'School' of Psychotherapy? Address delivered upon induction as a Fellow in the History Division of the APA, at the 108th annual meeting of the American Psychological Association, August 13, 2000, Washington, DC.
13. These include the quite different conceptualizations of Binet and Fere, Janet, Tissie, Bernheim, Forel, Moll, Dessoir, van Eden and van Renterghem, DuBois, Dejerine, F.W.H. Myers, Flournoy, and others.
14. The growth-oriented dimension is clearly established in William James's chapter on 'Multiple Personality' in E.I.Taylor, *William James on Exceptional Mental*

States. New York: Scribner's, 1982; in F.W.H. Myers's *The Subliminal Consciousness*, with an introduction by James Webb. New York: Arno Press, 1976; in Richard Maurice Bucke's *Cosmic Consciousness: A Study in the Evolution of the Human Mind*. Philadelphia, Innes & Sons, 1901; In Theodore Flournoy's *Spiritism and Psychology*, translated, abridged, and with an introduction by Hereward Carrington. New York ; London : Harper & Brothers, 1911; and in Jung. See Taylor, E.I., Preface to the reissue of C.G. Jung's *Psychology of the Unconscious*. Trans. Beatrice Hinkle, (orig. English edition, 1916). Supplement to The Bollingen Series, Princeton, NJ: Princeton Univ. Press, 2002.

15. Ann Taves, *Fits, Trances and Visions: Explaining Religion and Explaining Experience from Wesley to James*. Princeton, NJ: Princeton Univ. Press, 1999. See also my review of this work in the *International Journal for the Psychology of Religion*, 12:3, 2002, 205–207.

16. Murphy, M. and Donovan, S. *The Physical and Psychological Effects of Meditation: A Review of Contemporary Research with a Comprehensive Bibliography, 1931– 1996*, 2nd edition edited by Eugene Taylor. Sausalito, California: Institute of Noetic Sciences, 1997. We can find it also in the psychology of Jung, Maslow, Assagioli, and others.

17. See Frederick Streng, *Emptiness: A Study in Religious Meaning*. Knoxville: Abingdon Press, 1967; or more recently *The Problem of Pure Consciousness: Mysticism and Philosophy* , edited by Robert K.C. Forman. New York ; Oxford : Oxford University Press, 1990. Also, Taylor, E.I. Pure consciousness and the iconography of the transcendent. *AHP Perspectives* (Newsletter of the Association for Humanistic Psychology), August/Sept., 1999, 14–17.

18. Taylor, E.I., The evolution of William James's definition of consciousness, *Revision: Journal of Knowledge and Consciousness*, 1981, 4:2, 40–47.

19. Taylor, E.I. William James and the Spiritual Currents of American Pragmatism. Based on lectures commemorating the centenary of James's *Varieties of Religious Experience*. Delivered before The Swedenborg Society at Harvard University during the academic year 2001–2002. In preparation.

20. I have described the Western analytic tradition in terms of its roots in the so-called Judeo-Christian, Greco-Roman, Western European, and Anglo-American definition of reality in Taylor, E.I. *Shadow Culture: Psychology and Spirituality in America*. Washington, DC: Counterpoint, 2000. The alternative reality tradition in the West is described both there and in Ellwood, Robert S., *Religious and Spiritual Groups in Modern America*. Englewood Cliffs, NJ: Prentice Hall, 1973.

21. Parsons, Keith (ed.) *Science Wars: Debating Scientific Knowledge and Technology*. Amherst, NY: Prometheus Books, 2003. Also, Brown, J.R. *Who Rules Science?* Cambridge: Harvard Univ. Press, 2001. And Taylor, E.I. A hermeneutic analysis of hermeneutic analysis: Review of Graumann and Gergen *Historical Dimensions of Psychological Discourse*. *Contemporary Psychology*. Sept. 1998.

22. Taylor, E.I., Review of Peter Gay's *Freud: A Life for Our Time*. In *Commonweal*, March 21, 1989; see also Taylor, E.I., Buddhism and Western psychology: A biographical memoir. In S. Segal (ed.) *Psychology Encounters Buddhism*. Albany: SUNY Press, 2003. In press.

23. Morgan, George Allen (ed.) *Speech and Society: The Christian Linguistic Social Philosophy of Eugen Rosenstock-Huessy*. With comprehensive bibliography by Lise van der Molen. Gainesville: University Presses of Florida, 1987.

24. Taylor, E.I., Aikido: The evolution of a martial art into a spiritual discipline. *Somatics*, 1:2, Spring, 1977, 8–12.

25. *Varieties*, centenary edition, p. 300.

Chapter 2

Psychologies as ontology-making practices

William James and the pluralities of psychological experience

Sonu Shamdasani

What is the contemporary relevance of *The Varieties of Religious Experience* for the study of psychology and its history? Already in James's time, the project for a unitary science of psychology, vigorously pursued from many sides, was collapsing into a chaos of ever increasing fragmentation, coupled with attempts to assert the ascendence of particular agendas for psychology through the hegemonic control of institutions. A hundred years later, this fragmentation has only increased. The disciplines of the psychology of religion and subliminal psychology which James vigorously championed collapsed and all but disappeared. Meanwhile through historical studies, the status of the terms 'psychology' on the one side and 'religion' on the other have increasingly come in for intense scrutiny, and the question has been raised as to whether these terms have any stable referents, or, on the other hand, whether their unitary designation is not designed to paper over the diversity and multiplicity of the conceptions and practices that they designate. In the light of these concerns, I would like to address the contemporary status of James's text by characterising his method of studying psychological experience, and by inquiring how this can help us comprehend the varieties of psychologies and the experiences which they generate. But first, we need to ask . . .

What was psychology?[1]

In 1899, James remarked that the 'air has been full of rumours', and that 'we have been having something like a "boom" in psychology in this country'.[2] At the end of the nineteenth century, many figures in the West sought to establish a scientific psychology that would be independent of philosophy, theology, biology, anthropology, literature, medicine and neurology, whilst taking over their traditional subject matters. The very possibility of psychology rested upon the successful negotiation of these disciplinary crossings. The larger share of the questions that psychologists took up had already been posed and elaborated in these prior disciplines. They had to prise their subjects from the preserves of other specialists. Through becoming a science, it was hoped that psychology would be able to solve questions that had vexed thinkers for centuries, and to replace superstition, folk wisdom and metaphysical speculation with the rule of universal law. The result would amount to nothing less than the completion and culmination of the scientific revolution. Several decades of work in science studies have demonstrated that there is no singular atemporal essence to science or notions such as 'the scientific method', or in other words, that 'Science' with a capital 'S' does not exist. As Isabelle Stengers notes, 'it is pointless to search for a noncontextual, general definition of the difference between science and non-science'.[3] However, this is not to erase all differences between disciplines classed as sciences and those that are not. Rather, as Stengers notes, it is to affirm that the question of the scientificity of a particular discipline 'only takes on meaning in the precise context in which it is posed'.[4]

There has been much discussion concerning the scientific status of psychology. Given the sacramental significance of the word 'science', it may be fruitful to speak more generally of ontology-making practices, which would include all disciplines that aim to construct general, universal ontologies.[5] The value of such a term is that it may help one to avoid falling into pre-given demarcations. The task is then one of differentiating and comparing the procedures of different ontology-making practices. Much of this work is already going on in science studies today.

In 1874, Franz Brentano proclaimed that psychology was the '*science of the future.*' It was to psychology that 'more than all other theoretical sciences, the future belongs', and which 'more than all others will form the future'.[6] To make this possible,

> We must strive to achieve here what mathematics, physics, chemistry and physiology have already accomplished ... a nucleus of generally recognized truth to which, through the working together of many forces, new crystals will then soon adhere on all sides. In place of *psychologies* we must seek to place a *psychology*.[7]

Brentano's imperative sums up the aspirations of the 'new psychology' to form a unitary scientific discipline, modelled after how it imagined sciences like physics and chemistry to function. The mode in which psychologists sought to emulate – or simulate – the form of the prestigious sciences varied. However, the basic aspiration was to form a unitary science. Embedded within this conception was a distinction between two kinds of knowledge about human beings. The first was the scientific knowledge to which psychology aspired. This was to provide a certitude equivalent to the periodic table in chemistry. The second was 'all the rest', ie. all other means by which human beings had sought to understand themselves – philosophies, myths, religions, literatures, arts, moral systems, and so on. At best, this was seen to amount to a few lucky guesses. Psychology was to create a fundamental general ontology which would ultimately subsume all other forms of knowing about human beings. In this regard, James wrote to Hugo Münsterberg in 1890:

> The truth is that psychology is yet seeking her first principles, and is in the condition of Physics before Galileo or Newton. Nerve physiology has some

laws, even of a quasi elementary sort; but of a law connecting body and mind, or indeed of what is the elementary fact of mind, we have not at present even the beginning of an hypothesis which is valuable.[8]

Thus for James, psychology's will to science implied that its business was to be one of discovering and formulating universal laws, and that these had yet to be found. Two years later he concluded his *Psychology: A Briefer Course* by saying:

> When, then, we talk of 'psychology as a natural science' we must not assume that means a sort of psychology that stands at last on solid ground. It means just the reverse; it means a psychology particularly fragile, and into which the waters of metaphysical criticism leak at every joint ... it is indeed strange to hear people talk triumphantly of 'the New Psychology', and write 'Histories of Psychology', when into the real elements and forces which the word covers not the first glimpse of clear insight exists. A string of raw facts, a little gossip and wrangle about opinions, a little classification and generalization on the mere descriptive level; a strong prejudice that we have states of mind, and that our brain conditions them: but not a single law in the sense in which physics shows us laws, not a single proposition from which any consequence can causally be deduced. We don't even know the terms between which the elementary laws would obtain if we had them. This is no science, it is only the hope of science ... But at present psychology is in the condition of physics before Galileo and the laws of motion, of chemistry before Lavoisier and the notion that mass is preserved in all reactions. The Galileo and the Lavoisier of psychology will be famous men indeed when they come, as come they some day surely will.[9]

One might to do well to ask whether there could be a better description of the state of psychology today: gossip, wrangle, prejudices, but no single generally recognized law. Nevertheless, the frequency with which psychologists were likened (or likened themselves) to Galileo, Lavoisier and Darwin increased dramatically.

James's questioning of the presumption of writing histories of psychology before psychology was successfully founded bears consideration. From early on, histories of psychologies played an important part in attempting to define and construct the discipline of psychology and to demarcate it from other fields.[10] Throughout the twentieth century, histories of psychology have continued to play this role, whether intentionally or unwittingly. But what does the history of psychology consist in, if one leaves open the question as to whether psychology was ever founded? Rather than writing the history of the foundation of a discipline, one is writing the history of attempts by individuals in different disciplines to effect certain transformations in these disciplines through evoking the rubric of psychology.[11]

When challenged by James Ladd in 1892 concerning his assertion in *The Principles of Psychology* that psychology was a natural science, James replied that

I have never claimed that psychology as it stands to-day, *is* a natural science, or in an exact way a science at all. Psychology, indeed, is to-day hardly more than what physics was before Galileo, what chemistry was before Lavoisier. It is a mass of phenomenal description, gossip, and myth, including, however, real material enough to justify one in the hope that with judgement and good-will on the part of those interested, its study may be so organised even now as to become worthy of the name of natural science at no very distant day ... I wished, by treating Psychology *like* a natural science, to help her become one.[12]

There was a fine line between hoping that psychology would turn into a science by treating it like one, and – as was more generally the case – assuming that it already was a science, simply because it was talked about in a simulation of scientific rhetoric by sufficiently many people. Nevertheless, James invoked a distinction between a rational and practical science of the mind. Representatives of the former would be those German 'prism, pendulum, and chronograph-philosophers' whose methods 'could hardly have arisen in a country whose natives could be *bored*'.[13] By contrast, 'what every jail-warden, every doctor, every clergyman, every asylum-superintendent, ask of psychology is practical rules'.[14] It was James's increasing dissatisfaction with the meagre yield of laboratory psychology that led him to stress this distinction. It was towards a psychology that fulfilled this practical imperative that he was increasingly inclined. In conclusion, he argued that if one had to choose between the two forms of psychology, 'The kind of psychology which could cure a case of melancholy, or charm a chronic insane delusion away, ought certainly to be preferred to the most seraphic insight into the nature of the soul'.[15] In effect, psychology as a 'practical science of the mind' represented a psychology grounded in pragmatism as opposed to the positivist epistemology of experimental psychology. The *Varieties* represents the articulation of precisely such a psychology, and it is within this context that the question of religion – which had no place within the radically self-restricted domain of experimental psychology – arose.

Psychology's 'will to science' fuelled a profusion of activities. However, whilst there was no shortage of attempts to form the one general psychology, it became clear pretty soon that the sought-for unity was ever receding. The proliferation of variously styled psychologies demonstrated that there was little consensus as to what could be considered the aims and methods of psychology. In 1894, James wrote to Carl Stumpf: 'From all the psychologies either published or about to appear, there ought to be some sedimentary deposit of truth – I devoutly hope that it may be clearly discernable by all!'[16] A few years later, James lamented: 'there *is* no "new psychology" worthy of the name. There is nothing but the old psychology which began in Locke's time, plus a little physiology of the brain and senses and theory of evolution, and a few refinements of introspective detail'.[17] Thus the 'novelty' lay in the rhetorical mode in which psychology was increasingly presented. Not for the first time, an 'epistemological break' was to be created simply through proclaiming that it had taken place.

In 1900, the Berlin psychologist William Stern surveyed the new psychology. Aside from an empirical tendency and the use of experimental methods, he saw little in the way of common features. There were many laboratories with researchers working on special problems, together with many textbooks, but they were all characterized by a pervasive particularism. He noted that the psychological map of the day was as colourful and checkered as that of Germany in the epoch of small states, and that psychologists

> often speak different languages, and the portraits that they draw up of the psyche are painted with so many different colours and with so many differently accented special strokes that it often becomes difficult to recognize the identity of the represented object.[18]

Stern concluded: 'In short: there are many new psychologies, but not yet the new psychology'.[19] Thus the singularity of the term 'psychology' should not mislead one into thinking that such a discipline was ever successfully founded. Or that there is an essence to 'psychology' that could encompass the various definitions, methodologies, practices, world-views and institutions that have used this designation. Rather it indicates the massive significance that psychologists gave to being seen to be talking about the same thing. Indeed, psychology has come to mean many disparate and incommensurable things precisely because it had always been made up of them.

The formation of psychologies consisted in a parallel constitution of psychologies and their objects of study. The formation of an epistemological object consists in a process of purification, and fixity: taking an aspect of life and rendering it a suitable object of study, through imbuing it with the attributes of universality, ahistoricity, distinguishing between essential and non-essential attributes, and so on.[20] As we shall see, such aspects of this filtration of the ontology-making process were commented on by James himself.

For James at the time of the *Varieties*, psychology remained in a condition of aspiring to be a science. Hence none of its results – including those of his own psychology – had been sufficiently established to be universally binding. Thus psychologies could be considered to be optional ontologies, which had yet to join up with the general ontology which James considered science to be. The increasing gulf between the initial aspirations of the new psychology and the chaos and disunity that ensued forms one of the critical contexts of the *Varieties*. As we shall see, James's reformulation of psychology in the *Varieties* and after can in part be seen as a response to this.

Does religion exist?

One example of the dual constitution of psychologies and their objects of study is the psychology of religion. The formation of this discipline did not come about simply through applying the methods and conceptions of an existing discipline to a new area of study, or to 'naturally given' phenomena: rather, it was through constituting religion as an epistemological object that psychology aimed to constitute itself. The ubiquity of the term 'religion' and the longevity of so-called great world religions has led to the widespread notion that religion can be considered a *sui generis* category. From this perspective, it is surprising to consider that the modern concept of religion only emerged in the second half of the nineteenth century, and, furthermore, there are good grounds for dating its invention.

Contemporary scholars have questioned the status of the category 'religion', and posed questions as to whether it has any stable referent, and further, the uses which the term has served. Timothy Fitzgerald has argued that 'Religion cannot reasonably be taken to be a valid analytical category since it does not pick out any distinctive cross-cultural aspect of human life'.[21] Rather, he argues that the category of religion is itself a theological category, which he characterises as a liberal ecumenical theology. Thus the constitution of category of religion has led to the uncritical imposition of Judeo-Christian assumptions on non-Western data. In a similar vein, Richard King argues that the notion of religion is a 'Christian theological category' with a particular genealogy. He argues that 'the way the term has been employed results in the privileging of certain features of Christian and post-Christian Western culture and locates "other cultures" within an implicitly theological framework that transforms them as much as it attempts to make sense of them'.[22] Religion has generally been defined in a differential manner, that is to say, through being contrasted and set aside from the non-religious. Thus the formation of the concept of religion should not be seen as separate from the formation of a concept of the secular. Such an argument clearly has consequences for the history of the psychology of religion: the attempt to form a 'secular' science of the 'sacred' through constituting these very distinctions.

The questioning of the status of the term 'religion' thus converges with the questioning of the status of the term 'psychology'. If one can no longer assume that these terms have stable referents, one has to study carefully the uses that they serve in particular texts, practices and institutions. In reading the *Varieties* today – justly viewed as foundational in the psychology of religion – one has to consider how the text looks *after* 'religion' and *after* 'psychology'. What happens to the reading of the *Varieties* when we drop these terms, or rather, attentively track the work being done by them? If psychology never actually existed as a unitary enterprise, one has to look to its use in particular texts to determine its meaning, even in the case of a particular thinker.

I will first consider the consequences that follow from the suspension of the term 'religion' in the reading of the *Varieties*. One may commence with James's definitions of religion. In his work, one finds restricted and general conceptions of religion. In 1895, he proposed the following definition:

> when from now onward I use the word [religion] I mean to use it in the supernaturalist sense, as declaring that the so-called order of nature, which

constitutes this world's experience, is only one portion of the total universe, and that there stretches beyond this visible world an unseen world of which we know nothing positive, but in its relation to which the true significance of our present mundane life consists.[23]

Traces of this restricted use of the term are to be found in the *Varieties*. In his chapter on 'The divided self', James writes: 'To find religion is only one out of the many ways of reaching unity; and the process of remedying inner incompleteness and reducing inner discord is a general psychological process, which may take place with any sort of mental material, and need not necessarily assume the religious form'.[24]

The *Varieties* begins with a generalised definition of religion: 'Religion, therefore, as I now ask you arbitrarily to take it, shall mean for us *the feelings, acts and experiences of individual men in their solitude, so far as they apprehend themselves to stand in relation to whatever they may consider the divine*'.[25] Additionally, James adds that 'we must interpret the term "divine" very broadly, as denoting any object that is god*like*, whether it be a concrete divinity or not'.[26] Thus we find a tension and oscillation in James concerning the term 'religion'. The source of this may be clarified if one simply considers the consequences of dropping the category in the reading of the *Varieties*. The question that follows is, what is it then a study of? Varieties of what? *It then may be considered to be a study of states of transformation*, based on a corpus of first-hand testimonials generally utilising Christian phraseology and iconography. This may explain the oscillation between the generalised and restricted concepts of religion in the text: the study of states of transformation (placing the emphasis on the subtitle of the book, 'A Study in Human Nature') would incline him to the generalised definition, whilst the specifically Christian conceptions in the transformation narratives would incline him to the restricted definition. The question of Protestant bias is one that James is more aware of than some critics give him credit for. In his preface to Starbuck's *Psychology of Religion* (1899) he wrote: 'The Volksgeist of course dictates its special phraseology and most of its conceptions, which are almost without exception Protestant, and predominantly of the Evangelical sort'.[27] (However, the shaping effect of the 'Volksgeist' is a theme that remains undeveloped in James.)[28]

Considering James in this manner has some unexpected consequences. For over a century, criticisms have been made of James's conception of religion, along the lines of: James is not Durkheim, or Weber, or Freud, or a post-colonial feminist cultural critic and so on. Such criticisms tend to counterpose other conceptions of religion or approaches to the topic.[29] A great number of such criticisms of James's treatment of religion dissolve as being as obsolete as the category of religion. If one accepts the legitimacy of James's attempt to study states of transformation in individuals, then the fact that he ignores institutional religion, the history of the church, dogmas and theologies, etc., appears to be simply beside the point. The text then becomes more contemporary than a number of the criticisms that have been directed towards it.

Psychology, or how to make our ideas vague

If the *Varieties* may fruitfully be considered to be a study of states of transformation, how does James intend to study them? In other words, what is the role
and status of the term 'psychology' in the text?

In the introduction to the *Varieties*, James notes that he had initially intended
the lectures to consist of two parts, a descriptive part on 'Man's religious
appetites' and a metaphysical part on 'Their satisfaction through philosophy'. The
growth of the psychological matter led to the second being 'postponed entirely'
aside from a brief statement of his philosophical conclusions. Reading this at face
value has led many commentators to consider the *Varieties* as a work of
'psychology' (however understood), and to neglect its imbrication in his
philosophy of radical empiricism. Eugene Taylor has cogently demonstrated
the inseparability of James's psychology from radical empiricism and
demonstrated that far, from abandoning psychology, James's later work in part
constituted a critique of the metaphysical basis of the new psychology, so as to
reformulate it.[30] David Lamberth has excellently shown that James's descriptive
psychology in the *Varieties* is closely connected with his unfinished philosophical
project, and the manner in which this is subsequently articulated in *A Pluralistic
Universe*.[31] Following Lamberth's reconstruction, I would like to go further and
suggest that these two projects are in several important respects inseparable.
Indeed, many paragraphs in which James is developing radical empiricism
seamlessly interleave the discussion of the cases he introduces. Thus the nature of
the descriptive psychology which James employs in the *Varieties* warrants closer
consideration.

In this regard, James's mode of lengthy citation – which is strikingly out of
temper with the predilection for paraphrase in the humanities today – is
significant. In 1903, James wrote to his Italian translator, Guilo Cesare Ferrari:
'The book was written round the documents. I got them first, and poured in my
connective remarks like a sort of galantine jelly to enclose them, and I confess that
I should dislike to have any of them sacrificed.'[32] This form of composition is not
incidental for two reasons. First, the documents are presented in an evidential
manner. Whilst relying on first-hand testimonials, James makes available all the
documentation on which he is basing his reading. The material is made public,
and is therefore fully available for other researchers to judge James's constructions
against the material he is using. This is in line with what he considered to be a
necessary requirement for psychology to be a science. Second, it highlights the
minimalism and secondary status of James's connective remarks. Descriptive
psychology is now deliberately set in a minor key.

In the *Varieties*, James articulates his criticism of genetic explanation.[33]
Elsewhere, he expresses his dislike of symbolic interpretation.[34] By contrast, the
mode of 'descriptive psychology' which James pursues in the *Varieties* may be
characterised as an attempt to bring to formalised articulation different attitudes
and possible ways of living life. The narratives that James compiles show

experiences of transformations of the self and its experience of the world. Here, his descriptive psychology simply provides comparative, formalised articulation of these and sorts them into a serial order.

In his reply to Pratt's questionnaire on the subject of religious beliefs in 1904, James spoke of his 'hospitality towards the religious testimony of others'.[35] This may be taken as a leitmotif of James's approach. His characterisation of the religion of the healthy-minded and the sick-minded characters is marked by this hospitality: whilst his sympathies are clear, no standpoints are dismissed.[36]

Two further features of James's descriptive psychology here may be highlighted. The first is the delimitation of explanation. As James puts it, psychology can describe, but not explain. For example, when discussing the shift of excitement, James notes:

> Now if you ask of psychology just how the excitement shifts in a man's mental system, and *why* aims that were peripheral become at a certain moment central, psychology has to reply that although she can give a general description of what happens, she is unable in a given case to account accurately for all the given forces at work.[37]

If psychology cannot explain, what then is the status of psychological language and description? He goes on to describe these shifts in terms of things being 'hot' and 'cold' to us, and how they form centres of dynamic energy. However, there is no attempt here to link this to an underlying neurophysiology – as he had attempted in certain sections of *Principles* – these centres are now simply metaphoric. He writes of his language use: 'Whether such language be rigorously exact is for the present of no importance. It is exact enough, if you recognize from your own experience the facts which I seek to designate by it'.[38] Thus the purpose of psychological language here is *evocation*. What is proffered by way of explanation – hot, cold, centres of dynamic energy, the 'hackneyed symbolism of a mechanical equilibrium' and so on – is not presented in an ontological sense, but in a metaphorical one. The use of language in a non-ontological manner shifts the status of psychology. It no longer sets psychology above what it sets out to study, in imitation of how sciences are imagined to function. Psychological language is not privileged in any way as a form of translation over the languages it studies – in this case, the first-hand testimonials. Richer and more articulate descriptions take the place of explanations. James makes this suspension of ontological language explicit in the following statement:

> When I say 'Soul', you need not take me in the ontological sense unless you prefer to; for although ontological language is instinctive in such matters, yet Buddhists or Humians can perfectly well describe the facts in the phenomenal terms which are their favourites.[39]

This suspension explains how James can go on to use such terms as 'consciousness' in his late writings even after his banishment of consciousness in 'Does consciousness exist?' His later usages do not represent a contradiction or recantation, rather they represent a different form of usage.

The second aspect to which I wish to draw attention are moments where James stands outside psychology and looks at its assumptions and modes of operation. In his discussion of conversion he refers to the 'vague and abstract language of psychology' as constituting 'our own symbolism'.[40] He then compares the views of psychology and religion:

> Psychology and religion are thus in perfect harmony up to this point, since both admit that there are forces seemingly outside of the conscious individual that bring redemption to his life. Nevertheless psychology, defining these forces as 'subconscious', and speaking of their effects as due to 'incubation', or 'cerebration', implies that they do not transcend the individual's personality' and herein she diverges from Christian theology, which insists that they are direct supernatural operations of the Deity.[41]

Here, he suspends the ontological hypostatisations of psychology, and looks on it as a system on a par with Christian theology, without privileging either. Each can be described from the outside as a self-enclosed symbolic system with their ontological postulates.

These elements of James's descriptive psychology are developed in 'The energies of men'. In its quest for what makes possible the renewal of energy, this essay can be considered a continuation of the *Varieties*. James opens this essay by distinguishing between structural and functional psychology. This corresponded to the difference between the analytical and the clinical points of view in psychological observation. Clinical conceptions are vaguer and more adequate, more concrete and of more practical consequence. He champions the value of functional psychology, and in particular, the 'vagueness' of its language use:

> The terms have to remain vague; for though every man of woman born knows what is meant by such phrases as having a good vital tone, a high tide of spirits, an elastic temper, as living energetically, working easily, deciding firmly, and the like, we should all be put to our trumps if asked to explain in terms of scientific psychology just what such expressions mean. We can draw some child-like psychophysical diagrams, and that is all. In physics the conception of 'energy' is perfectly defined. It is correlated with the concept of 'work'. But mental work and moral work, although we cannot live without talking about them, are terms as yet hardly analyzed, and doubtless mean several heterogeneous elementary things . . . it is obvious that the intuitive or popular idea of mental work, fundamental and absolutely indispensable as it is in our lives, possesses no degree whatever of scientific clearness to-day.[42]

The 'psychology' already present in 'intuitive or popular' ideas is championed over 'scientific clearness'. The task then would be one of making this implicit 'psychology' more explicit. Thus functional psychology simply renders everyday language use more articulate, rather than attempting, as does structural psychology, to translate it into the terms of an underlying fundamental ontology.

One may pose the question: have structural, ontological psychologies always actually been functional psychologies, in James's terms, albeit impoverished ones, enabling people to transform their experiences and the languages for talking about them, despite their aspirations to form general universal ontologies? The conceptual frameworks of structural psychologies, whilst intended to have an explanatory power above that of everyday language, have been metaphorised and reabsorbed into the latter. Viewed functionally, the 'laws' of structural psychology become practical maxims and aphorisms. All that is left today of Mesmer's system of animal magnetism is the metaphoric description of personalities as 'magnetic' and 'mesmerising' – linguistic fossils of a grand monistic medical physics. A similar fate is now befalling psychoanalysis.

The question that then arises is whether this characterisation of James's procedure in the *Varieties* and after may have a wider validity in characterising the workings of psychologies. To take up this up, one needs to consider the question of the malleability of experience in James.

James and contemporary mind-cure

Given the multiplicity of disciplines and practices that have gone under the name of psychology, it is hazardous to attempt general statements and characterisations of 'psychology'. Thus in the following I am principally, though not exclusively, concerned with the psychotherapies: those contemporary mind-curers who form the modern-day analogue and indeed the heirs of the mind-curers studied by James in the *Varieties* under the rubric of the religion of the healthy-minded.[43]

From the outset of his interest in hypnosis, James was struck by the variability of trance states and the difficulty of constructing theories identifying the essential characteristics of the trance. He concluded his 1886 'Report on hypnotism' (written with Gouverneur Carnochan) by noting:

> Our experience has impressed upon us the variability of the same subject's trance from one day to another. It may occur that a phenomenon met with one day, but not repeated, and therefore accounted a mere coincidence, is really due to a particular phase of the trance, realized on that occasion, but never again when sought for.[44]

Thus any attempt to make an epistemological object out of the trance was beset by its variability. The following year, he concluded 'Reaction-time in the hypnotic trance', by writing: 'The only lesson of the facts I report seems to be that we should beware of making rash generalizations from few cases about the hypnotic state. That name probably covers a very great number of different neural conditions'.[45] If the hypnotic state was actually a name for different conditions, its use would serve to conceal the fact that these conditions might call for distinct explanations – which was James's critique of the concept of the unconscious.

In *Principles*, James discussed the conflict between the late nineteenth century hypnotic schools, which constituted the genesis of modern psychotherapy. Concerning differing theories of the trance state, he wrote:

> The three states of Charcot, the strange reflexes of Heidenhain, and all the other bodily phenomena which have been called direct consequences of the trance-state itself, are not such. They are products of suggestion, the trance-state having no particular outward symptoms of its own; but without the trance-state there, those particular suggestions could never have been successfully made.[46]

Whilst conceived in a realist mode, psychological theories actually created new forms of experience, due to the impressionability of the trance state. This enabled any theory to be 'realised'. James trenchantly points out the pitfalls that this held for the possibility of developing an objective account of hypnosis:

> Any sort of personal peculiarity, any trick accidentally fallen into in the first instance by some one subject, may, by attracting attention, become stereotyped, serve as a pattern for imitation, and figure as the type of a school. The first subject trains the operator, the operator trains the succeeding subjects, all of them in perfect good faith conspiring together to evolve a perfectly arbitrary result.
>
> With the extraordinary perspicacity and subtlety of perception which subjects often display for all that concerns the operator with whom they are en rapport, it has hard to keep them ignorant of anything which he expects. Thus it happens that one easily verifies on new subjects what one has already seen on old ones, or any desired symptom of which one may have heard or read.[47]

His discussions of theories of trance are not solely concerned with one phenomenon, but with the malleability of experience to conceptual reframing in general. This malleability explains the endless generation of multiple psychological and psychotherapeutic systems producing 'perfectly arbitrary results' – a history of psychotherapy in a nutshell. It explains the inevitable failure of such systems to form a universal psychology and general ontology. For James, the hypnotic schools had led to a potentially limitless proliferation of contradictory systems, each appealing to individual testimony as their proof.[48] His critique focused on their means for verification. There was no theory that could not be 'verified' by the procedures being used.

It is important to note that James's conception of the malleability of experience and its receptivity to conceptual remodelling is not part of a human-natural science division. Rather, it is an aspect of a more generalised modelling. As early as 1881, he wrote:

> While I talk and the flies buzz, a sea-gull catches a fish at the mouth of the Amazon, a tree falls in the Adirondack wilderness, a man sneezes in Germany, a horse dies in Tartary, and twins are born in France. What does that mean? Does the contemporaneity of these events with one another and with a million others as disjointed, form a rational bond between them, and unite them into anything that means for a world?
>
> Yet such collateral contemporaneity, and nothing else, is the real order of the world. It is an order with which we have nothing to do to get away from it as fast as possible ... we break it into histories, and we break it into arts, and we break it into sciences; and then we begin to feel at home. We make ten thousand separate serial orders of it, and on any one of these we react as though the others did not exist. We discover among its various parts relations that were never given to sense at all (mathematical relations, tangents, squares, and roots and logarithmic functions), and out of an infinite number of these we call certain ones essential and lawgiving and ignore the rest. Essential these relations are, but only for our purpose, the other relations being just as real and present as they ... the miracle of miracles, a miracle not yet exhaustively cleared up by any philosophy, is that the given order lends itself to the remodelling. It shows itself plastic to many of our scientific, to many of our aesthetic, to many of our practical purposes and ends.[49]

Psychologies have shown themselves remarkably successful at remodelling the chaos of the collateral contemporaneity of experience into serial orders. There are few aspects of experience that have not been multiply traversed by the encompassing arcs of rival psychological systems. Yet what is one to make of the collateral contemporaneity of psychologies, and what is the status of the appeal to individual testimony as their evidential support?

Revelation and validation

To take up these questions, one may consider James's discussion of mysticism in the *Varieties*. For a number of contemporary scholars, the status of the term 'mysticism' is as problematic as the term 'religion'.[50] Again, one can bracket out the problems surrounding the generic category of mysticism, and consider the types of experiences that James is studying: namely, experiences that are authoritative over the individuals who have them. In other words, James is concerned with experiences that are considered to be self-authenticating, such as states of transformation. Of such experiences, James writes: 'No authority emanates from them which should make it a duty for those who stand outside of them to accept their revelations uncritically'.[51] James's attitude towards such experiences is twofold: on the one hand, he affirms the reality of the experiences in question, but on the other, refrains from taking the conclusions drawn from them as legislative. He adds that those who don't have revelations must decide that as the various revelations corroborate incompatible theological doctrines, 'they neutralise each other and leave no fixed result'.[52] Thus if we embrace any one of them 'we do so in the exercise of our individual freedom'.[53] James here seems to sharply distinguish between what should be regarded as constituting general ontology – and hence recognised by all – and the optional ontologies (or 'overbeliefs', in James's expression) wherein everyone should be left free to make one's own choices.

The theories of the various schools of psychotherapy provide a set of narratives concerning the cause of illness or distress and how its resolution may be effected, with plot templates in the form of case histories. These transformation narratives are in turn linked to what are claimed to be universal models of human functioning. The self-authenticating nature of the transformative experiences undergone by individuals is taken as the proof of the ontologies in question. Thus we are faced with the transformations of experience generated by the psychotherapies on the one hand, and, on the other, by the positing of ontologies (forces, mechanisms, structures of the chronically overpopulated inner world) in the continued pursuit of a unitary science. This has led to the efflorescence of multiple optional ontologies, which have been embraced by large-scale social groupings. However, in the main, these tend to the monistic form, akin to the absolute idealism critiqued in *A Pluralistic Universe*. As James suggests, those who have not had such experiences should be under no obligation to accept the legislative universalism of such revelations.

For James, evaluation is by way of pragmatism. In the *Varieties*, this features as the judgement of the validity of religious experiences. Pragmatism is often understood in an individual sense. However, it is important to note that the judgement of validity in the *Varieties* is not by the subjects themselves (which is not James's primary concern) but by others. Valuation concerns what *we* should make of their experiences. It is important to stress this social dimension of pragmatism. As James states in *Pragmatism*:

> The truth of an idea is not a stagnant property inherent in it. Truth happens to an idea. It becomes true, is made true by events. Its verity is in fact an event, a process: the process namely of its verifying itself, its veri-fication. Its validity is the process of its valid-ation.[54]

A process of validation or verification is a way of describing how *practices* establish their truths. In his discussion of pragmatism's conception of truth, James stresses that truth in science requires 'consistency with previous truth and novel fact'. Theories that work are those that 'mediate between all previous truths and certain new experiences'.[55] Thus the degree of rigour of the verification process of a particular ontology-making practice would consist in the extent to which it successfully enables this consistency and mediation.

As we have seen, James's critique of the hypnotic schools – which formed the template of modern psychotherapeutic schools – focused on the failings of their means of verification. The inability to provide any check or comparative framework, would, from this perspective, constitute a lack of rigour. However, viewed from a functional perspective, the multiplicity of systematised articulations of experience offered by psychologies is to be welcomed. James suggests as much in the *Varieties* in his consideration of the multiplicity of religious formations:

> Is the existence of so many religious types and sects and creeds regrettable? To these questions I answer 'No' emphatically. And my reason is that I do not see how it is possible that creatures in such different positions and with such different powers as human individuals are, should have exactly the same functions and the same duties. No two of us have identical difficulties, nor should we be expected to work out identical solutions.[56]

The same would then apply for the varieties of psychologies, understood in functional terms. They may be understood as vehicles which have provided systematised articulations of experience. Paradoxically, it is the very failure of psychologies to establish a general ontology, in a structural sense, that has given such functional utility to the efflorescence of optional ontologies which the self-same psychologies have generated.

Notes

1. Parts of this section were elaborated in the context of a work in progress with Mikkel Borch-Jacobsen on the historiography of psychoanalysis, whom I would like to thank. On the formation of modern psychology, see my *Jung and the Making of Modern Psychology: The Dream of a Science* (Cambridge, Cambridge University Press, 2003).
2. William James, *Talks to Teachers on Psychology and to Students on Some of Life's Ideals* (Cambridge, MA, Harvard University Press, 1983), p. 14. References to James's work are given to the Harvard edition, with the exception of the *Varieties*, where references have been given to *The Varieties of Religious Experience: Centenary Edition*, with a foreword by Micky James and new introductions by Eugene Taylor and Jeremy Carrette (London, Routledge, 2002).
3. Isabelle Stengers, *Power and Invention: Situating Modern Science*, trans. P. Bains (Chicago, University of Minnesota Press, 1998), p. 81.
4. Ibid., p. 82.
5. The stress on *practices* of ontology-making is linked to what Andrew Pickering describes as the shift from a representational to a performative tense in science studies (*The Mangle of Practice: Time, Agency and Science*, Chicago, Chicago University Press, 1995).
6. Franz Brentano, *Psychologie vom empirischen Standpunkt* (Leipzig, Felix Meiner, 1925), p. 36.
7. *Ibid.*, p. 2.
8. 27 August, ed. Ignas Skrupskelis and Elizabeth Berkeley, *The Correspondence of William James, Volume 7, 1890–1894* (Charlottesville, University Press of Virginia, 1999), p. 89.

9. James, *Psychology: Briefer Course* (Cambridge, MA, Harvard University Press, 1984), pp. 400–1.

10. See for instance, Max Dessoir, *Outlines of the History of Psychology* (New York, Macmillan, 1912); James Mark Baldwin, *History of Psychology: A Sketch and an Interpretation*, 2 vols (London, Watts & Co., 1913).

11. On this question see Roger Smith, 'Does the history of psychology have a subject?' *History of the Human Sciences* 1, 1988, pp. 147–77; on the historiography of psychotherapy, see my review of Stanley Jackson, *Care of Psyche: A History of Psychological Healing*, Medical History, 47, 1, 2003, pp. 115–17.

12. James, 'A plea for psychology as a "natural science"', *Essays in Psychology* (Cambridge, MA, Harvard University Press, 1983), p. 270.

13. James, *The Principles of Psychology* (Cambridge, MA, Harvard University Press, 1981), p. 92.

14. James, 'A plea for psychology as a "natural science"', p. 272.

15. Ibid., p. 277.

16. 24 January, *The Correspondence of William James, Volume 7, 1890–1894*, pp. 485–6.

17. James, *Talks to Teachers on Psychology*, p. 15.

18. William Stern, 'Die psychologische Arbeit des neunzehnten Jahrunderts, insbesondere in Deutschland', *Zeitschrift für pädogigische Psychologie und Pathologie*, 2, 1900, p. 415.

19. Ibid.

20. On the denial of historicity to material objects and entities, see Bruno Latour, 'The historicity of things', *Pandora's Hope: Essays on the Reality of Science Studies* (Cambridge, MA, Harvard University Press, 1999), pp. 145–73.

21. Timothy Fitzgerald, *The Ideology of Religious Studies* (Oxford, Oxford University Press, 2000), p. 4.

22. Richard King, *Orientalism and Religion: Post-colonial Theory, India and 'The Mystic East'*, (London, Routledge, 1999), p. 60.

23. James, 'Is life worth living?', *The Will to Believe* (Cambridge, MA, Harvard University Press, 1979), p. 48.

24. James, *Varieties*, p. 139.

25. Ibid., pp. 29–30.

26. Ibid., p. 32.

27. James, *Essays in Morality and Religion* (Cambridge, MA, Harvard University Press, 1982), p. 103.

28. On the relation of the *Varieties* to contemporary 'religious-like' movements, see Clifford Geertz, 'The pinch of destiny: religion as experience, meaning, identity, power', in *Available Light: Anthropological Reflections on Philosophical Topics* (Princeton, Princeton University Press, 2000), pp. 167–86; and Ramón del Castillo, 'Varieties of American Ecstasy', in *Streams of William James*, 5, 2, European Perspectives on 'The Varieties of Religious Experience', Guest editor Felicitas Kraemer, pp. 1–4, forthcoming. This volume also contains papers presented at the centenary conference.

29. On criticisms of James, see Carol Zaleski, 'Speaking of William James to the cultured among his despisers,' in Donald Capps and Janet Jacobs, (eds) *The Struggle for Life: A Companion to William James's 'The Varieties of Religious Experience'* (Society for the Scientific Study of Religion, Monograph Series 9, 1995) pp. 40–60.

30. Eugene Taylor, *William James on Consciousness beyond the Margin* (Princeton, Princeton University Press, 1996). See also his contribution to this volume.

31. David Lamberth, *William James and Metaphysics of Experience* (Cambridge,

Cambridge University Press, 1999), pp. 97–145. See also his contribution to this volume.

32. 25 February. *The Varieties of Religious Experience* (Cambridge, MA, Harvard University Press, 1985), appendix, p. 553.

33. *Varieties*, pp. 13ff. On this question, see Jeremy Carrette, 'The return to James: psychology, religion and the amnesia of neuroscience', introduction to the centenary edition of the *Varieties*.

34. (Apropos of Freud.) James to Flournoy, 28 September 1909, Robert Le Clair (ed.), *The Letters of William James and Théodore Flournoy*, (Madison, University of Wisconsin Press, 1966), p. 224.

35. Reproduced in Donald Capps, '"That shape am I": The bearing of melancholy on James's struggle with religion', Donald Capps and Janet Jacobs (eds), *The Struggle for Life: A Companion to William James's 'The Varieties of Religious Experience'*, pp. 105–6.

36. It is important to note that James's concept of character in the *Varieties* is not purely subjective, as subsequent psychologies would conceive it. Character here stands for a particular outlook on life, a particular philosophy.

37. James, *Varieties*, p. 155.

38. Ibid.

39. Ibid., p. 154.

40. Ibid., p. 166.

41. Ibid., p. 167.

42. James, 'The energies of men', *Essays in Religion and Morality* (Cambridge, MA, Harvard University Press, 1982), p. 144.

43. On the significance of late nineteenth-century mind-cure in the genesis of modern psychotherapy see Eric Caplan, *Mind Games: American Culture and the Birth of Psychotherapy*, (Berkeley, University of California Press, 2001).

44. James, *Essays in Psychology*, p. 197.

45. Ibid., p. 203.

46. James, *The Principles of Psychology*, 2 (Cambridge, MA, Harvard University Press, 1981), p. 1201.

47. Ibid., pp. 1201–2.

48. At the same time, James valued the therapeutic utility of hypnotism. On 26 November 1890, he wrote to his sister Alice James, 'If I were you, I would seriously try *hypnotism*, which might do you good.' *The Correspondence of William James, Volume 7, 1890–1894*, p. 114. In his review of Pierre Janet's work, James contended that the 'possible application to the relief of human misery' was the 'really important part of these investigations.' ('The hidden self,' p. 265). In the *Varieties*, James criticised the over-extension of the word 'suggestion': 'the word "suggestion", having acquired official status, is unfortunately beginning to play in many quarters the part of a wet blanket upon investigation, being used to fend off all inquiry into the varying susceptibilities of individual cases. "Suggestion" is only another name for the power of ideas, *so far as they prove efficacious over belief and conduct*' (p. 91). In 'The energies of men' James offered the following definition of the action of suggestion: 'It throws into gear energies of imagination, of will, and of mental influence over physiological processes, that usually lie dormant' (p. 139).

49. James, 'Reflex action and theism', *The Will to Believe*, pp. 95–6. This generalised notion of the plasticity of experience is not grounded in ontological distinctions, such as the distinction proposed by Ian Hacking between 'interactive kinds' and 'indifferent kinds', *The Social Construction of What?*(Cambridge, MA, Harvard University Press, 1999), which risks falling back into a classical dichotomy

between the 'human' and 'natural' sciences, and one might add, into the dualisms which James sought to overthrow with radical empiricism.

50. See Richard King, *Orientalism and Religion: Post-colonial Theory, India and 'The Mystic East*, p. 60.
51. James, *Varieties*, p. 327.
52. Ibid., p. 396.
53. Ibid., p. 397.
54. James, *Pragmatism* (Cambridge, MA, Harvard University Press, 1975), p. 97.
55. Ibid., p. 104.
56. James, *Varieties*, p. 376.

Part II

James, psychology and religion

Chapter 3

Listening to James a century later

The *Varieties* as a resource for renewing the psychology of religion

David M. Wulff

A century after William James sailed to Edinburgh to deliver his long-aborning Gifford Lectures, his *Varieties* remains the one great classic in the psychology of religion. The *Varieties* has been reprinted far more frequently than any other book published before or since in the field, and it has been translated into more languages than any other. Moreover, in a 1970 analysis of 25 books that appeared in the field between 1950 and 1967, the *Varieties* proved to be the most frequently cited work (Grønbaek, 1970), just as in a subsequent survey of college courses on the psychology of religion, it was reportedly assigned more often than any other source (Vande Kemp, 1976). The *Varieties* alone has inspired deluxe, leather-bound editions, complete audio recordings, companion volumes (Begbie, 1909; Capps and Jacobs, 1995; see Wulff, 1995), and celebratory gatherings like this one today. A half century after the *Varieties* was published, Lawrence Grensted (1952, p. 51) remarked that the *Varieties* has 'deservedly become a classic. Few scientific books have been as brilliantly written or as widely read, and [its] influence was immediate and lasting. Still, fifty years later, [these lectures] form the necessary starting point for any serious study of the subject'.

Today, a century after its publication, we are compelled to acknowledge that, in spite of such high regard, the *Varieties* has in reality had little specific influence on the psychology of religion that followed in its wake. Scholars continue to be grateful for the prestige that James lent to the ever-struggling field and for the mellifluous prose that they are happy to quote, but from his generation to the present one, the *Varieties* has been viewed as an eccentric, even 'spooky' volume (Gale, 1999), given especially its emphasis on exceptional and often admittedly pathological phenomena. James's use of personal documents as his chief source of evidence was highly praised by Harvard psychologist Gordon Allport (1942), yet even this rare and articulate proponent of idiographic methods disdained them when it came time to do his own research on human religious propensities.

Some have argued that the *Varieties* is itself too much a personal document to provide foundations for a general psychology of religion (e.g. Strout, 1971), although an occasional individual scholar has deeply resonated with it (e.g. Hutch, 1995) and one found James's fundamental typology of the healthy-minded and sick soul a useful framework for a book-length study of the work of

30 major authors in American literature (Strandberg, 1981). Others have noted the *Varieties*'s limited Protestant Christian perspective (Goodenough, 1965), its confusing multiplicity of purpose (Wulff, 1997), its studied indefiniteness (Bruns, 1984), and its disorienting style (Ruf, 1991).

But James's great work was undercut mainly by changes in the *Zeitgeist*: the growing religious conservatism that followed the devastations of World War I, on the one hand, and the radical shifts in the intellectual climate introduced by behaviorism and positivism, on the other. The collective outcome was a greatly reduced interest in personal religious experience and a corresponding decline in the psychology of religion as a whole (Wulff, 1998). When the field underwent a revival starting around 1950, academic proponents were, with few exceptions, still in the thralldom of positivistic principles. Those who might have had reservations about these principles understood nevertheless the necessity of following them if the psychology of religion was to gain legitimacy in the eyes of other psychologists. Thus investigators pursued as faithfully as they could a program of empirical research centering on hypothesis testing through objective measurement, statistical analysis, and cautious generalization, all in relation to religion as it is ordinarily understood and practiced. James's disdain for statistical generalization and his advocacy of a qualitative, proto-phenomenological approach to exceptional religious states naturally seemed anachronistic and irrelevant.

In recent decades, however, we have been witness to radical shifts in the intellectual climate, and particularly in the philosophy of science, which have profoundly called into question the assumptions, methods, and goals of positivistic psychology. 'Critical psychologists' have systematically revisited the history of psychology, pointing out the social, political, and economic factors that, from the start, have often preempted scholarly ones in the shaping of commitments and agendas (Fox and Prilleltensky, 1997). Meanwhile, the long-sought-after goal of a unified psychology has all but been abandoned in the face of an increasingly fractionated discipline. Within the wider framework of postmodern thought, a growing number of psychologists are embracing the field's new pluralism and orienting themselves in such terms as social constructionism, hermeneutics, phenomenology, and narrative and discursive psychologies. Only slowly, however, are the implications of these perspectives working their way into mainstream psychology; psychologists of religion, concerned as they are about 'getting respect' (Batson, 1986), may be even more reluctant to embrace them.

I wish to argue today that we are at a propitious and critical moment for psychologists of religion to rethink their agendas and methods, even in radical ways, and that James's *Varieties* may provide essential leads in these reconsiderations. Like the *Varieties*, the psychology of religion has over the years pursued three separate agendas: (1) identifying and describing 'religion', the heart of which James equates with religious experience; (2) developing theories for understanding the origins and meaning of religious experience, content, and expression; and (3) investigating the correlates or consequences – the 'fruits', as James puts it – of religious attitudes and experience. These three tasks are natural and obvious ones, parallel to personality psychology's threefold agenda of accounting for the *structure* of the individual personality (in the present), its *development* (in the past), and its *dynamics* (in the immediate and more distant future). Psychology and the sciences on which it draws have come a long way since James's day, of course, but it is my view that lingering positivistic commitments and unacknowledged religious agendas have limited in significant and regrettable ways the psychology of religion's pursuit of these three tasks.

Identifying and describing religion

Let us consider first the challenge of defining religion and describing its manifestations in individual lives. Definitions of religion may be sorted into three types: (1) *conventional*, or lexical, definitions, which indicate actual historical usage; (2) *nominal* definitions, which are assigned for certain instrumental purposes and in particular contexts; and (3) *real* definitions, which claim to specify the unchanging nature of religion, typically by listing its essential features. Early comparativists and philosophers of religion thought it possible to arrive at a real definition of religion. But from the failure of these scholars to reach a consensus, the first generations of psychologists of religion concluded that definitions of religion are ultimately arbitrary – that is, nominal rather than real. So, too, James. In a long prefatory comment in the *Varieties*, he rejects as foolhardy any effort to establish a final and indisputable definition of religion's essence. Religion, he writes, 'as I now ask you arbitrarily to take it, shall mean for us the feelings, acts, and experiences of individual men in their solitude, so far as they apprehend themselves to stand in relation to whatever they may consider the divine' (1902, p. 34). This nominal definition sets the stage, then, for James's phenomenological exploration of the idiosyncratic inner worlds of exceptional religious experience.

Later in the twentieth century, however, as positivism worked its way into psychology and, by extension, into the psychology of religion, the defining of religion took a new twist. In accord with the positivist demand for operational definitions of all research variables, psychologists of religion set about to develop scales for measuring individual differences in religiousness. But rather than solving the problem of defining religion, operational definitions were in reality 'a means of getting around' the problem (Hood *et al.*, 1996, p. 7). In time, however, especially with the development of factor analysis, some empirical researchers came to see their scales and factor analytic results as a solution after all – or, if not the final answer, at least as a means toward attaining one. Just as factor analysis seems to many personality researchers to have finally revealed *the* fundamental dimensions of personality, for all time and all cultures – the so-called Big Five Factors of personality – so there is hope that modern empirical methods will eventually yield a similarly realist understanding of religion.

Meanwhile, James's definition is still widely quoted – but without the important introductory qualification: that it is arbitrary and intended for the occasion of his lectures. Moreover, whereas James's 'whatever they may consider the divine' explicitly includes whatever is considered 'most primal and enveloping and deeply true' (p. 34), whether or not it is theistic, those quoting his definition today frequently come round to equating it with God. And in contrast to James's frequent references to diverse religious traditions stand contemporary scales and factors that were derived from – and hence are only usable with – traditional Protestant Christians. James himself has been criticized for his use of Protestant categories, but at least he expressed regret that personal documents were not available in greater abundance from persons representing other traditions.

The growing tendency today for many to prefer the term 'spirituality' over 'religion', equating spirituality with deep, inner experience that may have no other-worldly object at all, and religion with conventional, usually theistic creeds and rituals, could draw contemporary psychologists of religion closer to James's point of view. Instead, however, these researchers have set about to operationalize spirituality as well, but so far with statements that sound awfully close to those of conventional religiosity measures. The problem is that, whereas most persons on the street today *do* think that religion and spirituality have somewhat different if hard-to-specify meanings, they also see them as overlapping to a large degree; most participants in North American surveys consider themselves to be *both* religious *and* spiritual. It is that distinct minority of unconventional participants who think of themselves as spiritual but *not* religious that initially gave the term 'spirituality' its contemporary currency. But conservative religious researchers and their sponsoring agencies are promoting it as well, for it sounds less sectarian and more scientific – and hence research on it is more fundable by government agencies, more publishable by secular publishers and organizations, including the American Psychological Association, and more saleable to a wide range of consumers.

I recommend that we return to James's good example. He defines religion largely as it was originally understood, according to the late historian of religion, Wilfred Smith (1963), as *experience* rather than as the reified systems of others' beliefs. Spirituality, it is clear, is for James a very close synonym, although he most often uses it in the *Varieties* in its adjectival form, spiritual. He refers, for example, to 'spiritual emotions', 'spiritual capacity', and 'spiritual vitality'. For James, the spiritual refers to the heart of the religious life when it is authentic – that is, when it is grounded in genuine, first-hand experience. When religion becomes an 'affair of outer works and ritual and sacraments' (p. 173), in contrast, it is at risk of losing its grounding. But it is just these conveniently observable and quantifiable factors that have most often served psychologists of religion to operationalize religion.

The religiousness or spirituality that James valorized cannot be so easily quantified. Indeed, the only way to take it into account, he says, is through personal documents – unless one can write about it at first hand, from one's own experience, which James claimed he could not. In either case, one is in the realm of qualitative data collection and analysis, with which most psychologists today have little familiarity. Qualitative data *have* been collected by psychologists of religion from time to time, as in the case of Walter Pahnke's famous Good Friday experiment, following which the participants were interviewed and then asked to write about their experiences. But as is commonly the case, Pahnke started with a specific hypothesis – that the entheogen psilocybin would trigger phenomena akin to classic mystical experience. Moreover, the qualitative data he collected were reduced to quantified ratings, which were subjected in turn to inferential statistical analysis. Such a strategy is what Kidder and Fine (1987) characterize as qualitative research with a 'little q'. 'Big Q' research, in contrast, starts not with an hypothesis but with a question, or an even less formulated questioning attitude; it is open-ended and inductive, concerned with gaining new insights rather than deductively confirming existing suppositions. Furthermore, it avoids the reduction of the data to preexisting categories or to numbers, seeking instead to allow the contours, textures, and meanings of the participant's experience to reveal themselves as faithfully as possible.

James's qualitative approach is of the Big Q variety, although James shows little of the preoccupation with methodology that is understandably typical of Big Q researchers today. Introspection, he observes in *The Principles of Psychology* (1890), was the leading method in psychology, and James used it with extraordinary sensitivity and skill. But as a professed outsider to religious experience, he was compelled in the *Varieties* to resort to a vicarious phenomenology instead, one based on generously quoted personal documents written by persons deep in the religious life. Beyond personal documents, his only explicit methodological device is the so-called method of serial study, according to which a phenomenon is illuminated by placing it in its series, from the mildest hint to the fullest expression. In conjunction with this comparative approach, then, James applied his own astute observations and reflections.

Few, if any, psychologists of religion today may hope to approximate James's level of perspicacity, but the virtual explosion of interest in qualitative methods in recent years opens up opportunities to follow in his footsteps as never before. Published in the last few years, for example, are several substantial handbooks on qualitative research methods (e.g. Denzin and Lincoln, 2000), the some 50–volume series on specific qualitative methods brought out by SAGE, and a growing number of books on qualitative research specifically in psychology. One such book, to illustrate, features grounded theory, phenomenology, case studies, discursive analysis, Foucauldian discourse analysis, and memory work, while also bringing into discussion such allied topics as social constructionism and hermeneutics (Willig, 2001). It would be an interesting exercise to take note of the various ways that James anticipated these contemporary frameworks – in his explicit acknowledgment, for example, of the inescapable influence of an investigator's personal point of view and of a time's accumulative experience and perspective, which together, he says, qualify all insights as provisional. But for our purposes, I simply want to emphasize the new opportunities and resources for building on the methodological foundations that James laid one hundred years ago and thus for returning religious experience to the prominence that he gave it.

The search for religion's origins

James thought that the second task he set for himself in the *Varieties* – reaching 'existential judgments' about the causal origins of religious experience – to be a particularly difficult one, given that introspection reveals little about such causes and that scientists then knew nothing about the cerebral correlates of the subconscious processes that were James's chief theoretical construct. Ignorance of such correlates forced him, he says, to resort to the use of mechanical or spatial metaphors while yet recognizing their illusory character.

Yet even if we truly understood the origins or conditions of a phenomenon, James argued, such understanding would not provide a sufficient basis for judging the phenomenon's value – its significance, importance, or meaning. James is famous for his sharp rebuke of unidentified contemporaries who resorted to what James called *medical materialism* – the discrediting of religion by tracing one or another of its manifestations to known bodily disturbances. All states of mind, even the scientist's and the atheist's, are dependent on organic conditions, James points out. The significance of such states, he added, can only be judged by their fruitfulness in individual lives.

Today, of course, we know a great deal more about the structure and functioning of the brain, and recent research has even uncovered consistent correlates of certain religious states. But unlike James's contemporaries, especially the French psychopathologists, at least a few neuroscientists today are inclined to see such correlates as evidence *for* the veridicality of religious experience if not even the existence of God. Most prominent is the work of Newberg and d'Aquili (Newberg, d'Aquili and Rause, 2001; d'Aquili and Newberg, 1999) based on brain-imaging of meditating Buddhists and Franciscan nuns at prayer. They report uncovering 'solid evidence that the mystical experiences of our subjects – the altered states of mind they described as the absorption of the self into something larger – were not the result of emotional mistakes or simple wishful thinking, but were associated instead with a series of observable neurological events … In other words, mystical experience is biologically, observably, and scientifically real' (Newberg, d'Aquili and Rause 2001, p. 7). Later in their book, Newberg, d'Aquili and Rause acknowledge that their neurological model 'proves nothing about the ultimate nature of Absolute Unitary Being.' Yet they hasten to add that 'our work has convinced us that the mystics, at the very least, are not delusional or psychotic: They are certain beyond a shadow of a doubt that their experiences are real' (p. 151).

Even without the illogic in these statements – for 'emotional mistakes' must also be associated with neurological events and hence are 'scientifically real,' too, and psychotics often find their experiences compellingly real—James, if he were living today, might well be tempted to coin a new, parallel phrase: *medical spiritualism*. In this case, the finding of neurological correlates is thought somehow to provide support for religious convictions and even 'a biological framework within which all religions can be reconciled' (Newberg, d'Aquili and Rause, 2001, p. 168). Such convictions have spawned a new field, neurotheology, as if neuroscience can now cast light on the nature of God. The temptation to draw conclusions about the veridicality of experience from knowledge of the bodily correlates of such experience is clearly a timeless one, and James remains a helpful commentator on it.

The quest for religion's fruits

If there is any part of James's agenda in the *Varieties* that researchers in our time have adopted, it is his emphasis on evaluating religion in terms of its fruits. Like James, who wished through his lectures to convince sophisticated contemporaries that religion has a vital function in human lives, psychologists of religion in the last third of the twentieth century dedicated themselves to fostering a positive image of religion, especially among their fellow psychologists. Whereas James, however, evaluated religion in terms of its most important representatives – the saints who combine in approximately equal measure a temperamental disposition toward exceptional states and basic human intelligence – today's researchers have followed the Clark School's model of sampling ordinary piety. Disturbed by the consistent early findings that religiosity tends to be accompanied by negative social attitudes – authoritarianism, ethnocentrism, dogmatism, and prejudice – these researchers found a solution in distinguishing different types of religiosity – most famously, the distinction between the intrinsic, or genuine, religious orientation and the extrinsic, self-serving orientation. The later, inauthentic type, they predicted and largely demonstrated, is responsible for religion's association with negative social attitudes, although the indiscriminately pro-religious, who endorse both extrinsic and intrinsic items, are more prejudiced still.

In the last couple of decades, however, the search for religiosity's correlates has shifted away from social attitudes to the more individualistic, even narcissistic dimensions of health, both mental and physical. Being religious, especially through participation in a religious community and religious services, is reported to be associated with a lower rate of mortality and higher scores on measures of physical and psychological well-being (Plante and Sherman, 2001). Some researchers (e.g. Koenig, 2002) are confident enough in these associations to recommend that doctors and therapists encourage their patients to become more religiously involved – a distinctly extrinsic point of view, we might note.

Although James was himself interested in the sometimes dramatic personal gains offered by religion, especially for those sufferers he called sick souls, his defense of religion finally rests on its capacity to transform the world. He had little positive to say of that majority of persons who are religious simply out of habit, and he acknowledged that those who are intensely religious are prone to aggression and intolerance; but without the saint's uncommon virtues – loving tenderness, equanimity, patience, generosity, simplicity, truthfulness, and self-sacrifice – says James, the world would be an infinitely worse place in which to live.

It is time, I believe, for psychologists of religion to return to James's question, but addressed now in relation to the world in which *we* live. Most conspicuously, there is September 11, when a small number of radical Islamic fundamentalists exploited modern technology to take down the World Trade Center and the thousands of people who were unable to flee it. Today's resurgent fundamentalism, evident in various religious traditions, is a phenomenon of momentous consequences – some, like 9/11, conspicuous and catastrophic, others more private and quietly insidious.

Three weeks ago, for an example of the latter, a 29-year-old member of a small religious sect near where I work was sentenced to life in prison for starving his 10–month-old son to death. The man's sister had delivered a 'leading', as they call it, according to which God had found the man's wife to be prideful and vain. To atone for these sins, their young son was no longer to receive solid food but only his mother's milk. Pregnant with another child, the mother was apparently unable to produce enough milk to sustain the boy's life. He died from severe malnutrition after 51 days. What is unusual about this case is not, unfortunately, the death of the child after being denied the essentials of life – over the past 30 years hundreds of children have died in the United States for lack of medical care or food because of their parents' religious convictions (Asser and Jenny, 2002) – but the fact of serious legal charges against the parents and the boy's aunt and the initial conviction (Parker, 2002).

At about the same time, American newspapers reported from the state of Utah the case of a 20-year-old woman who, pregnant with a third child, had fled with her one- and two-year-old children from her polygamous husband's household, which consisted of three wives and their 20 children. A member of a breakaway Mormon sect known as the Fundamentalist Church of the Latter Day Saints, the woman had, as a 16-year-old, been threatened with the loss of her salvation if she did not marry her 32-year-old husband-to-be rather than the young man she loved. At issue in this case is the sexual abuse of the 16-year-old girl and the neglect and mistreatment of 20 children, who were often supervised by but one adult (Liptak, 2002). I cite it, however, for another reason: the sheer number of children in a single family that promises to produce many more. In the same issue of the *New Year Times* describing this case, which was brought to light by a custody battle, was an article reporting startling and deeply disturbing evidence of global warming. Average temperatures in the state of Alaska have risen 7 degrees over the last 30 years, to the point that the permafrost on which houses and roads are built is no longer permanent. In addition to crumbling houses and sagging roads there are dying forests – 35 million trees have succumbed to a beetle infestation prompted by the higher temperature – catastrophic fires, and possible disruption of marine life. Alaska, it is said, is more affected by global warming than any other place in the world (Egan, 2002).

Each of us, it is estimated, contributes 20 tons of carbon dioxide to the atmosphere in a lifetime. Thus the family in Utah, in a community with thousands of other adherents, promises to add more than one million pounds of this greenhouse gas, and that's without taking into account the generations to follow. This disposition, often on theological grounds, to produce large numbers of children is not limited to small sects like this one, however, but can be found in larger religious groups throughout the world, including the orthodox Church of the Latter-Day Saints, the fastest-growing religious body in America.

It is obvious that the growth of technologies and the soaring world population have greatly increased the potential for destructiveness, whether intentional or not, of religious sentiments and teachings. Questions that were once largely academic – say, what factors bring about religious conversion? – have correspondingly a new urgency. What was it, investigators want to know, that brought about the conversion to Islamic militancy of the 24-year-old, apparently irreligious Tunisian who on April 11 blew himself up in a truck he parked in front of an ancient synagogue in Tunisia, killing 19 people, including 12 German tourists? But there are new questions, too, such as why martyrdom is so attractive to suicide bombers in Israel. We may also wonder how belief in a sister's reported message from God could survive over 51 days of watching one's beloved son waste away and die.

Unlike contemporary researchers, who have either ignored the dark side of religion or rationalized it as irreligion in disguise, James recognized it for what it is – a constant and integral potential. Given the magnification of this negative potential today by modern technologies, the population explosion, and widespread fundamentalist sentiments, it is time for psychologists of religion, among others, to recognize it as well. Should psychologists of religion finally embrace a more adequately encompassing understanding of religion, one that fully takes into account its profound ambivalences, and then bring to it a new openness to qualitative methods, they may well find themselves as innovators rather than imitators in the broader field of psychology, perhaps earning them at last the respect they have long yearned for.

References

Allport, G. W. (1942). *The Use of Personal Documents in Psychological Science*. New York: Social Science Research Council.

Asser, S., and Jenny, C. (2002). Child-abuse Cases: Repeal Religious-exemption Clauses. *The Providence Journal*, June 19, B6.

Batson, C. D. (1986). An Agenda Item for Psychology of Religion: Getting Respect. *Journal of Psychology and Christianity*, 5, 6–11.

Begbie, H. (1909). *Twice-Born Men: A Clinic in Regeneration*. New York: Fleming H. Revell.

Bruns, G. L. (1984). Loose Talk about Religion from William James. *Critical Inquiry*, 11, 299–316.

Capps, D., and Jacobs, J.L. (eds). (1995). *The Struggle for Life: A Companion to William James's The Varieties of Religious Experience*. West Layfayette, IN: Society for the Scientific Study of Religion.

D'Aquili, E., and Newberg, A.B. (1999). *The Mystical Mind: Probing the Biology of Religious Experience*. Minneapolis: Fortress Press.

Denzin, N.K., and Lincoln, Y.S. (eds). (2000). *Handbook of Qualitative Research* (2nd edn.). Thousand Oaks, CA: SAGE.

Egan, T. (2002). Alaska, No Longer So Frigid, Starts to Crack, Burn and Sag. *The New York Times*, June 16, 1.

Fox, D., and Prilleltensky, I. (eds). (1997). *Critical Psychology: An Introduction*. London: SAGE.

Gale, R.M. (1999). *The Divided Self of William James*. Cambridge: Cambridge University Press.

Goodenough, E.R. (1965). *The Psychology of Religious Experiences*. New York: Basic Books.

Grensted, L.W. (1952). *The Psychology of Religion*. London: Oxford University Press.

Grønbaek, V. (1970). Die heutige Lage der Religionspsychologie. *Theologische Literaturzeitung*, 95, 321–327.

Hood, R.W., Jr., Spilka, B., Hunsberger, B., and Gorsuch, R. (1996). *Psychology of Religion: An Empirical Approach* (2nd edn.). New York: Guilford.

Hutch, R.A. (1995). Over My Dead Body: A 'Common Sense' Test of Saintliness. In D. Capps and J.L. Jacobs, *The Struggle for Life* (pp. 147–162).

James, W. (1890). *The Principles of Psychology* (3 vols). Cambridge, MA: Harvard University Press, 1981 (original edition 1890).

James, W. (1902). *The Varieties of Religious Experience: A Study in Human Nature*. Cambridge, MA.: Harvard University Press, 1985 (original edition 1902).

Kidder, L.H., and Fine, M. (1987). Qualitative and Quantitative Methods: When Stories Converge. In M.M. Mark and L. Shotland (eds), *New Directions in Program Evaluation* (pp. 57–75). San Francisco: Jossey-Bass.

Koenig, H.G. (2002). *Spirituality in Patient Care: Why, How, When, and What*. Philadelphia: Templeton Foundation Press.

Liptak, A. (2002). Polygamist's Custody Fight Raises Many Issues. *The New York Times*, June 16, p. 14.

Newberg, A., d'Aquili, E., and Rause, V. (2001). *Why God Won't Go Away: Brain Science and the Biology of Belief*. New York: Ballantine Books.

Parker, P.E. (2002). Robidoux Guilty of Son's Murder: Sect Leader Faces Life in Prison. *The Providence Journal*, June 15, A1, A5.

Plante, T.G., and Sherman, A.C. (eds). (2001). *Faith and Health: Psychological Perspectives*. New York: Guilford Press.

Ruf, F.J. (1991). *The Creation of Chaos: William James and the Stylistic Making of a Disorderly World*. Albany: State University of New York Press.

Smith, W.C. (1963). *The Meaning and End of Religion: A New Approach to the Religious Traditions of Mankind*. New York: Macmillan.

Strout, C. (1971). The Pluralistic Identity of William James: A Psychohistorical Reading of *The Varieties of Religious Experience*. *American Quarterly*, 23, 135–152.

Strandberg, V. (1981). *Religious Psychology in American Literature: A Study in the*

Relevance of William James. Madrid: Jose Porrua Turanzas; Potomac, MD: Studia Humanitatis.

Vande Kemp, H. (1976). Teaching Psychology/Religion in the Seventies: Monopoly or Cooperation? *Teaching of Psychology*, 3, 15–18.

Willig, C. (2001). *Introducing Qualitative Research in Psychology: Adventures in Theory and Method*. Buckingham, UK: Open University Press.

Wulff, D.M. (1995). An Annotated Bibliography on William James's *The Varieties of Religious Experience*, with a List of English-language Editions, Audio Recordings, and Translations. In D. Capps and J. L. Jacobs, *The Struggle for Life* (pp. 281–305).

Wulff, D.M. (1997). *Psychology of Religion: Classic and Contemporary* (2nd edn.). New York: John Wiley & Sons.

Wulff, D.M. (1998). Rethinking the Rise and Fall of the Psychology of Religion. In Arie L. Molendijk and Peter Pels (eds), *Religion in the Making: The Emergence of the Sciences of Religion* (pp. 181–202). Leiden: Brill.

Chapter 4

The *Varieties*, the principles and the psychology of religion
Unremitting inspiration from a different source

Jacob A. Belzen

The paradoxical reception of the *Varieties* within the psychology of religion

There is hardly a book so well known among psychologists of religion, so widely associated with the field among the general populace, and so much read as a specimen of the psychology of religion, as *The Varieties of Religious Experience* by William James (1902/1982). The very celebration of the occasion of its publication unites us in the present volume, and rightly so, for there is no second book to be mentioned with such a status in the psychology of religion: the *Varieties* is without doubt our classic and our bestseller number one. For many years, when delivering a lecture in a more general series, and when trying to evoke interest in the psychology of religion, I encourage my audience to read it in order to get an idea of what psychology of religion is, or what kind of work is being produced by psychologists involved in this subdiscipline. I am willing to admit, however, that this proposal of mine is a kind of rhetorical trick, a hint that functions very much in the way of the *captatio benevolentiae* in the formal classic rhetoric. For in many respects – and I sincerely deplore having to make this observation or to draw this conclusion – the *Varieties* is not at all representative of the work psychologists are doing, and neither is the work representative of the field as a whole; on the contrary, good reasons could be advanced to doubt that the *Varieties* is a specimen of a psychology of whatever kind at all. Whilst I deplore having to make this observation, I would wish that other works in or from the psychology of religion were as readable as the *Varieties*, but alas, as with the majority of books on psychology, most other publications in the field are dull, or even boring, as most scientific works are. The *Varieties* is different, in many ways. However, I do not consider it my task to sing its praises, nor to analyze the reasons for its success, to raise interest in the psychology of religion with my audience or to recommend the study of the psychology, since all of that is unnecessary: the readers of this text are well acquainted with the *Varieties*, many of them may have read it more frequently, or perhaps even better, than I have. Therefore, I shall not put forward such-and-such reading of the work, no new interpretation, or whatever, but ask the perhaps slightly critical question of what the work has done to or has meant for the psychology of religion, and also whether, and if so, in what sense, the volume may be worthwhile for the subdiscipline today.

In general, I have the impression that the *Varieties*, in spite of its fame, has been ill treated within psychology of religion. First of all we should notice (a point put forward by quite a number of observers already, cf., e.g. Dittes 1973; Hood 1992, 2000; Wulff 1997), that the *Varieties*, as James's works on psychology in general, has not led to the establishment of an ever expanding body of theory, nor to the creation of any specific method or technique, and not to the development of a school either, in the sense of a coherent group of researchers or research projects, drawing on the same inspiration, using the same theories and methods, and working towards a common goal. It seems that the psychology of religion, as psychology in general, is just paying lip service to the honor and memory of the grand old man William James, without anyone's doubt, has been. This is a rather paradoxical state of affairs, with regard to methodology already nicely summarized some thirty years ago by James Dittes (1973), who wrote:

> His psychology is not employed by the field, and, far more importantly, his spirit does not inspire it. If William James is honored as the 'father' of the psychology of religion, it is in a very special sense, which can be interpreted in terms of ambivalence appropriate to the psychology of religion. He is revered as a great and distant hero but hardly heeded. He is the liberating Moses, who called down a plague on the houses of both the religious and the medical establishment and who led the psychology of religion into independent existence. But his recommendations as to how that independent existence should be conducted are ignored as thoroughly as the builders of the golden calf ignored those of the law-giving Moses. (pp. 328–329)

Also today, must of the so-called 'scientific study of religion' contradicts essential convictions of William James. Still many adhere to empiricism, objectivism and generalizibility as criteria of good scholarship in the psychology of religion. And where, in psychology in general, with still too little application within psychology of religion, new methodological vistas are being developed and tried out, there usually is no longer any reference to James and certainly not to his *Varieties*. As the compatibility of the *Varieties* with qualitative, interpretive and hermeneutical methods, under such headings as biographical analysis, N=1 methodology, case studies, document analysis, etc. is well known, I shall not deal with this issue any further. I want to point out a more theoretical issue with regard to which James has been equally ignored by numerous psychologists of religion, that is to say his observation that there exists no specific or elementary religious emotion. According to James, religious emotions are evidently distinguishable from other concrete emotions, but 'there is no ground for assuming a simple abstract "religious emotion" to exist as a distinct elementary mental affection by itself, present in every religious experience' (1902/1982, p. 28). James saw religious emotions as 'ordinary' emotions, taken from the common storehouse of emotions human beings dispose of and put in relation to a religious object. Given his clear statements, it is amazing that many psychologists of religion, even when they claim to be as phenomenologically oriented as James, have continued to work with the postulate of a specific religious emotion. In this respect, they are certainly no heirs to James, but rather to Rudolf Otto (1869–1937), the German historian of religion, who in his famous study *The Holy* (1917/1923) assumed the experience of what is sacred or holy to be a category all in its own ('*sui generis*', as he called it), a category for which he coined the neologism 'the numinous' (derived from the Latin 'numen', meaning something equivalent to the divine). Otto was part of a tradition, going back to the philosopher and theologian Friedrich Schleiermacher (1768–1834), who, trying to prevent the rationalistic and moralistic reduction of religion to worldview or to ethics, considered religion to be founded in a particular experience or feeling. As I shall point out in the next section, there are usually apologetic motivations behind this conception: the philosophers and thinkers in this tradition try to anchor religion in the mental constitution of the human being, thereby declaring it to be an element of human nature, which may then, of course, not be ignored or combated. But a century after James and so many others who have dealt with this issue (cf., e.g. recently Vergote 1996), it is amazing that this position is still being defended, precisely among those who – from a standpoint that is obviously positively inclined toward religion – claim to be phenomenologically inspired and to strive to stay close to the religious experience itself.

As an example of this still existing trend let me just refer to a recent psychological research, conducted on the European continent. In his empirical study *Religious Emotions and Religious Judgment*, Beile (1998) postulates the existence of religious emotions: emotions that would be only experienced in relation to God (p. 46). He is referring to work by Otto and Wyss (who is, however, a follower of Otto, and offers no independent viewpoints), and although he also refers to James, he seems fundamentally to misunderstand him. It is amazing how close Beile comes, in his descriptions and formulations, to James, yet without adopting his view, viz. that religious experiences are specific because of the specific context in which they occur and because of the specific intentions involved, but not because of any specific emotion that would be involved. The emotions experienced in a religious context are not religious in themselves, they are general emotions occurring in a religious context. (Obviously, it might be possible that there are emotions that function more often than other emotions in a religious context; but this is not what Beile's study shows nor what he wants to say.) It is peculiar how psychologists of religion, even when they claim to refer to James, can so fundamentally misinterpret him. On the other hand, however, many psychologists and contemporaries in general do side with him in reducing religious experience to emotional personal experiences, which are then considered to be the core and source of religion. In this regard, one would wish that psychologists of religion would have better read other phenomenologists of religion, like Otto, but also Van der Leeuw (1890–1950), Eliade (1907–1986) and many others, in order to get a better perspective on the multidimensionality of religion, on its richness in interwovenness with all kinds of aspects of life. Whatever religion is – I realize that its definition seems to be an impossibility, and also that the very word 'religion', as a Western invention, may be aptly fitted to cover the variety of forms to which it is supposed to refer, cf. Feil 1986, 1997; Haußig 1999; Kippenberg 2001 – it involves a phenomenon on a cultural level, including dimensions like organisation, ethics, specialists like priests or shamans, doctrine, *adat* (customary law), art or at least styling of places of gathering and/or of garments to be worn in liturgy, tradition, spirituality, etc., and is certainly not to be equated with or to be considered to be derived from emotion. As contemporary psychological research shows, it is rather the other way round: emotions are dependent on a cultural context, they are characterized by beliefs, judgments and desires – the content of which is not natural, but is determined by the systems of cultural belief, value and mores of particular communities. They are no natural responses elicited by natural features which a situation may possess, but socio-culturally determined patterns of experience and expression which are acquired and subsequently feature in specifically social situations (Armon-Jones 1986).

So, to conclude this first part of my argumentation, James seems to have been badly received within psychology of religion. He is being used, perhaps being abused, but not seriously listened to, neither methodologically nor theoretically: some people refer to him when they psychologistically reduce religious experience to religious emotions, but they ignore his conviction that religious emotions are religious because of the context in which they occur, and not because some emotions would be specifically religious in themselves or occurring only in religious situations. Furthermore, psychologists ignore his plea for methodological pluralism and they tend to forget his insistence that psychology cannot be conducted without maintaining fruitful relations to relevantly related disciplines like philosophy, phenomenology, history and others. The service rendered to the psychology of religion by James has been enormous: the fact that a celebrity such as he wrote about religion at the time that this subdiscipline strove to establish itself as an independent science, made religion acceptable as a subject to psychologists, and for decades psychologists of religion have been able to legitimise their research by reminding their colleagues of the *Varieties*. Besides, and perhaps even more important, this work is so well written, in such a lucid style, that it still brings support to the psychology of religion even today. On the other hand, the *Varieties* seems to fulfil for most psychologists of religion precisely the function I myself used it for so often: to capture the benevolence of the reader or the audience. James has been used as a flag, but appearances are deceptive: the cargo of the psychology of religion in general has not been what James's colors stood for.

On the psychology of religion in general

This situation being as it is, it is not to be expected that any further reference to the *Varieties*, or any new interpretation of it, will alter the course of either psychology in general or psychology of religion in particular. It is even to be doubted whether such strategies would render a service at all to the psychology of religion. Even today, at a time when religion and spirituality clearly are returning to psychology as objects of interest and research, psychology of religion is still often being looked upon with suspicion by psychologists in general. Not only is religion as a subject still embarrassing to many, but also the style found with people who call themselves psychologists of religion, and who to the field of 'religion and psychological studies' (which indeed is something other than psychology of religion), a style that is unempirical, that consists of interpreting texts, and that reminds us more of philosophy and/or literary studies than of psychology, is a cause of alienation to many psychologists in general. This is to be deplored, as psychology of religion is dependent on psychology for its viability and development. As this perhaps is a point that I should explain a little more, let me – before I get really provocative and suggest that we forget about the *Varieties* for a while – make explicit my understanding of psychology of religion.

As it happens, the enterprise of the psychology of religion is not a self-evident one, to say nothing of the fact that not too long ago certain first-rate thinkers declared it to be an impossible business. Still today the idea that religion and psychology have any connection at all has to be explained over and over to many people, not only outside the university but in the psychological laboratories as well. The fact is, however, that the connections between religion and psychology are extraordinarily numerous: religion can exert significant influence on the premises, the view of man and epistemology, on the theoretical orientation and methodology, on the way the issues are framed and the way things are organized in a psychology that labels itself a science (cf. Jones 1994, ter Meulen 1988, van Strien 1993). As a rule, certainly in its theoretical articulations, religion holds to a certain anthropology and consequently to an implicit psychology which can be made explicit and confronted or harmonized with present-day secular psychology. Psychology in turn can attend in its theories or in empirical research to the religious aspects of human conduct and experience; some parts of psychology are even specifically directed toward this end and are welcomed by some believers as furnishing insight or an instrumentarium, while others only wish to take suspicious note of it. In certain parts of the West we seem to be witnessing a historical–sociological development which consists in a tendency for psychology to take over various tasks and functions of religion and its representatives. According to some observers, psychology has even assumed the air of a (new) religion (Vitz 1994). Thus one could cite considerably more examples of various possible relations, on very different levels, between religion and psychology, without, however, necessarily having in view the *psychology of religion*. What is then psychology of religion, even taken in a narrow sense? After these initial remarks, no one should expect an all too straightforward answer (cf. Belzen 1995/1996); psychology of religion is a conglomerate of approaches, which, however, could be characterized tentatively as the effort to understand religion by means of psychology. Tautologically and simple as it sounds, I am convinced this circumscription will meet resistance from quite a number of people, but let me just proceed and explain a little further.

Psychology of religion is a subdiscipline of psychology, it is not religious psychology. The aim of psychology of religion is not to explicate psychological implications of any religious doctrine, not to advance or to increase religion, but to strive for insight into the empirical phenomena that go together under the label of religion. In principle, psychology of religion is neutral towards its object: it does not want to instigate, to promote or to defend religiosity, but neither does it want to destroy it. All of this can be done with the help of psychology, and examples abound, but the subdiscipline as such only wants to investigate. Therefore, psychology of religion is not a branch of theology, although it may be taught within theological training (which I would even recommend!). Being a part of psychology, its practice is not restricted to psychologists, however. Numerous people with another disciplinary training or institutional setting have made worthwhile contributions to the field (Belzen 2002), but in order to be regarded as a work in psychology of religion such research or publications will have to fulfill the requirements of psychology as a science. (Note, however, that these requirements are not being agreed upon by all psychologists.) Although being a subdiscipline of psychology, psychology of religion has – more often in the past than nowadays – been found with what the Germans call *Religions-wissenschaft*, with the conglomerate of scientific disciplines working on religion as an empirical phenomenon; a branch of scholarship sometimes called comparative religion, history of religion or perhaps best, sciences of religion. As there can be as many psychologies of religion as there are psychologies in general, it would be of no use to outline or even enumerate the different approaches, theories and methods found within psychology of religion. Let me remain on a more abstract level, and distinguish three kinds of psychology of religion:

1. When all kinds of theories or methods from psychology are being applied to religion, one might be allowed, in some sense, to speak of psychology of religion. Research instruments and research designs as developed within some of the major branches of psychology (like developmental psychology, brain psychology, social psychology, perception psychology, etc.) can all be used in research with religious subjects. All that concerns the human being can be involved in religiosity, and so there is no problem in taking concepts like the Oedipus complex, object relations, locus of control, social pressure, motivation, life satisfaction and subjective well-being, stress, adjustment, affective disorders, trauma and intervention, addiction, caregiving for disabled elders, abuse, burnout and the endless rest of what psychologists do research on, and to apply them to religion. The only critical remark to be

made here is that this procedure usually renders nothing specific about religion, usually we encounter in this category psychological work that does not have religion as its primary object of attention, but is focused on the elaboration of some psychological construct, method or theory. We have here forms of psychology that utilize religion, religious subjects or subjects in religious settings, as an example, but that do not focus on religion as such.

2. This focus is being found, however, with such endeavours in psychology that set out to explain religion (usually its existence, essence, origin and development). This type of psychology of religion is interesting, full of bold assertions and reasoning, and makes sometimes good (and controversial) reading. Here we find grand theories like Freud's and Jung's, but also more recent reasoning like sociobiological explanations of religion, or hypotheses about fear as the root of religion, about anxiety, guilt and deprivation, about religion as a habit, and lots of other hypotheses put forward with regard to religion's origin, maintenance and consequence. Problematic is often here the all-too-sweeping, and frequently reductionistic, character of the assertions: as if religion were nothing but, for example, longing for protection, or whatever the hypothesis concerned has put forward. Also, reasoning like this seems to transgress the boundaries of any competence psychology may have: it is not psychology's business to explain the origins or essence of cultural phenomena, other sciences may be better equipped for doing so, if at all. Next, there usually are all kinds of preconceptions involved, for example about the assumed universality of religion, which would then be certified by grounding it in some general feature of the human condition. The last reasoning may then be part of either an apologetic interest or of a critique of religion, when it is assumed that there are better solutions to the problems in the human condition than religion has to offer. (Sometimes one even finds the suggestion that the psychology as designed by theorist x or y (e.g. Jung, or some New Age thinker) would be more adequate to postmodern minds than old-fashioned religion – a rather arrogant, probably also ignorant, suggestion . . .).

3. Psychology can also strive to work with as few preconceptions as possible with regard to religion, and just try to understand religiosity as a function of the context in which it is found, if it is found. No universality of religion is assumed here, neither on the cultural nor on the personal level, but if religiosity is found with subjects from a particular (sub)culture, it – like other psychic phenomena – will be interpreted as depending on the cultural context, and the peculiarities of that culture will be explored and analyzed with the aid of psychological concepts (like narrative, habitus, activity, etc., cf. Belzen 1999a) in order to understand how the religiosity of a certain person or group has developed and how it functions. With this kind of psychology, religion as such is not explained, which is left as a task for anthropology or history. This kind of psychology needs and maintains close connections to neighboring disciplines such as those mentioned, and

sometimes seems to be no more than a psychological approach within such disciplines. The type of knowledge at which this psychology arrives will inevitably be limited and only valid in certain contexts. There is, on the other hand, no defense nor reduction of religion here: religion will be regarded as culturally pre-given, not to be utilized only as an example for a psychological theory about something else, but also taken seriously in its particularity.

The relationship between psychology of religion and psychology in general

However, with all these kinds of psychology of religion it is essential that they belong to and are part of the science of psychology. In other words: psychology of religion, in whichever way understood, is an application of 'ordinary' psychology to the specific domain that religion is. We should realize that this statement is not without its antagonists, although they may have been more numerous in the past than in the present (but cf., e.g. Vergote 1993 for a recent plea opposing the claim that psychology of religion would be an application of a more general psychology). It is, however, the position shared by James, whom the antagonists have nevertheless often claimed to be in favor of their position. There has been an old debate in, or rather on, the psychology of religion about the question of whether it would be necessary to develop a special psychology, next to an ordinary psychology, to be able to study religion. In this debate, some have assumed religion to be such a special reality, such a specific domain, that it would not be possible to study it with ordinary scientific tools. The variables, and the relationships among variables, e.g. the relation to the divine, would be unique, different from all other relationships, and therefore would require another approach than those of the psychologies studying relationships in general. This issue has been especially debated in Germany, where psychology of religion flourished until the Second World War (Belzen 1996), and where many religionists required psychologists of religion to develop particular theories and especially methods to conduct psychological research on religion (cf. Koepp 1920, pp. 21–22, 49–50). The debate never ceased, and is in some respects even still with us today. A distinction in four types of answers to the questions playing here, which has become well known, runs like this (cf. Dittes 1969; cf. also Hill 1999):

1. *Instancing* In events regarded by participants as religious, the same variables and relationships are found as in other events. This is a type of answer called 'parsimonious' by some, 'reductionistic' by others.
2. *Uniquely prominent relationships* Certain relationships among certain variables, which may exist outside religion, are particularly discernible within religious events. The relationships discerned in religion may hold in other situations, though in attenuated or masked or otherwise less observable fashion, so that their study in religion may help to illuminate other behavior.

This is analogous to the study of abnormal psychology, in which particular relationships (e.g. defensive reactions to anxiety) may be discernible and their study illuminating for normal behavior as well.

3. *Unique relationships* The basic variables in religious behavior are essentially those found in any behavior, but they interact with some variables within religion to provide relationships unlike those found elsewhere.

4. *Unique variables* The basic variables operating within religion are different and separate from those discerned outside religion.

Positions 1 and 4 are most extreme, of course. Position 1 resembles the first type of psychology of religion which I outlined above: with this type of research the focus very often is not on religion, but on the exploration of psychological variables as such, or on the validation of some theory about them. As such, however, this position remains within psychology, whereas position 4 disengaged itself from psychology: it rejects psychology as being inadequate for the exploration of the psychic dimension of religion, and requires the development of a new psychology, a psychology of a different type than that developed in the present academia. Very often this means a call for the development of a religious psychology, a type of theorizing about subjective processes involved in religion in a vocabulary derived from the religions themselves. Also some, perhaps extreme, adherents of esoteric traditions advance positions like this one, as well as some representatives of transpersonal psychologies. Most contemporary psychologists of religion belong to position 2 or 3, and this is also where William James would have been. James has been frequently misunderstood in this regard. From the facts that in his major textbook on psychology, the famous *Principles* of 1890, no chapter is devoted to religion, whereas he devoted an entire book to religion with the publication of the *Varieties*, observers have inferred that he would have developed two psychologies: one psychology, in the *Principles*, that would be able to deal with 'ordinary' life, and another psychology, in the *Varieties*, to be able to deal with religion. Yet this conclusion seems to be invalid in at least two respects. First of all, in the *Principles* James is dealing in many places with religion or religious issues. Religion is even so prevalent in the *Principles* that early reviews (among others by Stanley Hall, 1891) bemoaned both the text's religious content and its religiously toned metaphysics (Hood 2000, p. 533). Second, there are reasons to doubt whether the *Varieties* should be counted at all a specimen of a psychological work on religion. It might well be that James meant the lectures to have been precisely what the title says: an exploration of religious experiences, of course also of their emotional and personal dimension (remember that James thought emotion to be the basis of religion!), but from a philosophical perspective, aiming to be a contribution to philosophical anthropology, rather than to psychology. Let me just briefly remind you, first, that the *Varieties'* subtitle is 'a study in human nature'; second, that James apparently never intended it to be a psychological study: he states in the preface that he intended to give descriptive lectures on 'man's religious appetites' and metaphysical lectures on 'their satisfaction through philosophy', but that the psychological material he collected grew so unexpectedly that the book is now largely descriptive, and that he had no space left but for some suggestion of his philosophical conclusions, but that he hoped to state his position in a later work more clearly (James 1902/1982, pages xxxv, 520).[1] In any case, James did not develop two different psychologies in the *Principles* and in the *Varieties*; both are written from the same metaphysical and methodological presuppositions (cf. Hood 1992, 2000, 2002).[2]

If we just take a glance at the history of the psychology of religion, we see that innovations, developments and new approaches have, without exception, come into existence because of innovations and developments within psychological theories (either newly emerging ones or within some paradigm or another), not because anyone tried to construct a psychology that would be apt to deal with religion only. The effort to construct such a theory, while perhaps not impossible in itself, would place the theoretician involved outside the domain of psychology of religion: one may perhaps be doing something much more interesting or worthwhile than psychology of religion as such, but it would no longer be psychology, and by consequence no psychology of religion. If we take a well-known example like psychoanalysis or psychodynamic theories in general, we witness that interesting works in the psychology of religion came about because these theories were applied to religion. This is not to deny that innovations within psychoanalysis have come into existence since the innovators desired perhaps to work with theories that would be more adequate to conceptualize religion than the classical Freudian thought was. This certainly has been the case now and then, cf. for example, the rise of the object relations theories; but it is no argument against my more general thesis that psychology of religion is always an application of an 'ordinary' psychology to religion, and that innovations within the psychology of religion are dependent on innovations in those 'ordinary' psychologies. Psychology of religion is no enterprise on its own, and therefore the title of a book, about a decade ago, edited by Dunde (1993) is thoroughly misleading: in spite of what the title *Dictionary of the Psychology of Religion* suggests, the psychology of religion does not dispose of specific, own and unique theories, concepts or methods. Even the famous distinction between intrinsic and extrinsic religiosity (Allport and Ross 1967), a theme to which the largest portion of quantitative empirical research in psychology of religion has been related, is derived from more general talk about intrinsic and extrinsic motivation, and particularly from evaluative common-sense parlance about the 'formal religious' versus the 'authentically religious' personality as found in Allport's more general psychological theory (Allport 1937); so the distinction is not psychological in nature at all. Even Dunde's volume shows this point readily enough: not one single entry in the entire book refers to a psychological concept ('psychotherapy', 'soul/psyche' or 'psychoanalysis' are no psychological concepts); almost all of the entries refer to empirical religious phenomena (like ecstasy, faith, holiness, mysticism, etc.) – which should, of course, be studied by psychologists of religion (who don't do this enough! I complained in another place about their not doing this (Belzen, in press, a), and shall not repeat myself here).

On innovations in the psychology of religion

William James would have been among the first to admit that we need to develop such kinds of psychologies that are able to explore religion, but the kind of psychologies resulting from such efforts would still be homogenous in the sense that both religious and non-religious phenomena belong to their domain. This is also what James himself did: develop a psychology, and use it to illuminate religious phenomena. I think we should follow him on this track, and therefore my suggestion would be to turn to his psychology in general in order to achieve innovations in the psychology of religion rather than ruminate over and over again his *Varieties*. Let the *Varieties* remain what they are: *captatio benevolentiae*, appetizer, after which the real dinner still has to start. It is my conviction that James's psychological work in general still has a lot to offer to psychology, and therefore also to psychology of religion, today. In particular a second, almost perennial, debate in the psychology of religion could be settled by turning to James's *Principles*. Let me first expound this debate about the definition of religion. It has been observed before that most of the proposals to redefine the object of the psychology of religion are motivated by the desire to safeguard religion (or its equivalent as named by the new proposal concerned) and to consider it as an element of human nature (Belzen 1999a). In a plenary discussion at a symposium for European psychologists of religion a number of years ago (cf. Belzen and Lans 1986), one colleague suggested, for example, that the appropriate object for the psychology of religion would be the 'search for meaning', whether religious or not (Vergote and Lans, 1986, pp. 79–80). (Lans' reasons for this proposal were rather pragmatic: such an object would be more recognizable to colleagues, to organizations funding research, and to students without religious background.) This suggestion is indebted to a philosophical tradition that has become dominant since Kant and Schleiermacher and which aims at founding religion in some innate capacity of the human being. Well known, of course, has become the suggestion to found religion in emotion, whether a specific one or not. First suggested by Schleiermacher (with whom German theologians and psychologists of religion considered James to be compatible; the reason that they received – and even translated – him so readily, cf. Wobbermin 1906, pp. v–ix), this idea was elaborated magisterially by Rudolf Otto in his classic volume *Das Heilige* (1917/1923). As indicated already, Otto postulated a specific emotion that he called 'the numinous' which he considered to be a 'category *sui generis*'. After analyzing the numinous experience elaborately, Otto concluded that its emotional scheme is a formal a priori of man's affectivity, analogous to the Kantian a priori of reason. As a result of this emotional structure, the human being would be endowed with the sense of the Holy, in addition to being endowed with the categories of reason. Therefore, religion belongs to human nature.

When today some colleagues like Lans (in Vergote and Lans, 1986) propose that a person's search for meaning, that is, the innate tendency to make sense of an unceasingly, undifferentiated sensory input, would be the source and psychological kernel of religiosity, they are again founding religion in the person's psychic constitution, this time not in emotion, but in some cognitive faculty. This seems to be simply a variation of the tradition just mentioned, a tradition that has become dominant since the nineteenth century with the work of Darwin and his followers, who gave impetus to the idea of inherent sources of motivation, cognition and behavior. This tradition, suppressing the older empiricist tradition, ranging from the ancient Greeks to Hume (1711–1776) and Berkeley (1685–1753), postulated 'instincts' as the explanations of people being religious. Thus Le Bon (1903), at the turn of the century, proposed a 'religious sentiment' and McDougall (1909) understood religion to be an outgrowth of what he called the instincts of curiosity, fear and subjection.

The proposal to conceive of religion as founded in a more general human 'meaning-giving behavior', is a variation within this 'innate program' and articulated previously by another German scholar at the turn of the last century, Ernst Troeltsch (1865–1923), whose methodological reflections have been very influential in early *Religionswissenschaft* and psychology of religion alike (Troeltsch, 1905). Next to Kant's a prioris of scientific, ethical and teleological-aesthetical *Vernunft*, he postulated a 'religious a priori': a capability to recognize truth, even within the confusing diversity of contemporary opinions. This potential of consciousness is actualized in concrete evaluations of religious phenomena. The religious a priori is independent of the other Kantian a prioris, in the same way as religion cannot be deduced from logic, ethics or aesthetics. Whatever opinion one may have of the variations people have put forward in this line of thought, defensive motives seem to be involved. With someone like Schleiermacher this is clear enough even from the title of his publication: *Über die Religion: Reden an die Gebildeten unter ihren Verächtern* (On Religion: Speeches to its Cultured Despisers, 1799); many of the thinkers mentioned thus far started as theologians, as in a later era many psychologists of religion did; several authors in the wake of Troeltsch (e.g. Kalweit 1908) tried to use his reasoning to argue for the natural superiority of Christianity. Moreover, against the many criticisms that have been brought forward against particular forms of religion, and facing secularization and decline of church membership, quite a number of psychologists of religion obviously try to safeguard religion: Allport developed his distinction between 'extrinsic' and 'intrinsic' religion (Allport 1960) only when research indicated that religiosity correlated with ethical prejudices (cf. Allport 1962, p. 130). His differentiation restored peace of mind: 'intrinsic' religion did not show the – initially disturbing – correlation with prejudice. For the theologian and psychologist Batson, however, 'intrinsic' religiosity comes too close to evangelical fundamentalism; the 'quest' type he distinguished would not be characterized by what he perceives as the former's vices (Batson and Ventis 1982). Likewise, an increasing number of publications on mental health and psychotherapy try to show that, contrary to the disinterest of many psychologists, it is a failure to neglect or even oppose religion; these publications try to show which positive relationships (can) exist between religion and mental health, and how religion can be a beneficial factor in psychotherapy (Bhugra 1996; Randour 1993; Miller 2002; Shafranske 1996; Richards and Bergin 1997, 2000).

This assumption of founding religion in human nature can have odd implications as, for example, calling unbelievers nevertheless religious or assuming that non-religious persons would be less developed personalities. Certainly, contrary to the intentions, it might end as a very reductionistic enterprise, as, for example, when in the wake of the earlier discussion in sociology of religion on substantial versus functional definitions of religion, some psychologists of religion seem to redefine their object in order to call even attending a rock concert a modern type of, or equivalent to, attendance at a church service (Reich 1990). When, apparently, there is no religion, some theoreticians nevertheless speak of 'implicit' or 'invisible' religion. An earlier exponent of this reasoning was Erich Fromm, who defined religion as: 'any system of thought and action shared by a group which gives the individual a frame of orientation and an object of devotion' (Fromm 1950, p. 21). He himself showed the rather absurd consequences of this viewpoint, considering even the passion for money and sex or the desire for hygienic purity as instances of religion. Stretching the concept of religion in this way, these psychologists of religion might be in danger of losing their empirical object. In some contemporary corners of the psychology of religion, which draw more on psychoanalytic object-relations theories, one encounters, for example, the identification of 'faith' with a more general phenomenon like trust or confidence, considered to be indispensable for the human process of self-development (cf., for example, McDargh 1983). To some, religion and psychotherapy then almost become the same, both promoting personal integration by offering 'good relationships' with (a) God or a therapist respectively (cf., for example, Guntrip 1969; for a more general exposé, cf. Eugen 1981).

As I suggested earlier, it is my conviction that it would be better for psychology of religion to adopt a religiously neutral starting point and to drop assumptions such as human nature being inherently religious.[3] To my mind, theories and conceptions that (can) go together under the label of 'cultural psychology' provide useful tools for analyzing religiosity without being in need of questionable assumptions such as the innate character of human religiosity. At this point, I shall not try to elucidate what cultural psychology is – that would take us too far from what we are primarily dealing with. (I refer to Belzen 1997, 1999b, 2001 for exposés.) Let me just say that cultural psychology does not search inside the human being to investigate belief, feeling, reasoning and behavior, but rather tries to understand how the specific 'form of life' (Wittgenstein) in which the person is embedded constitutes and constructs feelings, thoughts and conduct. Cultural psychologists try to counterbalance the prevailing bias in psychology according to which psychological phenomena have their origin in intra-individual processes. They stress that psychological phenomena – such as attitudes, emotions, motives, perceptual outlook, forms of reasoning, memory and so on – are not just shaped by a surrounding culture, but are constituted by and rooted in particular cultural interactions. Culturally different settings require different activities, leading to different (cognitive) abilities, leading to different personalities and to different selves. Accepting that culture is a major shaping force in people's self-definition, conduct and experience requires a different kind of research than is usual in mainstream psychology of religion. The particular religious 'form of life' in which the human being is embedded can then no longer be neglected, in favor of searching some presumed inherent and invariable psychic structures. On the contrary, it is necessary to study people *engaging* in their particular 'form of life', not to take them out of it, by submitting them to experiments, tests or questionnaires. Further, it becomes necessary to study not the isolated individual, but also the beliefs, values and rules that are prevalent in a particular situation, together with the patterns of social relatedness and interaction that characterize that situation. In any case, it appears erroneous to try to study the 'individual mind' as such.

Cultural psychology was important a hundred years ago, when it had the founding father of academic psychology in Europe, Wilhelm Wundt, as its most famous representative. Developments in the twentieth century like phenomenology, social interactionism and, more recently, social constructionism and narrative psychology are clearly compatible with it. At present, cultural psychology is gaining ground rapidly again, as visible, for example, in an increasing number of publications and the establishment of scholarly infrastructure devoted to the field (cf., for example, the journal *Culture & Psychology*, published since 1995). Although James is usually not ranged under the forerunners or founding fathers of cultural psychology, many notions from his *Principles* are compatible with cultural psychological principles (perhaps precisely because this book was published at a time that psychology had not yet turned to the natural sciences as its model and had not yet locked itself into the 'laboratory'). I want to corroborate this claim by drawing attention to a recent development in the psychology of the self, one of the classic fields of psychology instigated by James, a development that is high on the contemporary cultural psychological agenda. I am referring to the emergence of the concept of the 'dialogical self' as proposed by Hermans and Kempen and as elaborated already in a number of theoretical and empirical investigations (cf., for example, the special issue of *Culture & Psychology*, 2001, 7 (3)).

In their elaboration of the self as dialogical, Hermans and Kempen first of all refer explicitly to the *Principles* of James in order to introduce the multifacetedness and the possibilities of the self. In contrast to Cartesian-inspired thinkers, James considered the self not as a unitary but as a multifaceted phenomenon when he discussed the 'rivalry and conflict of the different selves' (James 1890, p. 309). They also find support with James for the idea that some of the selves a person may have are not actual but simply possible selves (the self one would like to be or is afraid of becoming, cf. also Markus and Nurius, 1986). In the lengthiest chapter of the *Principles*, James distinguished four *constituents of the Self* ('constituents' may here be understood as 'classes' or 'categories'). The principal distinction is between the *I* on the one hand and the *empirical self* or *me* on the other hand. To the *me* belongs everything a human being may call 'mine', so not only the body, but also things like property, relationships, reputations. James divides this plurality into a *material self*, a *social self* and a *spiritual self*. To the material self belong our body, our clothes and what else we may own. The social self is the recognition we get from fellow human beings. (And properly speaking, as James himself notes, one would have to distinguish as many social selves 'as there are individuals who recognize [a person] and carry an image of him in their mind', p. 294.) By the spiritual self James understood 'a man's inner or subjective being, his psychic faculties or dispositions'. The *I*, finally, he circumscribed as: [it] 'cannot itself be an aggregate, neither for psychological purposes need it be considered to be an unchanging metaphysical entity like the Soul, or a principle like the pure Ego, viewed as "out of time". It is a *Thought*, at each moment different from that of the last moment, but *appropriate* of the latter, together with all that the latter called its own' (James 1890, pp. 400–401; italics and capitals original).

Combining these Jamesian thoughts with those of later theoreticians like George Herbert Mead (1863–1931), Michael Bakhtin (1895–1975) and Theodore Sarbin, Hermans and Kempen (1993) conceive of the self as a multiplicity of relatively autonomous *I* positions in an imaginal landscape. Drawing on Sarbin's (1986) proposal for a narrative psychology, assuming that in the self-narrative a single author tells a story about herself as actor, the authors conceive of the self as polyphonic: one and the same individual lives, or can live, in a multiplicity of worlds, with each world having its own author telling a story relatively independent of the authors of the other worlds. At times the various authors may even enter into a dialogue with one another. Moreover, the self, conceptualized in analogy with a polyphonic novel, has the capacity to integrate also the notions of imaginative narratives and dialogues. In their idea of the self, Hermans and Kempen no longer stipulate – in contrast to James and Mead – an overarching *I*, which would organize the several constituents of the *me*. Instead, the spatial character of the self leads to the supposition of a decentralized multiplicity of *I* positions that function as relatively independent authors, telling their stories about their respective *mes* as actors (Hermans and Kempen 1993). In their initial publication on the dialogical self, the authors point out three ways in which their conception differs from much of the received view in the West. In contrast to a conception of the self as individualistic, the *I* moves, in an imaginal space, from one position to another, from which different or even contrasting views of the world are possible. Second, the dialogical self is 'social', which does not mean that a self-contained individual enters into social interactions with other outside people, but that other people occupy positions in the multi-voiced self. The other person is a position the *I* can occupy and that creates an alternative perspective on the world (including the self). Finally, the conception of the dialogical self opposes the ideal of the self as a centralized equilibrium structure. Hermans and Kempen do not stipulate the self as the center of control: the different *I* positions in the self represent different anchor points, which – depending on the nature of the interaction – may organize the other *I* positions at a given point in time (Hermans, Kempen and van Loon 1992).

The dialogical self is a clear example of a cultural psychological elaboration of James's ideas about the self. It is being conceived of as evoked by culture, as structured by elements from culture, and as multiplex and changing because of a personal history within a culture at a certain sociohistorical stage. Elegantly drawing on several theories from the cultural psychological tradition, Hermans and Kempen present their Jamesian inspired conception of the self as a multiplicity of voices, as a decentralized multiplicity of *I* positions, telling stories about their respective *me*s. And important for the psychology of religion, this kind of theorizing allows for an alliance with recent development in international circles in psychology, as it allows for new ways of doing research on religion: questions about religion and the self may be asked in a new way. Moreover, this kind of cultural psychological theory enables us to get away from classic unhistorical and too little dynamic metaphysical assumptions about human nature as being inherently religious or not. As the self is being evoked and structured by a diversified cultural setting, and as religion may belong to such a cultural setting, we gain a new understanding of the emergence and development of human religiosity. When we view the self as an ensemble of relationships with 'actual' as well as 'imagined' others, from different realms, then also relationships with 'others' from history belong to the self, not only from one's personal past, but also from a mythical past or some spiritual realm. A person may maintain relationships with persons actually met, but also with persons known from stories, television, or pictures or from statues in a temple or other religious meeting place. To the extent that a person is religious, or is familiar with religious discourse and practices, she or he will be acquainted with stories about gods, spirits and saints; in other words, such a person will be familiar with religious signifiers, with whom she or he may or may not interact. Precisely to detect whether, why and to what extent one or several relationships with religious signifiers constitute an essential part of one's narrative construction of the world, what their place is in the more general organization of the self, and why, when and how such *I* positions will develop and where they will be moved to, are empirical questions that will be examined by a psychology of religion drawing on the theory of the dialogical self. Any psychology of religion employing the theory of the dialogical self will be a culturally sensitive psychology of religion, and not be in need of postulating any innate foundation for religious acting, knowing and experiencing. As I hope these few remarks make clear, the Jamesian-inspired conception of the dialogical self may also bring about innovative research in the psychology of religion (Belzen, in press, b).

Until the present day, James's work remains a source of inspiration. His conception of and way of doing psychology has proved to be inspiring throughout more than a century now. Even stronger: his *Principles* prove to be an unremitting source of inspiration to realistic developments in contemporary psychology (cf.

also the recent special issue of the journal *Theory & Psychology* (2002, *12* (2)) devoted to the dialogical self). As psychology of religion may only be advanced by orientation towards new developments in some part of psychology in general, my advice to psychologists of religion would be to also turn to James's *Principles*, or to psychologies that are elaborations of it, in order to find an approach that is different from the one dominant at present in psychology, to find new ideas and inspiration for developing forms of psychology of religion that are, again, as in James's founding days, valuable parts of the science of psychology. While his *Varieties* will continue to attract people to the psychology of religion, James's *Principles* will be available for further development into an interesting, relevant and modern psychology, a psychology that can and should be applied to religion, the perhaps most specifically human phenomenon found under the sun.

Notes

1.   Let me remind the reader that congenial contemporaries have also interpreted the *Varieties* in a similar way. Although, e.g., James Bissett Pratt (1908) did count the work among the psychology of religion, he pointed out especially that it was more than that: 'an attempt to see whether the facts studied may not be regarded as having some ultimate significance, and as bearing one way or the other on the deeper philosophical questions of religion' (p. 442).
2.   I guess that Hood would regard James to be a proponent of the third position outlined by Dittes; I am inclined to rank him with the second position (but this may be wishful thinking!) as I am probably more doubting with regard to the psychological value of the *Varieties*. I do think the work is phenomenological, but not in the sense of a phenomenological psychology as developed later in the twentieth century by, e.g., Husserl, Merleau-Ponty, Bühler, Van den Berg, Rogers and many others (Misiak and Sexton 1973), but in the sense of being descriptive and open minded in approach, perhaps to be called 'protophenomenology', at best (Wilshire 1968). Cf. also Spiegelberg (1972, 1982).
3.   To be clear: I do not assert that every psychologist of religion has the 'defense of religion' as her or his program, or starts from religious assumptions as dealt with in this chapter. Evidently, there are people publishing on, e.g. mental health and/or psychotherapy, who strive to stay strictly within a psychological framework only and who make no suggestions on a religious level to patients (cf., e.g. Rizzuto 1996; Strean 1994). Yet, in many related publications it is evident that at least one of the goals is to counterbalance (vulgarized psychological) views of religion as being neurotic, a damage to mental health, etc. One should also note, however, that very often patients themselves try to draw the therapist in some kind of religious discussion, i.e. they want 'more' than 'just' psychotherapy (cf. Kehoe and Gutheil 1993). The same trends could be witnessed within other fields of attention in psychology of religion.

References

Allport, G.W. (1937). *Personality: a psychological interpretation*. New York: Holt.
Allport, G.W. (1960). Religion and prejudice. In: *Personality and social encounter* (pp. 257–267). Boston: Beacon Press.

Allport, G.W. (1962). Prejudice: is it societal or personal? *Journal of Social Issues, 18,* 120–174.

Allport, G.W., and J.M. Ross (1967). Personal religious orientation and prejudice. *Journal of Personality and Social Psychology, 5,* 432–443.

Armon-Jones, C. (1986). The thesis of constructionism. In: R. Harré (ed.), *The Social Construction of Emotions* (pp. 32–56). Oxford: Blackwell.

Batson, C.D., and W.L. Ventis (1982). *The religious experience: A social-psychological perspective.* New York: Oxford University Press.

Beile, H. (1998). *Religiöse Emotionen und religiöses Urteil: eine empirische Studie über Religiosität bei Jugendlichen.* Ostfildern: Schwabenverlag.

Belzen, J.A. (1995/1996). Sketches for a family portrait of psychology of religion at the end of modernity. *Journal of Psychology of Religion, 4/5,* 89–122.

Belzen, J.A. (1996). Die blühende deutsche Religionspsychologie der Zeit vor dem Zweiten Weltkrieg und eine niederländische Quelle zur Geschichte der deutschen Psychologie. In: H. Gundlach (ed.) *Untersuchungen zur Geschichte der Psychologie und der Psychotechnik* (pp. 75–94). München-Wien: Profil.

Belzen, J.A. (1997). The historicocultural approach in the psychology of religion: perspectives for interdisciplinary research. *Journal for the Scientific Study of Religion, 36* (3), 358–371.

Belzen, J.A. (1999a). The cultural-psychological approach to religion: contemporary debates on the object of the discipline. *Theory and Psychology, 9,* 229–256.

Belzen, J.A. (1999b). Religion as embodiment: cultural-psychological concepts and methods in the study of conversion among 'Bevindelijken.' *Journal for the Scientific Study of Religion, 38* (2), 236–253.

Belzen, J.A. (2001). The future is in the return: back to cultural psychology of religion. In: Jonte-Pace, D. and W.B. Parsons (eds), *Religion and psychology: Mapping the terrain* (pp. 43–56). New York/London: Routledge.

Belzen, J.A. (2002). Developing scientific infrastructure: the International Association for the Psychology of Religion after its reconstitution. *Newsletter of Division 36 (Psychology of Religion) of the American Psychological Association, 27* (2), 1–12.

Belzen, J.A. (in press, a). In defense of the object: spirituality, culture and the psychology of religion.

Belzen, J.A. (in press, b). Culture and the 'dialogical self': towards a secular cultural psychology of religion. In: J. Straub, Carlos Kölbl, Doris Weidemann and Barbara Zielke (eds), *Pursuit of Meaning: Theoretical and Methodological Advances in Cultural and Cross-Cultural Psychology.* Cambridge: Cambridge University Press.

Belzen, J.A. and J.M. van der Lans (eds.), (1986). *Current issues in the psychology of religion.* Amsterdam: Rodopi.

Bhugra, D. (ed.) (1996). *Psychiatry and religion: Context, consensus and controversies.* London/New York: Routledge.

Dittes, J.E. (1969). Psychology of religion. In: G. Lindzen and E. Aronson (eds), *The Handbook of Social Psychology,* Vol. V (pp. 602–659). Reading, MA: Addison-Wesley.

Dittes, J.E. (1973). Beyond William James. In : C.Y. Glock and P.H. Hammond (eds), *Beyond the classics? Essays in the scientific study of religion* (pp. 291–354). New York : Harper and Row.

Dunde, S.R. (ed.) (1993). *Wörterbuch der Religionspsychologie.* Gütersloh: Mohn.

Eugen, M. (1981). The area of faith in Winnicott, Lacan and Bion. *International Journal of Psychoanalysis, 62,* 413–433.

Feil, E. (1986). *Religio. Band I: Die Geschichte eines neuzeitlichen Grundbegriffs vom Frühchristentum bis zur Reformation.* Göttingen: Vandenhoeck and Ruprecht.

Feil, E. (1997). *Religio. Band II: Die Geschichte eines neuzeitlichen Grundbegriffs vom Frühchristentum bis zur Reformation (ca. 1540–1620).* Göttingen: Vandenhoeck and Ruprecht.

Fromm, E. (1950). *Psychoanalysis and religion.* New Haven: Yale University Press.

Guntrip, H. (1969). Religion in relation to personal integration. *British Journal of Medical Psychology, 42,* 323–333.

Hall, G. Stanley (1891). Review of 'the principles of psychology' by William James. *American Journal of Psychology, 3,* 578–91.

Haußig, H.-M. (1999). *Der Religionsbegriff in den Religionen: Studien zum Selbst- und Religionsverständnis in Hinduismus, Buddhismus, Judentum, Islam.* Berlin/Bodenheim: Philo.

Hermans, H.J.M. and H.J.G. Kempen (1993). *The dialogical self: meaning as movement.* San Diego, CA: Academic Press.

Hermans, H.J.M., H.J.G. Kempen, and R.J.P. van Loon (1992). The dialogical self: beyond individualism and rationalism. *American Psychologist, 47,* 23–33.

Hill, P.C. (1999). Giving religion away: what the study of religion offers psychology. *International Journal for the Psychology of Religion, 9,* 229–249.

Hood, R.W. (1992). A Jamesean look at self and self loss in mysticism. *Journal of Psychology of Religion, 1,* 1–24.

Hood, R.W. (2000). American psychology and the Journal for the Scientific Study of Religion. *Journal for the Scientific Study of Religion, 39,* 531–543.

Hood, R.W. (2002). The mystical self: lost and found. *International Journal for the Psychology of Religion, 12,* 1–14.

James, W. (1890). *The principles of psychology.* London: Macmillan.

James, W. (1902/1982). *The varieties of religious experience: a study in human nature.* Harmondsworth: Penguin.

Jones, S.L. (1994). A constructive relationship for religion with the science and profession of psychology: perhaps the boldest model yet. *American Psychologist, 49* (3), 184–199.

Kalweit, P. (1908). Das religiöse apriori. *Theologische Studien und Kritiken, 81,* 139–156.

Kehoe, N.C. and Th. G. Gutheil (1993). Ministry or therapy: the role of transference and countertransference in a religious therapist. In M.L. Randour (ed.) (1993). *Exploring sacred landscapes: religious and spiritual experiences in psychotherapy.* New York: Columbia University Press.

Kippenberg, H. (2001). Was sucht die Religionswissenschaft unter den Kulturwissenschaften? In H. Appelsmeyer and E. Billman-Mahecha (eds), *Kulturwissenschaft: Felder einer prozeßorientierten wissenschaftlichen Praxis* (pp. 240–275). Weilerswist: Velbrück.

Koepp, W. (1920). *Einführung in das Studium der Religionspsychologie.* Tübingen: Mohr.

Le Bon, G. (1903). *The Crowd: a study of the popular mind.* London: T.F. Unwin.

Markus, H.R. and P. Nurius (1986). Possible selves. *American Psychologist, 41,* 954–969.

McDargh, J. (1983). *Psychoanalytic object relations theory and the study of religion: on faith and the imaging of God.* Lanham, MD: University Press of America.

McDougall, W. (1909). *An Introduction to Social Psychology.* Boston: Luce.

Meulen, R.H.J. ter (1988). *Ziel en zaligheid: de receptie van de psychologie en van de psychoanalyse onder de katholieken in Nederland, 1900–1965.* Nijmegen: Katholiek Studiecentrum.

Miller, W.R. (ed.) (2002). *Integrating spirituality into treatment: resources for practitioners.* Washington: American Psychological Association.

Misiak, H. and V.S. Sexton (1973). *Phenomenological, existential and humanistic psychologies: a historical essay.* New York/London: Grune and Stratton.

Otto, R. (1917/1923). *The idea of the Holy: an inquiry into the non-rational factor in the idea of the divine and its relation to the rational.* London: Oxford University Press (first German edition: 1917).

Pratt, J.B. (1908). The psychology of religion. *Harvard Theological Review, 1,* 435–454.

Randour, M.L. (ed.) (1993). *Exploring sacred landscapes: religious and spiritual experiences in psychotherapy.* New York: Columbia University Press.

Reich, K.H. (1990). Rituals and social structure. The moral dimension. In: H.-G. Heimbrock and H.B. Boudewijnse (eds). *Current studies on rituals: perspectives for the psychology of religion* (pp. 121–134). Amsterdam/Atlanta: Rodopi.

Richards, P.S. and A.E. Bergin (1997). *A spiritual strategy for counseling and psychotherapy.* Washington: American Psychological Association.

Richards, P.S. and A.E. Bergin (eds) (2000). *Handbook of psychotherapy and religious diversity.* Washington: American Psychological Association.

Rizzuto, A.M. (1996). Psychoanalytic treatment and the religious patient. In: Shafranske, E.P. (ed.). *Religion and the clinical practice of psychology.* Washington: American Psychological Association.

Sarbin, T.R. (1986). The narrative as a route metaphor for psychology. In: T.R. Sabin (ed.), *Narrative psychology: the storied nature of human content.* New York: Praeger.

Schleiermacher, F.D.E. (1799). *Über die religion: reden an die Gebieldeten unter ihren Verächtern.* Berlin: Reiner.

Shafranske, E.P. (ed.) (1996). *Religion and the clinical practice of psychology.* Washington: American Psychological Association.

Spiegelberg, H. (1972). *Phenomenology in psychology and psychiatry.* Evanston: North-Western University Press.

Spiegelberg, H. (1982). *The phenomenological movement: a historical introduction.* Den Haag: Mouton.

Strean, H. (1994). *Psychotherapy with the orthodox Jew.* New York: Jason Aronson.

Strien, P.J. van (1993). *Nederlandse psychologen en hun publiek: een contextuele geschiedenis.* Assen: Van Gorcum.

Troeltsch, E. (1905). *Psychologie und Erkenntnistheorie in der Religionswissenschaft: eine Untersuchung über die Bedeutung der kantischen Religionslehre für die heutige Religionswissenschaft.* Tübingen: Mohr.

Vergote, A. (1993). What the psychology of religion is and what it is not. *The International Journal for the Psychology of Religion, 3,* 73–86.

Vergote, A. (1996). *Religion, belief and unbelief: psychological study.* Amsterdam/ Leuven: Rodopi/Leuven University Press. (orig. publ. 1983).

Vergote, A. and J.M. van der Lans (1986). Introduction to the plenary debate: two opposed viewpoints concerning the object of the psychology of religion. In: J.A. Belzen and J.M. van der Lans (eds). *Current issues in the psychology of religion* (pp. 67–81). Amsterdam: Rodopi.

Vitz, P.C. (1994). *Psychology as religion: the cult of self-worship.* Grand Rapids: Eerdmans.

Wilshire, B. (1968). *William James and phenomenology.* Bloomington, IN: Indiana University Press.

Wobbermin, G. (1906). Vorwort. In: W. James, *Die religiöse Erfahrung in ihrer Mannigfaltigkeit: Materialien und Studien zu einer Psychologie und Pathologie des religiösen Lebens* (pp. III–XIII). Leipzig: Hinrich.

Wulff, D.M. (1997). *Psychology of Religion: classic and cantemporary* (2nd edn), New York: Wiley.

Chapter 5

Passionate belief

William James, emotion and religious experience

Jeremy Carrette

> If belief consists in an emotional reaction of the entire man on an object, how *can* we believe at will? We cannot control our emotions.
>
> William James *Principles of Psychology* [1890b] 1950: 321

With the development of new studies in social theory and psychology, William James's work on emotion has received renewed interest (Barbalet 1999; Frijda, Manstead and Bem, 2000; Williams 2001). As social psychologist Barbalet has argued: 'Recent interest in emotion encourages a return to James' (Barbalet 1999). However, few of these studies have considered how James's theory of emotion might inform and shape his understanding of religion in his work *The Varieties of Religious Experience* ([1902] 1960 Fontana). Given the fact that the *Varieties* is grounded on notions of religious emotion, it is surprising that James's theory of emotion has not received greater consideration when examining this major work. A number of commentators do make the connection in passing but never follow through the implications or explore the relationship in any great detail (Levinson 1981: 104–105; Myers 1986: 466–467, 608; Watts 1997: 247–249). Eugene Taylor did consider this question in his 2001 paper to the 109th American Psychological Association conference – where he usefully maps out the 'higher religious emotion' – but his concern is primarily with the mystical rather than with the problem of the social (Taylor 2001). Wade Clark Roof and Sarah McFarland Taylor also recognised the significance of James's early theory of emotion and the *Varieties* in an article for Capps' and Jacobs' 1995 collection on the *Varieties*. Considering James's early 1884 essay 'What is an Emotion?', Roof and McFarland stated: 'A review of James's theory of apperception is key to understanding and exploring the way he deals with feelings and emotions in *The Varieties* because it is this theory that informs his treatment of religion. ' (Capps and Jacobs 1995: 200). Unfortunately, while Roof and McFarland were accurate in their assessment of the importance of the theory of emotion for understanding the *Varieties*, they never explored James's theory of emotion beyond his initial 1884 essay and maintained a problematic reading of James's theory of emotion as simply based on sensory somatic processes, rather than on cognitive and social dimensions. This, of course, is not surprising, given the representations of James's work on emotion. Indeed, while there has been more interest in James's theory of emotion than any other of his psychological contributions, it also the case that there is no other theory that has been subject, as Damasio states, to such 'endless and sometimes hopeless controversy' (Myers 1986: 215; Damasio [1994] 1996: 129).

Roof and McFarland were more concerned to use James's theory of emotion to demonstrate an embodied religious perspective, rather than understand the concept of emotion, and thus missed the opportunity to examine this vital relationship between the theory of emotion and the *Varieties*. The renewed interest in emotion and the concerns of social psychologists to open the discussion have led to renewed interest in James's work. It seems appropriate, on the 100th anniversary of the publication of James's Gifford lectures, to consider how contemporary interest in his theory of emotion might provide a new reading not only of James's theory of emotion but also the *Varieties*.

This chapter seeks, therefore, to offer a 'corrective reading', to follow Peter Ochs's idea of textual interpretation, of James's theory of emotion in relationship to the *Varieties*, with particular concern to address issues from the perspective of the social psychology of emotion (Ochs 1999). The distinctive contribution of this paper is taking forward recent discussions of James's work on emotion into a close reading of his Gifford lectures. This task is all the more important since it is now agreed that it is too restrictive to understand James's theory of emotion in isolation from his wider work. In the *Varieties* James is methodologically concerned with the 'religious sentiment', or 'religious emotion', to the exclusion of social and institutional factors. He reads religion in terms of feeling (James [1902] 1960: 47–50) but, paradoxically, the theory of emotion as developed in the *Varieties* is caught up with a series of issues related to the social and cognitive dimensions of emotion. The *Varieties* therefore represents a development of his theory of emotion rather than a diversion from his earlier work, which, as we shall see, contains the possibility of integrating social context despite its popular representation as grounded in the perception of physiological states.

What is particularly interesting about the understanding of emotion in the *Varieties* is the way it challenges an individualistic approach to James or at least subverts the edges of such a discussion. There have been many studies questioning the psychological reductionism of James's position (for example, Jantzen 1989; Lash 1990), but few have linked such challenges to the theory of emotion itself. What I am suggesting is that at the heart of the *Varieties* is a model of emotion caught up in a social and cognitive analysis. This does not in itself correct James's individualism but certainly tapers the extremities of such a position. This chapter seeks to plot this relationship. However, before we explore James's work in any depth, I want to make a point about reading James.

Reading James: diversity and pluralism

James scholarship suffers, as the James archivist Eugene Taylor concurs, from reading aspects of James's work in isolation from his wider corpus of writing

(Taylor 1997: 2). The *Varieties* does not stand in isolation from his previous work and his work on emotion cannot be isolated from his wider concerns by simply reading his 1884 essay 'What is an Emotion?' A 'corrective reading' of James requires acknowledgement of the pluralism of his own work and the specific focus of each study. In this sense, the *Varieties* cannot be understood without considering his earlier work on psychological theory and his popular essays in *The Will to Believe* (James [1897] 1903). Indeed, *The Will to Believe* sets the tone for his consideration of religion and offers a corrective to readings of individualism in the *Varieties*. I wish to go further than this by suggesting that James's work on religious emotion contains, somewhat surprisingly, the seeds of a pre-given social analysis or social location of emotion. The fact that James highlights individual feelings in the *Varieties* does not mean that he thought social factors were not significant. By connecting the dots in James's wider work we find a more coherent pluralistic theory than is suggested by reading James's texts in isolation from each other.

The problem of finding a consistent position in James's work is due to the different groups James had in mind when writing, such that the *Varieties*, like *The Will to Believe*, is written to counter a scientific materialism and therefore assumes a strategy of experience and emotion against rationalism. For example, James is aware that his definition of religion according to individual feeling was 'arbitrary', it was, as he stated, constructed '*for the purpose of these lectures*' (italics in original) (James [1902] 1960: 48). He even concedes that he could drop the term 'religion' for conscience or morality (James [1902] 1960: 49) and perhaps even emotion. James gives precedent to the 'feelings of reality' in order to oppose rationalism (James [1902] 1960: 87). He wants to oppose the 'intellectualism' and domination of a 'logical' analysis in science, philosophy and dogmatic theology (James [1902] 1960: 416–417; 428–438). James, to some extent, is trying 'to defend feeling at the expense of reason' (James [1902] 1960: 414). James is not suggesting that emotion is '*better*', but rather that the subconscious and non-rational dominate in a particular psychological reading (89). What James wants to argue is that science and religion are both important 'keys for unlocking the world's treasure-house' (James [1902] 1960: 132). I wish to characterise James, as Gerald Bruns acknowledges, as holding 'loose ends', as refusing, what Hilary Lawson has recently characterised as 'closure' (Bruns 1984; Lawson 2001). As Bruns makes clear, in reading James's pluralistic universe: 'Things exist not in themselves but only in their versions, and a pragmatist differs from a rationalist by addressing the versions of things, not their logical "sorts" – which is why it is always a difficult question as to what, exactly, a pragmatist is talking about.' (Bruns 1984: 304). The *Varieties*, like James's theory of emotion, is a version and only by linking aspects of James's work together can we appreciate something of the elusive whole. It would seem that James's problem is not so much what he has written, but how he has written it and how we read James. As James is aware at the end of the *Varieties*: 'We must frankly recognise the fact that we live in partial systems, and that parts are not interchangeable in the spiritual life' (James [1902] 1960: 466).

James's theory of emotion is one particularly good example of the way he is read according to a specific 'closure' – a failure to appreciate the complex folds of his work. There is a tendency in the textbook formulation of James to assume a basic reading of his account of emotion found in his 1884 essay 'What is an Emotion?' without considering the modifications and context of his discussion. Writers such as Barbalet even go as far to suggest that James has been 'fundamentally misrepresented in the secondary literature' (Barbalet 1999: 261) while others, such as Levinson and Watts, argue that the peripheral or somatic model of emotion from 1884 is 'overstated' (Watts 2000: 46; Levinson 1981: 103–104). What I wish to show is how the *Varieties* is central to a wider social appreciation of emotion than is found in James's earlier work.

Exploring James's theory of emotion

James's theory of emotion is often stated by simply quoting one or two key sentences from his 1884 article for *Mind*, 'What is an Emotion?'. James states, for example: 'My thesis . . . is that *the bodily changes follow directly the PERCEPTION of the exciting fact, and that our feeling of the same changes as they occur IS the emotion.*' (James [1884] 1983: 170).

The classic example given is the sighting of a bear that causes the body to tremble and in turn produces the emotion of fear. Emotion is seen as the perception of the bodily sensation and in this sense James denies a simple cognitive understanding of emotion. But is there more to James's theory than this simple characterisation?

While it is perhaps not disputed that James, to a greater or lesser extent, formulated a model of emotion based upon the perception of bodily changes (the classic James–Lange model), it is far from clear the extent to which James understood this model to eradicate all other positions, which raises the question of whether James perhaps held a more complex assessment than is often attributed to him. There does seem to be some evidence to suggest that James did not hold an exclusively physiological model of emotion and that in subsequent development of his theory of emotion there were significant modifications. There is also evidence to support the idea that James's theory of emotion requires careful qualification in terms of the specific emotions under discussion and its relationship to other concepts in his work, such as his theory of consciousness and his model of the self. One of the strongest exponents for such a position is Jack Barbalet. In his excellent re-examination of James's work on emotion he suggests a careful reading of James in terms of his wider corpus of writing and the interconnection between his complex set of ideas. 'James' discussion of the relations between bodily sensations and emotion,' he argues, 'does not assert that all emotions derive from bodily sensations' (Barbalet 1999: 254).

James's early theory of emotion, according to Barbalet, refers rather to the 'standard' or 'coarser' emotions (James [1884] 1983: 170; [1890b] 1950: 449). He also argues that his theory of emotion is always a theory of 'emotional consciousness' which was only a 'part' of his theory of emotion (Barbalet 1999: 256). Barbalet seeks to rescue James's appreciation of the 'total 'situations'', 'relational circumstances' and the importance of 'history' in the understanding of emotion (Barbalet 1999: 257–258). He also goes on to show the importance of emotion for self-knowledge and decision-making in James's wider work (Barbalet 1999: 259–260). Barbalet also wants to emphasise the way James clarifies his position in response to critics in his 1894 essay 'The Physical Basis of Emotion' (Barbalet 1999: 257). What effectively Barbalet does is pick up the scattered qualifications and modifications dotted throughout James's work on emotion, which in turn allow for a more open-ended analysis. What is perhaps surprising, especially given his detailed reading of the theory of emotion, is the way he neglects to consider how the *Varieties* also develops the picture of emotion. None the less, Barbalet's attempt to highlight the wider and more complex shape of emotion in James's work does allow a more balance perspective. It reveals that James is in part responding to the psychological discussion of his time in reacting against 'associationist' models. More importantly, his work does seem to suggest a wider spectrum of emotion and concern for the 'social environment' (James [1884] 1983: 175).

Barbalet's avoidance of the *Varieties* when considering James's work on emotion takes on added importance when some scholars, such as Levinson, argue that the *Varieties* is a clarification of the earlier 'reductively physiological' model (Levinson 1981: 104–105). There is certainly a suggestion of what Levinson calls a 'cognitive variable' in the consideration of religious emotion as formed by the object of consciousness (Levinson 1981: 104). It is also this understanding that allows Watts to consider the physiological reductionism of James as 'overstated' (Watts 2000: 46). But if Barbalet is correct, then these so-called developments in James's theory of emotion were not so much developments as different contextual explorations of emotion. Gerald Myers seems to support such an idea when he suggests that 'beliefs, changes in consciousness, cultural conditioning factors, and expectations were not his main concern' in the earlier work (Myers 1986: 608). It is, none the less surprising, as Myers indicates, that the James–Lange theory is not discussed in the *Varieties* (James [1902] 1960: 467). Has James's position evolved or merely shifted in focus? What, we may ask, does the *Varieties* offer his theory of emotional consciousness?

Feelings and emotion

One of the problems in examining the nature of emotion in the *Varieties* is the semantic slippage between the use of the words 'emotion', 'feeling' and 'impulse' or 'instinct'. James states that his inquiry will focus on 'religious feelings and religious impulses' (James [1902] 1960: 26), but there is little distinction in

James's work between these terms and the idea of emotion. 'Feeling' seems to be understood as the experiential dimension of emotion, a kind of 'record of inner experience' which allows for a descriptive survey (James [1902] 1960: 28). The idea of emotion is slowly introduced into the text through a discussion of physiological or organic symptoms (James [1902] 1960: 31–36) and then moves back to religious sentiments and feelings when the experiential dimension is given emphasis, only to return to the broad category of religious emotion. The tension between these terms revolves around whether the object of consciousness in religious emotion is embodied and whether it is possible to have an abstract emotion or what James calls 'purely spiritual emotion' (James [1890b] 1950: 477). To put it simply, is religious emotion the feeling of a bodily event or is the object of consciousness disembodied emotion? The shifts between the language of emotion and feeling raise, at least, a question over whether there is continuity between religious 'feelings' of the *Varieties* and the James–Lange theory of 'emotion'. Gerald Myers confirms this tension between emotion and feeling in James's articulation of the James–Lange theory, acknowledging that James was dissatisfied about what he had to say on the question of feelings (Myers 1986: 237–241). Myers believes that such confusion was cause for much of the difficulties in understanding the object of consciousness in emotion and its physiological basis in James's work. 'If James,' as Myers states, 'had worked out more clearly the link between emotion and feeling, he might have avoided the unfortunate confusion not only in his elaboration of the James–Lange theory, but in his very formulation of it. ' (James [1902] 1960: 240). This distinction is significant because to separate emotion and feeling allows for 'a two-staged model' of bodily sensations and the feelings related to the sensation, something that allows for Watts's cognitive appreciation of James's account of religious emotion (Watts 1997: 249). However, putting such issues aside and assuming James's interchangeable use of the words 'feelings' and 'emotion', what, we may ask, does the *Varieties* offer to James's theory of emotion?

Varieties of emotion

The classic formulation of religion in the *Varieties* is developed through a consideration of individual feelings. James states that his study will be 'psychological' and not an examination of 'religious institutions' (James [1902] 1960: 26), but to say that something is 'psychological' does not mean that context and environment (the social) is not considered (see Carrette 2001). There is, as we have noted, a deliberate attempt by James to counter the medical materialism of the scientific community and this obviously shapes the experiential agenda of the *Varieties*. However, in making this move James shifts from a physiological basis of religious emotion to a distinctively cognitive and social model. As James argues, religion is not an 'aberration of the digestive function' or a 'perversion of the respiratory function' as some have argued (James [1902] 1960: 33–34). James concedes that there is no mental state that is not grounded upon physical correlates, but this, according to James, is not the sole force of religious emotion. '[T]here is not a single one of our states of mind, high or low, healthy or morbid, that has not some organic process as its condition. Scientific theories are organically conditioned just as much as religious emotions.' (James [1902] 1960: 36).

James, in accordance with his earlier model of emotion, grounds religious emotion in the body but, unlike the earlier work, he does not restrict emotions to the body in the *Varieties*. Religious emotion is not, as suggested in his 1884 essay, simply a somatic peripheral; it is rather a far more complex process. In the *Varieties* religious emotion is 'more' than just physiological processes. The key factor of religious emotion that James wants to preserve is the 'value' of religion against a reductive discussion of 'origin' – or, as he puts it, 'the bugaboo of morbid origin' (James [1902] 1960: 42). In order to avoid a discussion of origins James focuses his study on 'the immediate content of the religious consciousness' (James [1902] 1960: 34), which is the 'feeling' of a reality. It is the fruits, not the roots, that are of concern for James (James [1902] 1960: 41). Religious emotion holds with it something distinct from a perception of physical sensation.

In order to understand the theory of religious emotion in the *Varieties*, it is necessary to outline how James marks out the concept. First, James points out that there is 'no one essence' to religion (James [1902] 1960: 46). He acknowledges that religious emotions are 'organically conditioned' like any other emotion (James [1902] 1960: 36), but there is something more to (religious) emotion. Religious emotion is not different from other emotions, except in so far as it is 'directed to a religious object' (James [1902] 1960: 47).

> As concrete states of mind, made up of a feeling *plus* a specific sort of object, religious emotions of course are psychic entities distinguishable from other concrete emotions; but there is no ground for assuming a simple abstract 'religious emotion' to exist as a distinct elementary mental affection by itself, present in every religious experience without exception. (James [1902] 1960: 47)

Religion, according to James, draws on a 'common storehouse of emotions' and as there is no specific object or act that is religious, so there is no specific emotion that is religious. However, James does acknowledge that 'there is a state of mind, known to religious men, but to no others' (James [1902] 1960: 64), it is 'an absolute addition' or 'added dimension' (James [1902] 1960: 64–65). Religious consciousness is rich from the emotional point of view because of its imaginative power to transform lives (James [1902] 1960: 66–67). Religious emotion feels something, a presence or as if something were true. It is the feeling of a reality that, according to James, gives 'a new sphere of power' (James [1902] 1960: 64). Religion is different from morality precisely because of this emotional quality or what James calls the 'enthusiastic temper of espousal' (James [1902] 1960: 65). At one point James does seem to suggest that the reason for such a power is the 'allegorical meaning' (James [1902] 1960: 66). Life is made richer through an imaginative resource, which in turn suggests the importance of ideation or cognition in the emotional framing of religion. It is not clear whether emotion is the best way to frame religion, in so far as it suggests transitory states of consciousness. Religion might better be described, as James at times suggests, as an 'attitude' (James [1902] 1960: 67; 69). The key suggestion here is that the 'attitude', or mental outlook, shapes the emotional response. Both a physical and a mental process determine the emotion. The 'more' of religious emotion appears therefore to be some transcendent, cognitive or social dimension, what Taylor recognises as an 'elevated' state of consciousness (Taylor 2001).

The key question is 'how' the religious attitude is shaped. What is it that gives shape to the emotion or what is the object of religious consciousness? According to James, this is the reality of 'an unseen order' (James [1902] 1960: 69), but this unseen order is shaped by 'ideas'. James at this point is following a Kantian logic in the 'Ideas of Pure Reason', but what is important about this line of argument is that they 'have this power of making us vitally feel presences that we are impotent articulately to describe' (James [1902] 1960: 71). In religion there is a 'sense of reality' or a 'feeling' of 'something there' (James [1902] 1960: 73). With the exception of so-called mystical states, where James believes there is an 'absence of definite sensible images', most religious feelings are dependent on ideas (James [1902] 1960: 70). Such an assumption raises a separate set of philosophical questions, explored by Katz (1978) and others, as to whether it is possible to have a 'raw unmediated experience'. I do not wish to entertain these questions here, because I am concerned more with James's theory of emotion than discussions of mysticism as such – although there is an important relationship in terms of how an experience or a feeling is formed. The key issue is how James accounts for the emergence of a feeling without a specific object of consciousness. The theory of emotion here directly clashes with his Kantian philosophical agenda in the discussion of mysticism (see Jantzen 1989). We are far from the physical basis of emotion at this point and instead appear to be developing an interesting spectrum of emotions or at least an acknowledgement of different types of emotion.

In mysticism James seems to believe that feelings refer to something beyond ideas, but, somewhat in a tautology, he also believes that feelings are framed by ideas. James acknowledges, for example, that the 'more concrete objects' of religion, such as deities, are known 'only in idea' (James [1902] 1960: 69). There is a tension here. On the one hand James argues: 'The whole force of the Christian religion, therefore, so far as belief in the divine personages determines the prevalent attitude of the believer, is in general exerted by the instrumentality of pure ideas, of which nothing in the individual's past experience directly serves as a model.' (James [1902] 1960: 70). And, as he states a little later: 'The absolute determinability of our mind by abstractions is one of the cardinal facts in our human constitution. ' (James [1902] 1960: 72). Once James acknowledges that 'concrete' and 'abstract' ideas shape the religious emotion he is open to the question of the cognitive and social dimensions of emotion. James even concedes that 'conceptions and constructions are thus a necessary part of our religion' (James [1902] 1960: 416). Such a view does not seem to support the individualism that characterises so much of *Varieties*. It rather allows us to see the 214 narratives of religious experience in the *Varieties* as examples not just of individual experience alone but a social record of the way experience is shaped by ideas in different cultural contexts. The very cross-cultural project of James is confirmation of the way that religious emotion is in part socially determined and not simply a somatic event. Ideas, intellect or what James calls, 'over-belief' – the 'buildings-out performed by the intellect into directions of which feeling originally supplied the hint' – determine the emotion (James [1902] 1960: 415). According to James: 'Feeling is private and dumb, and unable to give an account of itself' (James [1902] 1960: 415). Feelings thus require a social cognition to give them 'public status'. Indeed, James suprisingly recognises that reason and intellect are necessary in religion to overcome what he calls 'unwholesome privacy' (James [1902] 1960: 415). None the less, such over-beliefs were 'absolutely indispensable' for religion and the 'most interesting and valuable' things about an individual (James [1902] 1960: 490).

Emotion and intellect

This interrelationship between feeling and intellect is crucial for understanding James's theory of religious emotion. The theme in fact continues to be explored after his Gifford lectures in his 1902 Summer School of Theology Lectures on 'Intellect and Feeling in Religion' (James 1988). On the one hand, there are suggestions in the *Varieties* that the relationship between emotion and intellect might offer a more balanced model of emotion. James, for example, is able to acknowledge that we 'construe our feelings intellectually' (James [1902] 1960: 416). Here there is a kind of co-dependency between emotion and intellect, something dominating current research in neuroscience (see Damasio [1994] 1996). It raises the question of whether intellectual beliefs are to some extent grounded upon emotions and this challenges the binary separation between the two. James certainly seems to think that abstract theology is based upon deeper emotional undercurrents (James [1902] 1960: 428–429). However, what is not clear is whether James is suggesting that emotion holds a series of inter-related components (physical, cognitive and social), or whether feeling and intellect are distinct.

At times the suggestion seems to be that feelings are framed by ideas (James [1902] 1960: 415), that there is a cognitive component to emotion, as Fraser Watts had suggested. But James's argument is more complex and philosophically determined than this psychological analysis would suggest. In other places in the *Varieties*, particularly the lecture on philosophy, and in the Theology Summer School lectures there is a distinct conflict between intellect and feeling (James 1988: 93). In the attempt to preserve individual feeling against institutional practices James asks: 'Are there realities beyond the individual which are pertinent only to him *as such*? Which well up *within*, and not without, him? Whose existence discredits *abstract* philosophizing?' (James 1988: 94). James wants to separate intellect from feeling while simultaneously seeking to acknowledge an inter-relationship between the two.

In James's model, religious feelings, or experiences, precede myths, dogma and creeds (James [1902] 1960: 416). The striking feature is that James believes feeling to be 'a deeper source of religion' (James [1902] 1960: 414), deeper than intellect or cognition. Feelings are thus seen as separate from ideas and, while this raises the question of whether feelings and emotions are distinct, it also raises the question of whether feelings can be separate from somatic factors. This question takes us to the heart of the problem of emotion in the *Varieties*. James's theory of emotion in the *Varieties* moves back and forth from assuming the possibility of disembodied emotions (feelings of something other) and separating the physical basis of emotion from feelings. What the *Varieties* does show, even if there are all sorts of conceptual problems between feeling and emotion, is that James offers a complex model of emotion in *Varieties* in line with Barbalet's social psychological reading of his early work.

Ribot and James on religious emotion

The possible breadth of the theory of emotion in the *Varieties* is not, as Barbalet has argued, inconsistent with his earlier work. For example, James's qualification in his1884 study makes this clear when he states: 'I should say first of all that the only emotions I propose expressly to consider here are those that have a distinct bodily expression. ' (James [1884] 1983: 169). In the *Varieties* James has clearly extended the discussion of emotion beyond the study of physical emotions to more complex states, which allows cognitive psychologists and social psychologists to reclaim lost dimensions of James's work. However, this corrective reading of James needs to take account of the fact that James's consideration of emotion in the *Varieties* is significantly influenced by the French philosopher/psychologist Théodule Ribot. Ribot's 1896 work *The Psychology of the Emotions* (*Psychologie des Sentiments*), while indebted to James's earlier work, broadens out James's model to include a discussion of religious sentiments.

In my view, James's discussion of emotion and religion cannot be understood without taking into account Ribot's work, especially his chapter devoted to the religious sentiment. While James only quotes twice from Ribot's study in the *Varieties* it none the less shapes the contours of his thinking. As James states in a letter to Ribot on 31 January 1901: 'I am writing some lectures for Edinburgh on the 'Varieties of religious experience' *quite on your method*', (Quoted in James 1985: 538). James's alignment of his method with Ribot's is confirmed not only in his use of Ribot's work in the *Varieties* but also in the broadening out of his theory of emotion.

James refers to Ribot first in relation to the sick soul (referring to Ribot's concept of 'anhedonia', a lack of zest for life). The second reference occurs in

James's final conclusions on the intellect and feeling when he cites Ribot's sense of the evaporation of religious emotion in the intellect (James [1902] 1960: 153, 479). Ribot may not be as important as Myers, Flournoy and Starbuck to the understanding of the composition of the *Varieties*, but he is important because Ribot's work shapes the discussion of emotion in two ways: first, by anticipating James's sick and healthy soul in depressive and exalted forms of emotion (Ribot [1896] 1911: 324) and, second, by plotting the relationship between the intellect and emotion in religious thinking in a similar fashion to James. James's discussion of philosophy and dogmatic theology echo Ribot's analysis (compare Ribot [1896] 1911: 316–318 and James [1902] 1960: 414–415). Ribot also sees mysticism as the 'highest point' of religious emotion (Ribot [1896] 1911: 318). The difference is that James, perhaps in tactical manner, plays down (rather than ignores) the social dimension of religious emotion that Ribot continually acknowledges, although it is intriguing to note that, a few years later, when James fills in Pratt's questionnaire on religious belief, James is more affirmative of a social reading of religion. He responded to the question about whether religion is understood as 'an emotional experience' by writing, somewhat surprisingly: 'Not powerfully so, yet a social reality' (James 1904: 123). It is precisely this shift that is significant in recognising Ribot's influence and appreciating James's context-specific accounts of religion.

The references to Ribot's work in the *Varieties* are not without significance. Ribot's study of emotion follows the physiological model of James and Lange, which he believed rescued the study of emotion from 'a state of stagnation'. But Ribot's following of the physiological model of emotions (as opposed to the intellectualist model) is not absolute. Rather Ribot puts forward a continuum of emotion ranging from the physiological to the intellectual. Ribot, like James in his later work, acknowledges that emotion must be located in particular contexts and not assume generalities. As Ribot states: 'To separate it [emotion] from social, moral, and religious institutions, from the aesthetic and intellectual movements which translate it and incarnate it, is to reduce it to a dead and empty abstraction'. (Ribot [1896] 1911: viii). What is particularly interesting is that Ribot believes that religious emotion is less physiologically determined than most others, that it is determined in part by intellectual, conceptual or abstract, factors, and that it is also 'social' in character (Ribot [1896] 1911: 310). He writes: 'Except the intellectual feelings themselves, no emotional manifestation depends more on the intellectual development than the religious sentiment, because every religion implies some conception of the universe – a cosmology and a system of metaphysic' (Ribot [1896] 1911: 311). What Ribot is aware of at this point is that cognitive and social factors influence emotion as much as physiological factors, particularly in the area of religion. However, as James also later argued, Ribot believed that the emotional element in religion could easily be effaced by the intellect, as seen in the work of theologians and religious philosophers (Ribot [1896] 1911: 317).

Intellect, feeling and religious practices

If James is following Ribot's method he is certainly less willing to concede the importance of the intellect to religious feelings. James polarises these two things more than Ribot because he wants to preserve feelings as prior to the emergence of thought in religion. The relationship between intellect and feeling is complex in both writers but each follows a similar path. The key difference is one of emphasis. James, while acknowledging a sort of continuum, always draws out – but does not deny – feelings over intellect and individual over social. Yet if you tease out James's work you can see his continual refusal to exclude the wider perspective of emotion. It is as if he refuses to be drawn on the issues in detail while pushing the individual experience and feeling in the narrative against medical materialism. Feelings are the way around the scientific and philosophical boundaries of abstract knowledge. He none the less concedes that individuals 'involuntarily intellectualise their religious experience', which seems to suggest that the cognitive and social environment powerfully influence the emotional world (James [1902] 1960: 439).

Ribot is more willing to acknowledge the social aspect of religion, because, ironically, it enables him to preserve the James–Lange model by grouping emotion into different classifications. He, unlike James, also stressed that when religion became philosophical doctrine it ceased to be religion. However, while Ribot has a tendency to disregard the 'individual and speculative belief' as religion, this is not the case with religious practices. The crucial feature of religious emotion for Ribot was that it maintained its social form in worship and ritual (Ribot [1896] 1911: 318). Ribot seems to take seriously the emotion engendered in religious practices in a way that James categorically avoids. James's work on worship and ritual is inadequately condensed and severely restricted in his lecture on 'Other Characteristics', concerning sacrifice, confession and prayer (James [1902] 1960: 439ff). James cannot avoid acknowledging religious institutions (ecclesiastical systems) or worship in his study, but he never finds a way to integrate these into this model of religious emotion (James [1902] 1960: 439–440). In his summary, he confirms the 'emotion-inspiring institution and belief' as standing alongside his 'palpitating documents' (James [1902] 1960: 480). He is unable to dispute that he himself attempts to devise some 'general facts' and 'formulas' from the 'privacies of religious experience' (James [1902] 1960: 416). He is forced to acknowledge wider forces even as he adopts a specific framework and admits to 'trying to reduce religion to its lowest admissible terms, to that minimum' in order to find a basis for all religious people (James [1902] 1960: 480). It is perhaps not surprising that his student James Pratt returns to such everyday practices in his own consideration of religious consciousness (Pratt [1920] 1924; see also Wulff 1997: 507). However, James's resolution to the question of religious emotion took him beyond such questions, and the theory of emotion as such, to the theory of the subconscious.

Religion, according to James – and one assumes religious emotion also – is driven by a consciousness of something 'more', which in psychological terms is seen as the subliminal or subconscious, or even a 'B-region' (James [1902] 1960: 457, 462, 484–487). James believed this notion was the 'doorway' for a science of religion. It stood alongside the religious questions as an area of enquiry, which acknowledged the limits of consciousness (James [1902] 1960: 487). Such a conclusion to the Gifford Lectures makes for some interesting reading in terms of James's theory of emotion. Having argued for the physical basis of emotion, James enters the field of religion by opening up the problem of the object of consciousness in religious emotion. Religious emotion is shaped by ideas, social contexts, and even something 'more' than consciousness itself. If the *Varieties* offers anything for James's theory of emotion, it certainly offers conceptual problems. The problem of the object of religious consciousness is the problem of the theory of emotion. If feeling is the feeling of something in consciousness, what is the object? Is it the body, the ideas, the rituals or something 'more' that is the object of consciousness? If James had attempted to carry forward his analysis of emotion with the precision of his earlier work the *Varieties* would perhaps hold greater insights into these questions, but we are left with the fragments, the 'partial systems', as James calls it in the conclusion to the *Varieties* (James [1902] 1960: 466).

Concluding comment: James's theory of emotion

What the *Varieties* demonstrates is that James's theory of emotion is always context specific. It is possible to recognise a wider social and cognitive analysis of emotion grounded in somatic factors. This position, as Barbalet indicates, is neither simply social constructivist or biologically reductive. James is seen to anticipate current thinking of emotion as somatic markers and the importance of emotion in rationality; as, for example, developed in Lazarus (1991) and Damasio ([1994] 1996). This sense that feeling is a prerequisite for belief determines much of James's work in the *Varieties* (James [1902] 1960: 414). It challenges the usual binary opposition between rationality and emotion and places renewed attention on the nature of religious experience.

I should emphasise in conclusion that I am not trying to make James into a social psychologist. I am rather responding to recent work in the social psychology of emotion and trying to think through such issues in relation to James's work on religious emotion in the *Varieties*. My argument is that James's theory of emotion highlights the tensions within James's work on religious emotion and that the *Varieties*, as David Lamberth has explained, was philosophically restricted with all the personal documents (Lamberth 1999: 97–98). Indeed, James concludes the *Varieties* by discussing pluralism and hope and pointing towards another book (James [1902] 1960: 500). It is these issues that fashion the open-ended work. Contemporary discussions of emotion do, as Barbalet suggests, require a return to James. Such discussion of emotion is important to the study of religion because it raises important issues about the politics of experience. It shows us that our emotions, complex and multidimensional as they are, do in part require us to reflect continually on the ethical issues of society and the context of our feelings.

Bibliography

Barbalet, J.M. 1999 'William James' Theory of Emotions: Filling in the Picture' in *Journal for the Theory of Social Behaviour* Vol. 29 No. 3 pp. 251–266.

Bruns, G.L. 1984 'Loose Talk about Religion from William James' in *Critical Inquiry* Vol. 11 No. 2 Dec. 1984 pp. 299–316.

Capps, D. and Jacobs, J.L. (eds) 1995 *The Struggle for Life: A Companion to William James's 'The Varieties of Religious Experience'* Society for the Scientific Study of Religion and Princeton Theological Seminary.

Carrette, J.R. 2001 'Post-Structuralism and the Psychology of Religion: The Challenge of Critical Psychology' in *Mapping Religion and Psychology* ed. Diane Jonte-Pace and William Parsons (Routledge) pp. 110–126.

Damasio, A.R. [1994] 1996 *Descartes' Error: Emotion, Reason and the Human Brain* Oxford: Papermac.

Frijda, N.H., Manstead, A.S.R. and Bem, S. (eds) 2000 *Emotion and Belief: How Feelings Influence Thought* Cambridge: Cambridge University Press.

James, W. [1884] 1983 'What is an Emotion?' in *Mind* Vol. 9 pp. 188–205.

— 1879/1880 'The Sentiment of Rationality' in James [1897] 1903 pp. 63–110.

— [1890a] 1950 *Principles of Psychology* Vol. 1 New York: Dover.

— [1890b] 1950 *Principles of Psychology* Vol. 2 New York: Dover.

— 1892 *Psychology: A Briefer Course* London: Macmillan.

— 1894 'The Physical Basis of Emotion' in James 1985 pp. 299–314.

— 1895–1896 'Notes for Philosophy 20b: Psychological Seminary – The Feelings' in James 1988 pp. 212–230.

— [1897] 1903 *The Will to Believe and Other Essays in Popular Philosophy* New York: Longmans Green.

— [1902] 1960 *The Varieties of Religious Experience* Glasgow: Fontana, Collins.

— 1902 'Summer School of Theology Lectures on Intellect and Feeling in Religion' in James 1988 pp. 83–100.

— 1904 'Answers to Pratt's Questionnaire' in *Psychology and Religion* ed. L.B. Brown (Penguin: London, 1973) pp. 123–125.

— 1985 *Essays in Psychology* Cambridge, Massachusetts: Harvard University Press.

— 1988 *Manuscript Lectures* Cambridge, Massachusetts: Harvard University Press.

James, W. and Lange, C.G. [1922] 1967 *The Emotions* New York: Hafner.

Jantzen, G. 1989 'Mysticism and Experience' in *Religious Studies* 25, September, pp. 295–315.

Katz, S.T. (ed.) 1978 *Mysticism and Philosophical Analysis* London: Sheldon.

Lamberth, D.C. 1999 *William James and the Metaphysics of Experience* Cambridge: Cambridge University Press.

Lash, N. 1990 *Easter in the Ordinary: Reflections on Human Experience and the Knowledge of God* Notre Dame: University of Notre Dame Press.

Lawson, H. 2001 *Closure: A Story of Everything* London: Routledge.

Lazarus, R. 1991 *Passion and Reason* Oxford: Oxford University Press.

Levinson, H.S. 1981 *The Religious Investigations of William James* Chapel Hill: University of North Carolina

Myers, G.E. 1986 *William James: His Life and Thought* New Haven: Yale University Press.

Ochs, P. 1999 *Peirce, Pragmatism, and the Logic of Scripture* Cambridge: Cambridge University Press.

Pratt, J.B. [1920] 1924 *The Religious Consciousness: A Psychological Study* New York: Macmillan.

Putnam, R.A. 1997 *The Cambridge Companion to William James* Cambridge: Cambridge University Press.

Reed, E.S. 1997 *From Soul to Mind: The Emergence of Psychology from Erasmus to William James* New Haven: Yale University Press.

Ribot, T.H. [1896] 1911 *The Psychology of the Emotions* London: Walter Scott.

Strout, C. 1971 'The Pluralistic Identity of William James: A Psychohistorical Reading of *The Varieties of Religious Experience* in *American Quarterly* Vol. 23, May, pp. 135–152.

Taylor, E. 1978 'Psychology of Religion and Asian Studies: The William James Legacy' in *Journal of Transpersonal Psychology* Vol. 10, No. 1. pp. 67–79.

— 1982 *William James on Exceptional Mental States* New York: Charles Scribner's Sons.

— 1996 *William James on Consciousness Beyond the Margin* Princeton: Princeton University Press.

— 1997 'Mysticism: The View from a Cross-cultural Comparative Psychology of the Subconscious' in *Studia Mysticorum: Newsletter of the Mysticism Study Group in the American Academy of Religion* Vol. 3: 1–2 Summer/Fall, pp. 2–3.

— 1999 *Shadow Culture Psychology and Spirituality in America* Washington: Counterpoint.

— 2001 'Let us Begin with Those 'Theoretic Raptures': William James on the Higher Religious Emotions' Unpublished paper presented at the 109th annual meeting of the American Psychological Association, 27 August 2001, San Francisco, California.

Taylor, E. and Wozniak, R.H. (eds) 1996 *Pure Experience: The Response to William James* Bristol: Thoemmes Press.

Watts, F. 1997 'Psychological and Religious Perspectives on Emotion' in *Zygon: Journal of Religion and Science* Vol. 32 No. 2. pp. 243–260.

— 2000 'The Multifaceted Nature of Human Personhood: Psychological and Theological Perspectives' in *The Human Person in Science and Theology* ed. N.H. Gregerson, W.B. Drees and U. Görman, Edinburgh: T&T Clark.

Watts, F. and Williams, M. 1988 *The Psychology of Religious Knowing* London: Geoffrey Chapman.

Williams, S. 2001 *Emotion and Social Theory* London: Sage.

Wulff, D. M. 1997 *Psychology and Religion: Classic and Contemporary* New York: John Wiley.

Part III

James and mysticism

Chapter 6

For an engaged reading

William James and the varieties of postmodern religious experience

Grace M. Jantzen

What are the varieties of religious experience in postmodernity? It is a safe bet that if William James were here today, that is a question he would be asking. One hundred years ago his concern with religious experience culminated in a discussion of saintliness and mysticism that became, for good and ill, the definitive treatment of the subject for the century that followed. Today, entering a new and violent century in which religion is declaring itself as a massive global and political force, James would surely be probing the religious consciousness of those who wage holy war, whether with hijacked aircraft or belts of explosives, or in the name of 'God bless America' or the right to occupy a 'Holy Land'. In the twenty-first century religion is conscripted on all sides to the service of oppression, terror and destruction. But is there also a variety of religious experience that works on the side of justice and of peace?

Although we can be confident that James would have been asking such questions, it is far less clear what answers he might have proposed. It is my belief that the reception and popularity of his work among analytic philosophers of religion have skewed his approach, so that, I shall argue, it has been bent into a mystification that other aspects of his work do not support. I propose first, therefore, to make some suggestions towards saving James from his admirers, using his affinities with Hegel and his development of pragmatism. I shall then take these hints further, reading James against himself, to seek a variety of religious experience that engages with the violent coming of postmodernity.

William James's chapters on mysticism have been endlessly reprinted in textbooks of philosophy of religion; and his four characteristics of mystical experience – ineffability, noetic quality, transiency and passivity – taken as definitive. A steady stream of writers have used his chapters as a basis for their struggle with the questions of whether or not mystical experiences are true or authoritative; and thus whether or not they are evidence for the existence of God (e.g. Katz 1978; Swinburne 1979; Davis 1989). And within the chapters themselves, James often seems to invite such a reading, as though what is at stake is the validity of truth claims which are to be evaluated from as neutral and objective a place as possible. In his introduction of the subject, he places himself as external to mystical experience, and promises to be 'as objective and receptive as I can' (James 1982: 379). Throughout, he is concerned about that in mystical experience which is 'suggestive of pathology' (386) or which could be reduced to 'nothing but suggested and imitated hypnoid states, on an intellectual basis of superstition, and a corporeal one of degeneration and hysteria' (413). James is convinced that there is more to mysticism than mental illness, and does his best to prove it; but the question of whether mystical experiences are deceptive or trustworthy is never far from his pen.

Even granting his claim that mystical experiences are energizing, and often a mark of strong characters with a highly practical and organized flair for getting things done – James discusses, among many others, Teresa of Avila who reformed the Carmelite order in Spain, and Ignatius Loyola who founded the Jesuits – James still struggles with the question of truth. He admits:

> If the inspiration were erroneous, the energy would be all the more mistaken and misbegotten. So we stand once more before the problem of truth ... You will remember that we turned to mysticism precisely to get some light on truth. Do mystical states establish the truth of those theological affections in which the saintly life has its root? (415)

He considers a range of examples, quoting from mystical writings less as a way of developing an argument than in an effort to elicit recognition (421). Finally he concludes, famously, that mystical states 'are and have the right to be absolutely authoritative over the individuals to whom they come' (422); yet 'non-mystics are under no obligation to acknowledge in mystical states a superior authority' (427). The two halves of this conclusion seem bafflingly contradictory: whatever has happened to objective truth? Surely a mystical experience either is from God or it is not. If it is, then must it not count as evidence for the existence of God not only to the experiencer but to all who recognize its occurrence? ... and so the arguments have gone on, often with recourse again to the alleged characteristics of mystical experience, especially ineffability.

I have argued elsewhere that these alleged characteristics are highly misleading if they are taken as definitive of mystical experiences; that the allegedly empirical case studies that James cites are in fact often distorted beyond recognition because they are removed from their social and literary context; and that the whole question of what counts as a mystical experience and who counts as a mystic has for centuries been a question in which is hidden a whole technology of power and gender (Jantzen 1995). The analytic philosophers of religion who have used James are mostly invested in the same gendered power, not least in their production of what counts as 'truth'; and therefore have, I would claim, mystified religious experience by configuring it as a private, subjective state of consciousness without political situation. And James, as I have said, leaves himself wide open to such interpretation.

But I have come to think that there is also a reading of James that subverts this account (and which I acknowledge not to have taken seriously enough in my previous work on him). It begins by recognizing that James's conclusion about the authority of mystical states has not just the two parts I cited, but a third, which is often overlooked. It is this:

> They [i.e. mystical states] break down the authority of non-mystical or rationalistic consciousness, based upon the understanding and the senses alone. They show it to be only one kind of consciousness. They open out the possibility of *other orders of truth*, in which, so far as anything in us vitally responds to them, we may continue to have faith. (423, emphasis mine)

'Other orders of truth'? What might James mean by this? Judging from the examples he gives in the chapters on mysticism, it might be that he is appealing to 'reasons of the heart', immediate intuitive certainty which is part of (or arises out of) a purely subjective state of consciousness which he calls 'mystical' but which (as he himself is well aware) could equally well be paranormal or even pathological. And if this is what he means, then all the questions about evidence and delusion come back all over again.

I think that sometimes James does indeed mean this; and that his preoccupation with the odd and hallucinatory, with alcohol and nitrous oxide and trances and voices and levitations and things that go bump in the night – preoccupations that mystics in the Christian tradition regularly warned *against* – can be understood as attempts to escape the Kantian strictures on knowledge of the noumenal. And in those terms it can't possibly work. Once one has accepted a Kantian epistemological framework, one cannot sneak around the categorial grid by treading lightly on the 'verges of the mind', since in Kantian terms the categories are always already operational, and structure the 'verges' of the mind as surely as its more central pathways (see Jantzen 1989; 1990).

But scholars of James on mysticism, myself among them, have often failed to pay attention to the chapters that follow. James did not end his lectures with mysticism. In his next lecture, in fact, he works at developing another perspective on the question of truth; and while I don't think it solves all his problems, I do think it points to a constructive way forward. In particular, I think it helps us with the most important question that James's legacy leaves to us, and with which I began: what are the varieties of religious experience in postmodernity, and how should they be understood?

In James's chapter on philosophy, he tries to apply to religious doctrines and religious experiences the philosophy of pragmatism which he was developing. He argues for an 'organic connection' between thought and conduct (James 1982: 442). If a theory or intellectual position makes no practical difference, has no consequence whatsoever upon how life is lived, then it is not just useless, it isn't even true. 'True', here, is conceived in terms of consequence: if a proposition is 'practically indifferent' then there can be no serious reason for calling it either true or false (444) – we are here only half a breath away from the logical positivism of half a century later: A.J. Ayer's verification principle, or Antony

Flew's parable of the gardener, and all the headaches they gave to philosophers of religion.

But that isn't quite where James wants to go. James's targets are the systematic theologians, who argue at length about the correct formulation of particular doctrines even though which formulation is adopted makes not the slightest bit of practical difference, does not help to meet human needs, and is in fact nothing but manufacture of words. Such people, James feels, are 'the vilest type of wretch under the sun' (446). The world looks to them – to us – for spiritual nourishment and discernment in the political and cultural nightmares of our time, and what do we have to offer? If systematic theologians (and James would surely include philosophers of religion) are spinning doctrines about religion or psychology or experience but are not concerned with how these doctrines are engaging with the pressing needs of the world, then 'they have the trail of the serpent over them.'

> One feels that in the theologians' hands ... verbality has stepped into the place of vision, professionalism into that of life. Instead of bread we have a stone; instead of a fish, a serpent. Did such a conglomeration of abstract terms give really the gist of our knowledge of the deity, schools of theology might indeed continue to flourish, but religion, vital religion, would have taken its flight from this world. (446)

The god of these thinkers, James says, is a 'metaphysical monster', an 'absolutely worthless invention of the scholarly mind' (447).

Strong language, this; indeed it is James at his most vehement. In the light of it one can only imagine his shudders at the ways in which his chapters on mysticism have been used to calculate the probabilities of metaphysical theism or the evidence for dogmatic claims. What James is pressing for, at least in these passages, is an engaged reading: an engagement not only with religion but with the wider world, so that the thinker about religion is characterized by practical compassionate discernment. It is a long way from the dilemma with which James is often credited: either mysticism can be trusted as giving direct knowledge of the divine, or it must be rejected in favour of an empirical epistemology grounded in sensory phenomena.

That dilemma had in fact been discussed in Hegel's *Phenomenology*, and it is no accident that James frequently appeals to it (no accident, either, that it is largely ignored by twentieth-century analytic philosophers of religion). In Hegel's terms the struggle is between champions of the Enlightenment, who reject faith and intuition and appeal to unbiased evidence available to any objective observer, and the 'naive consciousness' which accepts on faith its own immediate intuitions (Hegel 1977, *Phenom* #538f; p. 328f) – Hegel had in mind the German pietist movement. For the protagonists of the Enlightenment, such unquestioning faith is utterly perverse and irrational. But the pietist-turned-philosopher could point out that the Enlightenment assumption that there could be such a thing as detached, objective neutrality to which evidence of the senses is unambiguously available is not an assumption that bears scrutiny. The burden of Hegel's argument here is that there is no pure place, no point of unsituated knowledge. All truth claims are made from a social and political position. If the claimant is ignorant of his or her own perspective, or even denies that s/he has one at all, this only renders their claims all the more suspect. There is no neutral ground. Every claim, and every investigation of a claim, is always already from somewhere, with some prior assumptions and investments. (For an excellent discussion of Hegel on this point, see Pinkard 1996: 165–187.) What Hegel was after was a critical self-consciousness of one's assumptions and perspectives, ever and again bringing them to scrutiny in the light of shared ideals and values of beauty and goodness. Claims, including claims of religious experience (or its denial), are never simply private. They arise within a shared linguistic and cultural system and have implications and practical consequences for that system. Therefore any evaluation of religious experience must begin not from putative objectivity and detachment but from a critically aware engaged reading: engaged both in the mystical texts and in the social and political worlds of the writer and the reader. Indeed, as Gadamer has stressed in his Hegelian hermeneutic, the work of the intellectual is precisely to bring these levels of engagement into interaction with each other.

I don't want to pretend that Gadamer's (ultimately conservative) fusion of horizons is the same as Hegel's sociality, let alone James's pragmatism. But what all of them have in common is a recognition that an objective empirical[1] stance, whether about religious experience or anything else, is self-deception. There is no substitute for an engaged reading: engaged and critical. When James writes about 'other orders of truth' and of the need for religious experience and belief to be of some practical consequence, I think that at least some of the time he is reaching for Hegelian insights of critical sociality.

But I concede that this is to read James to some extent against himself. There is plenty in *The Varieties of Religious Experience* that is at odds with the engaged reading which in my view represents James at his best. First among the discrepancies is James's insistence on the essential privacy of religion and religious experience. As he defines his topic, he insists upon taking religion as 'the feelings, acts and experiences of individual men [*sic*] in their solitude, so far as they apprehend themselves to stand in relation to whatever they may consider the divine' (31). Although he recognizes also institutional religion (churches, synagogues, etc.), he never even seems to notice the political and social nature of religion. Mysticism, in particular, he says is 'essentially private and individualistic' (430). In his writings it is as if mystical experiences come upon people without warning and without antecedent in their cultural experience, inviting the interpretation that they are direct and unmediated experiences of the divine to the private individual.

Now, I suggest that what James was trying to do was to treat the question of religious experience without getting bogged down in questions of doctrine and denomination and religious affiliation. He was, after all, a psychologist; and he wanted to look at the question from a psychological point of view, not as a historian of religious institutions. But whether or not this was his intention in delimiting religion to individuals in their solitude, its *effect* was at odds with the critical sociality that must lie at the basis of any ethical pragmatism, and played directly into the hands of those who, in the twentieth century, were only too happy to remove from politics and public life the energy for reform often generated by religious experience.

It is also at odds with simple observation, as James's critics were quick to point out. If religious experiences were entirely unconnected to the experiencer's individual and cultural history, then it would be inexplicable why Catholics have visions of the Virgin Mary while Hindus have visions of Shiva dancing, but not the other way around. This fact has been appropriated, once again, by analytic philosophers of religion primarily interested in how the relationship between experience and interpretation affects its evidential value (Stace 1961; Katz 1978; Alston 1991). But I suggest that this preoccupation misses a key point, which comes to the fore if we think about religious experience in terms of engagement.

Although James sometimes represents the practical consquences of religious belief or experience as though it were a matter of the private moral behaviour of the individual, he is well aware that ethical pragmatism must be social in scope. The upshot is that religious experience both in its provenance and its effects is inseparable from social, cultural and political positions and interconnections. To put the point in terms that have become familiar since Foucault, any religious experience and any consequent action is socially constructed, always already formed by the cultural situation of the people concerned.

This is not a reductionist claim, any more than the parallel claim that any experience is inseparable from personal psychological history is reductionist. It does, however, move the question away from arguments about the evidential value of religious experience to a question of the relationship of religious experience to critical sociality. And that, I think, is a good move. I shall suggest something of its value for postmodernity below; but I want just to pause a moment on the preoccupation with evidence to ask some questions. Why – for whom, and for what purpose – is the question of evidence central? What questions does it leave unasked? Who does it silence? What political and cultural technologies of power remain unchallenged if religious experience is construed as private unsituated intensity? Whose interests are served by this construction? The point of the questions is that whatever answers might be attempted – and they need not all be nefarious – they show that even when the social construction of religious experience is ignored or denied, it is already operative within the denial itself.

If, then, we read James the pragmatist against James the proponent of solitary individualism, and take seriously the social and political situatedness of religious experience, how does this help us to understand religious experience in postmodernity? I want to suggest three points, all of them in need of greater elaboration and qualification than I can give them here.

First, it provides us with the means to take seriously the religious experiences and their practical consequences that announce the twenty-first century, and to recognize their social and political interconnections. The struggle between India and Pakistan, while involving more than religion, never involves less. The same is true for Israelis in their aggression against Palestinians, and for Muslims who proclaim a Holy War against the economic and military oppression perpetrated against them by the USA and its allies. And it is no less a part of the 'Crusade' – ostensibly against terrorism – announced by the USA, and then by others who appropriate its rhetoric for their own ends. In the USA 'God bless America' is regularly invoked by an administration acutely conscious of the religious sensibilities of the voting populace; and many a car has a bumper sticker of 'God bless America' on the front and 'Nuke 'em Now' on the back. It would be absurd to suggest that everyone caught up in these struggles has intense mystical experiences that conform to James's four characteristics. But it would be irresponsible and dangerous not to take seriously these varieties of religious experience in postmodernity, and the way that they are situated within and in turn reshape the social and political world. There can today be no doubt about the enormity of the practical consequences of religious experience. To refuse to engage with it, or to treat it only as a quarry of evidence for religious doctrines, would be to abdicate responsibility as scholars of religion in a way that I hope James would have been the first to deplore.

Second, as these examples show, 'religious' does not equate with 'benign'. This again is in tension with some themes of James's book, where he seems to imply that if a religious experience is not pathological then it must be good, and to be trusted. Rather, if religious experience takes shape within (and in turn reshapes) its social context, then if that context is deformed, whether through internal greed and lust for power or through economic or military oppression, the religious experience is bound to be affected by these deformities. Up to now, scholars of religion have looked to overtly religious rituals and doctrines to interpret and situate religious experience. I am not minimizing their importance; but I would urge that if we are trying to understand the varieties of religious experience in postmodernity then we also need to ask wider questions. Who benefits from these experiences? Who loses? Who is left out? Who gets hurt? What sorts of religious experiences are available in a xenophobic society? Or in a society that uses its power to force compliance upon the rest of the world, or on its own weaker members? Or in a society so ground down with oppression that there seems to be no future and no hope for its enraged and despairing youth? Or in a racist or sexist society?

But third, as we have learnt from Foucault, there is no structure of power without resistance. Societies are not monolithic. Hegel, while recognizing that social situatedness is inescapable, pressed for a *critical* sociality. And this also, I want to argue, is important for the varieties of religious experience in postmodernity. There are those who would argue that in the light of the devastating consequences of reactionary varieties of religious experience in modernity and postmodernity, it would be better to get rid of religious experience altogether: to be progressive is to be secular. But I don't think that response is adequate, for several reasons (all of which would merit further discussion). In the first place, secularism is itself a construct of modernity built upon highly dubious and quasi-religious premises that are increasingly called into question by progressive thinkers. Second, in purely practical terms, many of us are incurably religious: it would be naive to suppose that religious experience could be banished with the wave of a disapproving wand. Third, rejection of religious experience by critical and progressive thinkers would simply abandon the field to those who conscript religious experience to devastating and reactionary ends.

I suggest, therefore, that it is altogether more helpful to consider how constructive varieties of religious experience could be fostered and evaluated in an engaged and critical sociality. Where can we find the resources for a spirituality which is often deadened or distorted by the assumptions of global consumerism and the ugliness of modernity? Here again, I think, William James is helpful, though again only if to a certain extent read against himself. For he points to the need of taking seriously the lives and writings of mystics and holy men and women, both in Christendom and in other religious traditions. His book is full of extracts from these writers. Now, for the most part, they wrote from a context other than that of Western secular modernity, and with values and assumptions quite at odds with it. In consequence, reading, say, Christian medieval mystics in postmodernity, getting to grips with the alterity of their perspectives, enables us to see post/modernity otherwise, to have a place from which there can be critical engagement with the current varieties of religious experience. Medieval mystics have much to say about such postmodern concerns as time, desire, the stranger and the alien, despair, poverty and greed, nihilism, violence and gender, and how all of these are related to and reconfigure our conceptions of the divine. An engaged reading of medieval mystics therefore is an important resource for critical engagement with the pressing concerns of postmodernity.

But only if they are read somewhat differently from the way in which James himself reads them. For one thing, he culls extracts and snippets from their writings that (at least appear to) illustrate the points he wishes to make. An engaged reading of the sort I am advocating, by contrast, would need to study their lives and writings in depth, and with attention to their social and literary location; and rather than use them to illustrate preconceived points, try to discern what they themselves were getting at and why, in their context, it was important. Moreover as I have already said, James pays a lot of attention to the unusual and even bizarre, to intense subjective states; but for the most part this was not the central emphasis of the mystics themselves. Again, the sort of reading that I think is needed focuses less on subjective states and more on the goodness and beauty of the life and teaching in relation to the overriding concern of the mystics in question. James does not notice issues of sexism, racism, or other forms of political and economic oppression either in his own writing or in the mystics he reads: although he seems to have been concerned with the rights of women and Blacks in his personal life, one would not know it from his intellectual analyses. An engaged reading of the mystics in postmodernity must be alive to all of these issues.

While there are differences from James, therefore, in the approach I advocate both to the medieval mystics and to an understanding of the varieties of postmodern religious experience, we stand greatly in James's debt. For it was he who, more than most others, drew attention to the importance and varieties of religious experience; he who, at his best, looked for an engaged reading; he who saw that understanding religious experience is worth the strenuous efforts of scholarship and insight because they literally change the shape of the world. To honour him it is not required that we agree with him at every point, but that we engage in the next century in the question he asked of the last: how shall we understand the varieties of religious experience in postmodernity?

Note

1.   I am using 'empirical' here as shorthand for the epistemology that bases itself on sense perception, *not* as in James's much wider usage which broadens to include all experience and is sometimes shorthand for pragmatism.

References

Alston, William P. 1991. *Perceiving God: The Epistemology of Religious Experience* (Ithaca and London: Cornell University Press).

Davis, Caroline Franks. 1989. *The Evidential Force of Religious Experience* (Oxford: Clarendon).

Hegel, G.W.F. 1977. *Phenomenology of Spirit*. Trans. A.V. Miller. (Oxford: Clarendon Press).

James, William. 1982. *The Varieties of Religious Experience* (London: Penguin).

Jantzen, Grace M. 1989. 'Mysticism and Experience' in *Religious Studies* Vol. 25.

Jantzen, Grace M. 1990. 'Could there be a Mystical Core of Religion?' in *Religious Studies* Vol. 26.

Jantzen, Grace M. 1995. *Power, Gender and Christian Mysticism* (Cambridge: Cambridge University Press).

Katz, Stephen T., ed. 1978. *Mysticism and Philosophical Analysis* (London: Sheldon).

Pinkard, Terry. 1996. *Hegel's Phenomenology: The Sociality of Reason* (Cambridge: Cambridge University Press).

Stace, Walter Terence. 1961. *Mysticism and Philosophy* (London: Macmillan).

Swinburne, Richard. 1979. *The Existence of God* (Oxford: Clarendon).

Chapter 7

Asian religions and mysticism

The legacy of William James in the study of religions

Richard King

'Mysticism' and 'the mystical'

In the twentieth century the academic study of mysticism has been a key feature of debates within the study of religion, reaching its zenith in the 1960s and 1970s with a variety of debates about the nature and forms of mysticism, the question of a mystical common core to all religions and the status of drug-induced mystical experiences playing a prominent role in the field. Although generally given less significance some thirty years later, there are signs that the study of mysticism has not disappeared but is rather reformulating itself around the term that has increasingly come to replace 'the mystical' at the turn of the twentieth century, namely 'spirituality'. However, despite the relative lack of explicit discussion of 'mysticism' in much recent academic work within the field of the history of religions, the term and its associations remain deeply embedded within the intellectual history of Religious Studies, providing an influential 'mystocentrism' that remains at work throughout the field (Wasserstrom, 1999). Moreover, in the continued emphasis that is placed upon some (often poorly defined) notion of 'experience' as a core determining feature of human religiosity, the 'mystical' or 'the spiritual' retains a pre-eminent place within the history of religions as a field of study.

William James has, of course, been a crucial figure in the establishment of the modern academic study of mysticism and therefore also a key influence upon subsequent work on religious experience within the history of religions. As Michel de Certeau (1964, 1982) has argued, the term 'mysticism' is itself an offshoot of *la mystique*, and first came to the fore in early seventeenth-century France. The invention of 'mysticism' in the sense of the imagination of 'a Christian mystical tradition' is a feature of the early modern period and cannot be found prior to this time. Subsequently, as a result of colonial exploration and the European encounter with other cultures, the term 'mystical' was exported and applied to non-European contexts. In the nineteenth century, energized by the Romanticist fascination with all things Eastern, the term became particularly associated with tropes about 'the mysterious Orient' and led to the construction of highly stereotypical representations of Asian traditions as 'mystical' in nature (for further elaboration of these points see King, 1999).

The term 'mysticism', like its close relative 'religion', is part and parcel of the normalized inventory of concepts that we have inherited from our European cultural heritage in the Western world. It is through the uncritical application of such concepts cross-culturally that European-derived conceptions of the world and of human history have been reproduced and universalized in the modern period. In its adjectival form (in English the term 'mystical'), the concept has of course a much longer history than the modern term 'mystic-ism'. The ancient Greek term *mystikos* was used by the pre-Christian mystery religions of the Graeco-Roman empire in relation to the act of closing one's eyes or one's lips (that is remaining silent) with regard to the secrecy of their various rites of initiation. In early Christian literature, as Louis Bouyer (1990) has demonstrated, *mystikos* was used to denote three interdependent dimensions of early Christian practice: namely the allegorical, spiritual or 'mystical' interpretation of scripture, the mysterious transubstantiation involved in the Christian Eucharist, and finally mystical or spiritual insight into the nature of the divine, granted by the grace and presence of the Holy Spirit.

We also find in late Antiquity the notion of the Church as the 'Mystical Body' or *Corpus Mysticum* of Christ and from the sixth century onwards (following Pseudo-Dionysius), the notion of a 'mystical theology', that is an apophatic or negative approach to discourse about the divine, grounded in a recognition of the inability of all language and imagery to encapsulate the magnificence and transcendence of the Creator. Alongside this highly intellectual path of negation there were also less abstract and more affective strands represented by diverse figures such as Bernard of Clairvaux (1090–1153), Hildegard of Bingen (1098–1179) and Julian of Norwich (b. 1342), etc. These strands, though diverse, tended to place a much greater emphasis upon love and the senses as a means of encountering God.

A number of contemporary scholars in the field have also paid increasing attention to the gender politics involved in this complex history. The medieval period in particular seems to have brought forth a number of inspirational women and female-oriented movements like the Beguines in Europe. Mostly excluded from formal theological training and the abstract intellectualism of apophatic theology, many, though not all, of these women placed a great deal of emphasis upon visions as the source of their wisdom and authority and in some cases were persecuted and even executed for their claims. Modern feminist scholarship has become increasingly interested in the apparent resurgence of female spiritual activism during this period and the historical task of recapturing some of the silenced voices of these remarkable women has really only just begun (Bynum, 1982; Petroff, 1986; Beer, 1992; Jantzen, 1995). However, it would be anachronistic to imagine that any of these figures would have conceived of themselves as belonging to something called 'the Christian mystical tradition' since, as de Certeau demonstrates, this notion only began to emerge in the early modern period. Before that time there is no obvious construal of the term as a substantive that might usefully denote an identifiable phenomenon now captured by the category 'mysticism'.

William James and the modern study of mysticism

When we come to the modern period we find that the diverse uses of the term 'mystical', which I have very briefly outlined, become increasingly displaced by an emphasis upon mysticism as overwhelmingly experiential in nature, thereby recasting the term according to a post-Enlightenment and highly psychologized conception of 'experience'. At the same time, increasing emphasis has been placed upon the use of the term as a substantive 'mystic-ism' – now seen as denoting an identifiable and global phenomenon present in the various religious traditions of the world. William James has been a key figure in this use of the term, although in so doing we should note that he is as much a cipher of a wider cultural shift in the nineteenth century (Schmidt, 2003), precipitated by processes of modernization and the construction of the modern psychological subject, as he is one of the prime instigators of this trend within the academic study of religion.

James was especially interested in establishing the intellectual framework for an emerging field – the comparative science of religions. For the indologist Max Müller, the framework for this new science was to be found in the insights of comparative linguistics and the study of mythology, but for James the ground for this new science was to be provided by the emerging discipline of psychology. James's work attempted to establish a framework for psychological study of religion which remained sensitive to the possibility of the veridicality of such experiences. He remained critical of reductionist approaches which interpreted religious experiences either in terms of neurological functions of the brain or as repressed sexual desires projected in the form of an erotic encounter with the divine. An important dimension of James's approach was his sensitivity to what he called 'the mystical impulse' within humans and his openness to the possibility of 'unseen worlds' beyond the senses.

For James institutional and organized religion was 'second hand' in the sense that the true core of religion was to be found in individual religious experiences. Indeed, as William Barnard (1997, 12–13) has suggested, for James, the mystical is in many respects a broader and more significant category than the religious, referring to a wider range of mental states with significantly more transformative potential than what James considered to be more mundane and everyday 'religious' experiences. Indeed, in privileging the mystical over the religious, James is a thoroughly 'up-to-date' thinker, being an important precursor of the increasingly prevalent trend in contemporary Western culture to prefer 'spiritual' as opposed to 'religious' as a way of describing one's individual sense of the sacred. Nevertheless, accounts of such experiences – whether described as mystical or religious in nature – provided the primary data for James's psychological analysis of the subject matter. Today it is not uncommon for people to say that they are spiritual or that they have spiritual beliefs but that they are not religious, meaning of course that they do not affiliate with a particular religious institution or movement but still have some experience of the sacred. This association reflects modern shifts in Western understandings of religion since the Enlightenment and a tendency for many to distinguish between an inward and personal experience of the sacred (spirituality or mysticism) and allegiance to a particular form of organized religion. In a comparative context mysticism then has come to denote those aspects of the various religious traditions that emphasize unmediated experience of oneness with the ultimate reality, however differently conceived.

In his Gifford Lectures (1901–02, subsequently published as *The Varieties of Religious Experience*), James provides the classic example of the modern association of mysticism with mystical experience. From the very outset, James reads 'mysticism' in terms of what he calls 'mystical states of consciousness'. It is these that constitute for him, echoing Schleiermacher (1768–1834), the 'root and center' of personal religious experience. It is this intellectual sleight of hand at the beginning of his lectures on mysticism in the *Varieties*, where the shift from a concern with 'mysticism' to 'the study of mystical experience' occurs, that we find one of the defining moments in the emergence of the modern study of mysticism.

James's orientation is highly indebted for instance to that strand of Enlightenment thought that tended to locate 'the religious' within the *private* sphere of human existence and key figures such as Kant and Schleiermacher. His emphasis upon individual accounts of supposedly private experiences was of course at the expense of a broader consideration of the social and political dimensions of the mystical within the history of Christianity (see Jantzen, 1995; King, 1999). It is clear from a wider reading of James's work, however, that he resists the temptation to reduce 'mysticism' to 'mystical experiences' and that he was aware of the 'extra-experiential' dimensions of the phenomena under investigation. Crucial here is the transformative role of experience and its assessment in terms of its fruits in 'the religious life'. Thus James notes in a discussion of Hindu traditions:

> The Vedantists say that one may stumble into super-consciousness sporadically, without the previous discipline, but it is then impure. Their test of its purity, like our test of religion's value, is empirical: its fruits must be good for life. When a man comes out of Samadhi, they assure us that he remains 'enlightened, a sage, a prophet, a saint, his whole character changed, his life changed, illumined.' (James, 2002: 310. James's citation is from Vivekānanda (1896), *Raja Yoga*, London)

The significance of the wider context in which the experience occurs can also be seen in James's own discussion of the 'fruits' of the experience as a basis for determining its significance and in his discussion of 'saintliness' (Lectures XI–XII) and what he calls the 'more habitual and chronic sense of God's presence' in 'The Reality of the Unseen' (Lecture III, James, 2002: 59). However, the consequences of James's decision to underplay these aspects in his psychological account has had far-reaching consequences for the reception of his work among scholars of religion and the subsequent trajectory of mainstream debates within the comparative study of mysticism.

The mystical ladder

In classifying the various states of consciousness he wishes to consider, James constructs a hierarchy of such states – what he calls steps on 'the mystical ladder' (2002: 297), with highly rarefied and incommunicable experiences of unity at the zenith. In many respects James's mystical ladder replicates the move of apophatic theologians such as Pseudo-Dionysius (the author in fact who first coined the term 'hierarchy'), in downplaying the significance of sensory knowledge in authoritative apprehensions of the divine. In James's account, however, we find a radically new application of this hierarchy that, when applied back to the historical data he wishes to explore, translates that material according to a post-Enlightenment construal of 'experience'. The steps on James's mystical ladder no longer refer to stages on, say, the Christian pathway to God, or in the stripping away of images in order to praise the divine, but rather denote a hierarchy of transient 'states of consciousness'. This modern psychological construction of 'the mystical' would have made little sense to Dionysius or even to later apophatic theologians such as the fourteenth-century Dominican thinker Meister Eckhart.

Indeed, the modern 'reading back' of 'the mystical' in terms of privatized experience into pre-modern contexts has come under increasing criticism in some of the most recent scholarship in this field. Ineffability in modern debates about mysticism have been applied to the apparently indescribable nature of intense and private experiences rather than the traditional explications of the transcendental majesty of God. Medievalist Denys Turner, for instance, describes his work *The Darkness of God* (1995) as concerned with 'the retrieval of the medieval tradition of apophatic or "negative" mysticism ... from a contemporary "experientialist" misreading.' (Turner, 1995: 5). He further states that:

> I have drawn the conclusion from my study that in so far as the word 'mysticism' has a contemporary meaning; and that in so far as that contemporary meaning links 'mysticism' to the cultivation of certain kinds of experience – of 'inwardness', 'ascent' and 'union' – then the medieval 'mystic' offers an anti-mysticism. For though the Christian Neoplatonist used that same language of interiority, ascent and 'oneness,' he or she did so precisely in order to deny that they were terms descriptive of 'experiences'. (Turner, 1995: 4)

Similarly, in her feminist analysis of Christian mysticism, Grace Jantzen (1995) points to the shifting meanings of 'the mystical' throughout history, highlighting both the power struggles involved in all attempts to define the category and the ways in which women have been excluded by men from positions of authority in this process. In my own work I have attempted to offer an analysis of the colonial implications of the notion of 'the mystic East', arguing that the representation of Hinduism and Buddhism as 'mystical' has functioned to reinforce Western stereotypes of Eastern religion and culture as world-denying, amoral and lacking an impulse to improve society (King, 1999). This has allowed the West to define itself as progressive, scientific and liberal in contrast to the superstitious, tradition-bound and 'underdeveloped' Third World nations of Asia. In this regard the stability of the category of the mystical and the way in which it is adopted has itself become subject to critical analysis as emphasis has shifted towards the power relations involved in attempts to classify particular religious figures, movements or traditions as mystical in nature.

James and subsequent debates within the study of mysticism

James's characterization of mysticism has had an unprecedented influence upon contemporary scholarship in this field within Religious Studies. As is well known, in the *Varieties* James characterizes mystical experiences in terms of four basic attributes: ineffability, noetic quality, transiency and passivity. As Bill Barnard has pointed out, this characterization was heuristic in nature and was never intended by James to be prescriptive or definitive accounts of 'the mystical' as James was 'less concerned with the descriptive task than he was with creating a workable explanation of mystical experience' (Barnard, 1997: 63). In offering this account James was also not arguing for some kind of transcultural common core that might be said to underlie the different forms of mystical experience. James's main preoccupation (in the *Varieties* at least) was to sketch out the bare bones of a theoretical framework for the study of human experience in all of its variegated dimensions. James makes his own rejection of what might today be called 'essentialist' characterizations of religion as early as the second of his Gifford Lectures (2002: 26). 'Most books on the philosophy of religion try to begin with a precise definition of what its essence consists of ... Meanwhile the very fact that [these definitions] are so many and so different from one another is enough to prove that the word 'religion' cannot stand for any single principle or essence, but is rather a collective name.' Nevertheless, for the sake of bringing into view the phenomena for his psychological analysis, James states that he will ignore the institutional aspects of the religious:

> Religion, therefore, as I now ask you arbitrarily to take it, shall mean for us the feelings, acts and experiences of individual men in their solitude, so far as they apprehend themselves to stand in relation to whatever they may consider the divine ... In these lectures, however, as I have already said, the immediate personal experiences will amply fill our time, and we shall hardly consider theology or ecclesiasticism at all. (James 2002: 29–30)

Although there is clearly much that one can say of a critical nature about James's definition with the benefit of one hundred years of hindsight, not least its androcentric and theocentric biases, we should also remember that James saw his own demarcation of the subject matter as an arbitrary and heuristic characterization, articulated for the sake of providing a psychological account of the phenomena that he wished to classify as 'religious experience.' This point has not always been sufficiently grasped by later writers who, though heavily influenced by James, have not also always adopted his heuristic and pragmatic approach to category formation. That James was a highly gifted and nuanced thinker, unwilling to rest in easy absolutisms, is a feature noted for instance by one of his fiercest critics, the psychologist James Leuba. In criticizing James for what he calls his 'over belief in a superhuman consciousness' Leuba makes the following comments about the fertile and diverse strands within James's thought:

> It is fortunate for science and philosophy that this passage [on the limits of reason in explaining the sense of divine presence] does not represent William James completely. It expresses only one, or perhaps two, of the several moods or attitudes of this gifted writer: the mood of the scientist acutely conscious of defeat and limitation and partly discouraged; and the mood of the romantic soul, lover of adventure and mystery. (Leuba, 1929: 293-4)

Much of the subsequent academic literature on the study of mysticism, particularly in the 1960s, 1970s and 1980s, has been similarly concerned, as James was, with questions of taxonomy. How many different types of mysticism are there? Some writers, most notably Aldous Huxley, argued that mysticism represented a *philosophia perennis* – a common core or thread running through the major world religions. Other writers, such as R. C. Zaehner, rejected this view, arguing that the doctrinal differences between these texts, traditions and figures were too profound to be ignored or simply pushed under the carpet.

The question of the relationship between mystical experiences and their interpretation also became one of the central preoccupations of scholars of mysticism in the latter half of the twentieth century. For Walter Stace (1960) and Ninian Smart, mystical experiences were phenomenologically the same cross-culturally but differed because of the specific interpretations or doctrinal ramifications that were subsequently applied to them by the mystics themselves. However, scholars such as Steven Katz rejected any attempt to drive a wedge between experience and its interpretation. Katz argues that it is not just the interpretation but the *experience itself* that is conditioned by the cultural background of the mystic. Christian mystics have Christian mystical experiences and Buddhists have Buddhist ones. This should not surprise us, Katz argues, since this is precisely what the cultures and traditions of these mystics condition them to experience (1978: 26–7). According to Katz, it is not possible to have a pure or unmediated experience. There is no such thing, he argues, as an experience that is free from interpretation or any recognizable content. Katz therefore describes his work as a 'plea for the recognition of differences'. There is no perennial philosophy or cross-cultural unanimity between mystics of different religious traditions.[1]

It is probably fair to say that Katz's position has become the dominant view within the field since the 1980s. Most of the positions taken in this debate, however, can be seen to be implicit within James's own early attempts to provide a psychological framework for the cross-cultural study of mysticism. *The Varieties of Religious Experience* is often read as if it presupposed a perennialist position.[2] James's early contribution to this debate, however, was decidedly ambivalent. In the *Varieties*, James suggests at one point that mystical states offer 'a pretty distinct theoretic drift' towards optimism and monism (322). However, later in that same discussion, he acknowledges that the apparent unanimity of mystics in fact disappears upon more careful analysis (329–30).[3] James's pluralistic philosophical tendencies and temperament pulled him in the direction of diversity, an inclination reinforced as he became more aware of differences between religious traditions from the work of specialist scholarship of the time. This stance becomes most clearly articulated in his late article 'A Pluralistic Mystic' where James revels in the discovery that mystical experiences do not necessarily lead one to a monistic world-view (Twiss, 1995: 133; Barnard, 1997: 29–34). John E. Smith notes that although he significantly underestimated the importance of social and political factors in religious traditions, 'James did not view mysticism as a unified, transhistorical form of religious experience, but rather as one of several distinctive forms depending on the variety of religious traditions in the background.' (Smith, 1983: 276).

We can see then that much of the late twentieth-century debates on the question of a common core and Steven Katz's plea for a recognition of cultural differences is little more than a re-statement of the internal dynamic and debate going on within James's own thinking upon this matter and his growing preference for an account that pays attention to the pluralistic nature of mysticism as a phenomenon. Similarly, in the classic debate between Aldous Huxley (1954, 1956) and R.C. Zaehner (1961) about the truth-bearing status of drug-induced mystical experiences, we find that James's approach had already outlined the basic terms of this debate at the beginning of the twentieth century.

The debate about the possibility of a 'pure consciousness event' within the study of mysticism continued to rage well into the 1990s with a number of critical responses to Steven Katz's position, focusing particularly upon his claim that it is not possible to have an unmediated experience, devoid of conceptual or cultural baggage.[4] However, even these interventions (e.g. by Sallie B. King, 1988 and Robert Forman, 1990) have made important contributions but have generally failed to challenge the narrowly experientialist framing of the discussion. Consider, for instance, Robert Forman's autobiographical appeal to his own experience of a 'pure consciousness event' which he puts forward as an empirical refutation of Katz's view (Forman, 1990). Forman's response, along with his other work in the field, such as his study of the medieval Dominican Meister Eckhart, remains firmly located within a modernist framework of interpretation with an emphasis placed upon a psychological analysis of individual accounts of mystical experiences.

One wonders what James himself would have made of the debate about the existence or not of 'pure consciousness events' (PCEs). On the one hand James's response to Forman would seem reasonably clear – the mystic's insight can only be authoritative for the individual undergoing the experience. Katz therefore has no reason to accept Forman's account as authoritative. However, James's sensitivity to 'the mystical impulse' in humans and his interest in personal accounts of human transformation would have made him highly receptive to Forman's attempts to argue for the reality of PCEs, at least on a phenomenological level. However, we should be careful not to confuse this later discussion of PCEs with James's own notion of 'pure experience', grounded as it was in his radical empiricism, and denoting the entire range of our experiential processes prior to their division into subject and object. It is not immediately clear that James's pluralistic philosophy of radical empiricism renders his notion of 'pure experience' (which is not particularly associated with mystical states of rapture) compatible with Forman's non-dualistic 'pure consciousness event' (see Dilworth, 1969; Zaleski, 1993–4). What Forman, Katz and James all share in common, however, is an epistemological problematic largely inspired by Kant and responses to him.[5] A century after the establishment of the comparative study of mysticism as a field, many of the key scholars in the field continue to articulate a series of theoretical positions that are pre-figured *in* and in fact largely pre-determined *by* the modernist psychological paradigm within which James constructs the subject matter.

James and 'oriental mysticism'

In the modern era mysticism has also been closely associated with the notion of spirituality and also with the religions of Asia. As a result of European colonial exploration the term 'mystical' and its various cultural connotations was increasingly applied in non-European contexts and cultures. In the eighteenth and nineteenth centuries in particular, energized by the Romanticist fascination with all things Eastern, we find the emergence of a number of tropes relating to 'the mystic East' or the 'mysterious Orient'. Thus was born some of the most enduring and powerful stereotypes of Asia with whole traditions and peoples described as 'mystical' and 'other-worldly' in contrast to the rational and 'this-worldly' West (see King, 1999). Today it is not uncommon for people to say that they are spiritual or that they have spiritual beliefs but that they are not religious, meaning of course that they do not affiliate with a particular religious institution or movement but still have some experience of the sacred. This association reflects modern shifts in Western understandings of religion since the Enlightenment and a tendency for many to distinguish between an inward and personal experience of the sacred (spirituality or mysticism) and allegiance to a particular form of organized religion. In a comparative context mysticism then has come to denote those aspects of the various religious traditions that emphasize unmediated experience of oneness with the ultimate reality, however differently conceived.

The important archival work of such scholars as Eugene Taylor (1978, 1986) and David Scott (2000) have thrown considerable light upon the literary and philosophical influences upon James with regard to his appreciation of Asian religious traditions. Alongside the mediated influence of inspirational figures like the American transcendentalist Ralph Waldo Emerson, and James's interaction with scholars of Asian religions, all of which I do not have sufficient time to discuss, we can point to the significance of two key South Asian figures in James's reading of the Hindu and Buddhist traditions. They are Swāmi Vivekānanda (1863–1902) and Anāgarika Dharmapāla (1864–1933). Both, particularly the former, were crucial in the crystallization of James's understanding of Asian traditions. This no doubt stemmed from their apparent significance as 'living sources' of their respective traditions. In this sense they provided contemporary doorways into these ancient religions in a manner that seemed to offer some kind of equivalence to the personal accounts of mystical experiences that provided the raw data for James's analysis in the *Varieties*. Vivekānanda, founder of the Ramakrishna Mission, an organization devoted to the promotion of a contemporary form of the Hindu school of Advaita Vedānta, promulgated a thorough-going non-dualistic philosophy and placed particular emphasis upon the spirituality of Indian civilization as a curative to the nihilism and materialism of modern Western culture. In Vivekānanda's hands, prevailing Orientalist notions of India as 'other-worldly' and 'mystical' were embraced and praised as India's special gift to humanity. In so doing Vivekānanda became a focal point for the Indian people to unite under the banner of a universalistic and all-embracing Hinduism.

Anāgarika Dharmapāla, like Vivekānanda, was a modernist reformer in South Asia, though in this case with reference to the Theravāda Buddhist traditions of Sri Lanka. Indeed H.L. Seneviratne (2000) has even gone so far as to argue in his recent book on the subject that Dharmapāla effectively founded a new religion – a kind of neo-Buddhism, strongly influenced by its encounter with Protestant missionary activities and the emergence of an indigenous urban middle-classed elite. Dharmapāla reads Buddhist history through the lens of Western Orientalism and in his very rejection of Protestantism replicated its emphasis upon scripture, social reform, a this-worldly work ethic and a disdain for the 'village superstitions' which he saw as corrupting accretions to the pure teachings of the Buddha.

Both Vivekānanda and Dharmapāla attended the First World Parliament of Religions in Chicago in 1893. Both were a great success, resulting in a number of subsequent tours of Europe and North America where their reputations as key representatives of the Hindu and Buddhist traditions became firmly established. James met Vivekānanda in March 1896 when the latter made one of three visits to Harvard University and delivered a lecture on 'The Vedanta Philosophy' to the Graduate Philosophical Society (Taylor, 1986). Similarly, James met Dharmapāla during the latter's third visit to America in 1902–04, when he decided to attend one of James's psychology lectures at Harvard. James, clearly already well aware of Dharmapāla's credentials, is said to have asked the man in the saffron robes to take the chair, remarking that 'You are better equipped to lecture on psychology than

I.' At the end of the session James declared that 'This is the psychology everybody will be studying twenty-five years from now' (cited in Scott, 2000: 335). Sadly, James's optimism about the cross-cultural nature of future work within psychology turned out to be radically over-optimistic, with most practitioners within the field recoiling from any real cross-cultural engagement with 'the East', preferring instead to characterize themselves in secularist terms as a 'hard science'.

Of the two Asian figures, it was Vivekānanda who was most influential in the popularization of notions of 'Indian spirituality' at the end of the nineteenth century. In India, he became a key figure in the development of neo-Hinduism or neo-Vedānta, that is a modernist and reformist trend within Hindu circles, heavily influenced by Orientalist and Theosophical conceptions of India. It was Vivekānanda who first popularized the idea of yoga as an Indian contribution to science – 'the science of supra consciousness' and of yoga as the unifying symbol of the Indian nation (Van der Veer, 2000: 73). In reading the Hindu and Buddhist traditions through the mediating lenses of figures such as Vivekānanda and Dharmapāla, James and his contemporaries failed to appreciate the sense in which such 'living sources' were themselves implicated in a complex series of translations and reinventions of their own traditions, characterized by anti-colonialist, nationalist and modernist sentiments. In effect, the fundamental reconfiguration of South Asian society and subjectivity during this period – as played out in the life and works of Dharmapāla and Vivekānanda, that is their involvement in the complex processes of modernization going on in South Asian societies at that time – is for the most part lost on James when he cites them as authorities for interpreting the Hindu and Buddhist traditions. Both figures, like James, are heirs to the European Enlightenment, though refracted through the colonial experience. Their reformist spirits and eagerness to engage with Western modes of authoritative knowledge made them highly amenable to a psychological reinterpretation of their own traditions.

The shared involvement of Vivekānanda, Dharmapāla and Western scholars such as James in the colonially dependent processes of modernization in the late nineteenth and early twentieth century can be seen from the following comment by Eugene Taylor (1986: 378): 'Although from another country, Vivekānanda fitted readily into a larger movement of interest in inner experience and character development that was at that time a conspicuous part of American folk culture. From this strata of society he made many friends.' What is not fully appreciated in Taylor's discussion here is the sense in which all participants in this 'dialogue' between cultures were united by their shared involvement in the processes of modernization and the emergence of the modern psychological 'subject'.

Translating yoga in terms of modern psychology

There are, however, a number of problems with the representation of ancient yogic traditions as forms of mysticism in the modern sense of the term. First, it should be appreciated that the history of yoga in South Asia represents a vast panoply of different traditions, practices and world-views. This is necessarily occluded by Dharmapāla and Vivekānanda since their very authority as modern representatives of the Hindu and Buddhist traditions required a selective reading of history. Second, as Sonu Shamdasani argues in this volume, James is primarily interested here in the study of 'states of transformation'. He is not a social theorist like Durkheim and we should not expect him to prefigure the social and the institutional aspects of the phenomena he is studying. However, it behoves scholars of mysticism to move beyond the self-determined limits of James's psychological analysis. Although the traditional practice of yoga clearly involved the prolonged application of 'psychosomatic' techniques designed to transform one's perspective upon reality, it is not clear that the emphasis that is placed upon different 'levels of attainment' within yogic literature is well represented if read exclusively in terms of post-Enlightenment notions of 'private experience'.

The Buddhist path, traditionally conceived, is not so much concerned with the cultivation of so-called 'altered states of consciousness' but is rather about the development of analytical insight or wisdom (*prajñā*), equanimity (*upekṣā*) and calm (*śamatha*). Even *śamatha* – calm – is not about the attainment of a transient or altered state of consciousness, but is rather a quality of continued mental and emotional stability to be applied throughout one's life. In the traditional Buddhist system of eight or nine *jhānas* – briefly discussed by James in the *Varieties* (2002: 311) – the higher levels of attainment correspond directly to cosmological realms into which one can be reborn and should not simply be read as referring to transient psychological states in the modern sense. The goal for many traditional practitioners was precisely to be reborn in one of these realms in a future life. In other words *psychology and cosmology cannot be so easily disentangled when analysing these historical materials.* Moreover, for texts like the *Yoga Sūtra* it is our everyday consciousness that is characterized by constant fluctuation or 'alteration'. The goal of yoga then is precisely to eradicate such transient states, not cultivate them (Yoga Sutra 1.2 – *citta-vṛtti-nirodha*). There are some South Asian philosophical schools that offer an analysis that is more amenable to James's phenomenological reading of such concepts, most notably the Yogācāra school of Buddhism, with its rendering of traditional Buddhist cosmology in terms of stages of meditative awareness (Shaw, 1987). Even in this case, however, we must be careful not to translate ancient Yogācāra thought into modern psychological terms, thereby erasing important historical and philosophical differences between the two (see King, 2000: ch. 7). To interpret classical yogic texts in general as if they provide accounts of 'mystical states of consciousness' comparable to the personal testimonies documented in Starbuck and James's other examples is to ignore the didactic, propadeutical and systematizing function they perform within their respective traditions. As Robert Sharf notes with regard to Buddhist meditative handbooks such as the *Visuddhimagga* (Theravāda), these works are 'first and foremost scholarly compendiums, compiled by monks of formidable learning who were attempting to systematize and schematize the confused and often conflicting descriptions of practices and stages scattered throughout the canon' (Sharf, 1995: 238). Such texts are frequently making prescriptive and polemical points and have often had more of a liturgical function. It is misleading to read them as if they provide us with straightforwardly phenomenological accounts of 'altered' states of consciousness in the modern sense of the phrase.

Attention to the social and institutional history of yoga also highlights the limitations of an exclusively psychological approach to such phenomena. Historical and ethnographic work establishes quite conclusively that before the suppression of their networks by the British Raj at the end of the eighteenth century, ascetics and renouncers were often deeply involved in the social, economic and political activities of Indian communities, often acting as soldier mercenaries, traders and money lenders. Most significantly, a century before Vivekānanda's construction of the 'spiritualized ascetic', it had not sat easily with the colonial agenda of the British, being increasingly displaced by the *Pax Britannica* at the end of the eighteenth century and culminating in the unsuccessful but protracted Samnyasi Rebellion of the late eighteenth century (van der Veer, 1988; Pinch, 1996). Widespread involvement of groups of ascetics in such activities of course does not accord well with prevailing Orientalist conceptions of other-worldly *sādhus*, nor does it sit easily with the 'spiritualizing' agenda of reformists such as Vivekānanda. The study of mysticism as a multi-disciplinary exercise, however, must take account of this history if it is to avoid trading in ideal forms and reified stereotypes.

The representation of yoga as a system for the transformation of the individual through the cultivation of altered states of consciousness is a partial reading that ignores the social, institutional and cosmological dimensions of traditional yogic traditions. It only became possible to represent yoga in this fashion because of the reconstruction of the social, economic and political infrastructure of South Asia brought about by the complex processes of European colonization and the 'modernization' of India. The new forms of subjectivity that emerged in South Asia in the nineteenth and early twentieth centuries were highly influenced by European-derived notions such as 'religion', 'mysticism' and 'spirituality'. Through the complex interactions precipitated by European colonialism and Asian responses to such influences, 'yoga' became nationalized, partially 'detraditionalized', and its introspective dimensions increasingly emphasized. This aided the secularization of yoga in the twentieth century and also rendered it more readily exportable to the West, leading eventually to the development of what Paul Heelas (1996) has called the 'self-spiritualities' associated with the New Age and to the commodification and marketing of yoga as a physicalized therapy and aid to 'lifestyle enhancement' in a late twentieth-century capitalist context (Lau, 2000). At the turn of the twenty-first century this has also resulted in the development of new forms of *capitalist spirituality* with a highly individualistic and consumerist orientation (see Carrette and King, 2005).

The psychological framing of yoga also dovetails too easily with modern notions of the atomistic and autonomous individual. The fundamental problem with the way in which James and subsequent 'psychologically oriented' scholars have framed discussions of 'mysticism' and 'spirituality' has been that statements about the non-dualistic and non-conceptual nature of ultimate reality (for instance) become translated into a post-Enlightenment intellectual framework where such accounts are invariably read as referring to extraordinary and transitory experiences of a private and individual nature. This represents the translation of such traditions according to a modern regime of governmentality, grounded in the dominance of the 'psy disciplines' of the Western world as a means of understanding modern subjectivity (Rose, 1998).

It is going too far to say that there is *no* discussion of consciousness and different mental states in the literature of the various yogic traditions of South Asia. On the contrary, there are many highly technical and systematic accounts of 'consciousness' and the mind (often viewed as separate 'functions' in many South Asian systems of thought). We should be careful, however, not to read such texts as if they were psychological treatises in the modern sense. The specific socio-cultural context in which South Asian yogic systems arose did not necessitate the development of a specific 'secularized' discipline known as 'psychology', as understood in the contemporary Western world. This is not so much because South Asians did not separate 'psychology' from 'religion' (as it is often put), since to frame the point in this way is to take modern Western cognitive categories as the normative pattern for discussing world history. Rather, we should acknowledge that the world-views of traditional South Asian yogic traditions (including those labelled 'Hindu', 'Buddhist', 'Jaina', and 'Sufi') considered the analysis of consciousness and the development of a 'wholesome' (Buddhist: *kuśala*) orientation toward the world to be inseparable from a consideration of one's existential relationship to that world.

Yoga in these contexts was not a form of psychotherapy (although it was often claimed to have therapeutic consequences for the practitioner and the wider society), nor was it an ancient form of psychoanalysis (although it did provide analytical insights about the workings of the individual mind). Similarly, the overarching world-views of modern Western academic psychology and traditional South Asian yogic systems result in a different orientation and framing of the analysis of consciousness (Sanskrit: *citta*, *vijñāna*, *jñāna*, etc). One can find evidence of all of these elements within the pluriform traditions of yoga practised throughout South Asia, but they have not traditionally constituted its fundamental *raison d'être*, which has overwhelmingly been the pursuit of enlightenment and liberation (*mokṣa*) from an apparently endless cycle of rebirths (*saṃsāra*).

This realization does not mean that there is nothing to be gained from an engagement between the two, but it does mean that we cannot simply map one system of thought in terms of the presuppositions and concepts of another without anachronism and distortion occurring. What made the modernizing projects of Vivekānanda and Dharmapāla of such interest to James was that both figures effectively re-mapped long-established and complex systems of thought and practice in a way that rendered them amenable to modern, post-Enlightenment debates about the nature of experience and human consciousness.

One does not have to look very far to see some of the consequences of an uncritical reading of the history of yoga as seen in highly individualized 'spiritualities of the self', and the commodification and transformation of ancient yogic traditions and practices into a secularized system of therapy, physical exercise and/or mood enhancement in a late capitalist context (Lau, 2000; Carrette and King, 2005). We certainly cannot lay the blame for all of this at the feet of figures such as James, Vivekānanda and Dharmapāla. The history of the transmission of yoga to the West is far too complex for such an analysis to be helpful (consider, for instance, the role of Iyengar in the popularity of a highly physicalized form of haṭha yoga in the West in the late twentieth century). Moreover, in the case of James, he can hardly be held responsible for the less nuanced ways in which his work has been received and subsequently utilized by following generations. Nevertheless, it is important to acknowledge the crucial role played by figures such as James in laying the intellectual foundations for such later developments.

Conclusion

It is important to acknowledge the crucial contribution made by William James to the emergence of the psychology of religion and the comparative study of contemplative systems and practices in the modern period. James set the terms for debates within the study of mysticism in the twentieth century and his impact upon the field has been quite remarkable. However, from the point of view of a balanced history of religions, it is important to acknowledge the limitations of James's experientialist paradigm for a broader historical and multidisciplinary analysis of such phenomena. James shows some evidence of being aware of some of the limitations of his work in this regard, although this recognition has often been lost in the enthusiasm that later writers have shown in applying James's psychological analysis uncritically to complex and multi-dimensional traditions and practices within the study of religions.

In so far as scholars of religion continue to construe 'the mystical' in narrowly psychological terms they continue to orbit around the same post-Kantian agenda in which much of James's own work can be located. There is need, if you like, for a new 'Copernican revolution' to occur in the comparative study of mysticism and spirituality. Such an approach would need to pay attention to the discursive formations and political construction of the field itself, and no longer rest uncritically upon post-Enlightenment notions of 'the religious' as pre-eminently 'private' and experiential in nature. There are signs that the particular epistemological *cul-de-sac* ensuing from the late twentieth-century debates about 'pure consciousness events' has lost much of its appeal within mainstream academic circles, and scholarship within the field has increasingly turned its attention towards the social, historical and political contexts of the mystical. It is time to challenge the narrow psychological framing of 'the mystical' as established by James and inherited (often in a less nuanced manner) by scholars of Religious Studies. This critique is vital if the study of mysticism, spirituality and 'contemplative systems' (however such a field might be conceived in the future) is to reconfigure itself in terms of the shifting interdisciplinary formations of twenty-first century scholarship. James would have expected nothing less of us as intellectual heirs, admirers and yet critical readers of his work.

Notes

1. Contrary to perennialists such as Huxley and Stace, Katz argues that when a Buddhist speaks of emptiness and Meister Eckhart discusses the nothingness of the Godhead they are not saying the same thing at all. Buddhists reject the idea of an all-powerful creator deity, while Eckhart as a Dominican theologian takes this presupposition for granted. Whereas Buddhists believe that there are no absolute beings or entities (since everything is empty of independent or inherent existence), Christians like Eckhart believe that the world is such only because it is created by God – the absolute first cause of everything. Even the claim that the experience of underlying reality is ineffable does not necessarily imply a common core since if one cannot truly speak about the ultimate reality, how can one be sure one is speaking about the same ultimate reality?
2. Perennialism as a position is attributed to James in Katz, 1978: 1–2 and Proudfoot, 1985: 121. For a counter view see Twiss, 1995: 152–3, 133.
3. Fundamentally for James this was because mystical experiences exceed the limits of our intellectual capacities. See Lecture XVIII (Philosophy) for discussion of this. Moreover, as James notes in his discussion of the mystical feeling, since it 'has no specific intellectual content' it is capable of forming 'matrimonial alliances' with a variety of different views (2002: 329).
4. It is clear for instance that Katz's stance leaves no room for the unconditioned awareness of reality that is presumed in Buddhist notions of enlightenment (*bodhi*), the Taoist ideal of uncultivated spontaneity (*tzu-jan*) and the non-conceptual state of meditation (*nirvikalpa samādhi*) advocated by many Hindu schools of thought, such as yoga and Advaita Vedānta. Scholars of these traditions have sometimes proven reluctant to rule out the fundamental goals of such Asian traditions, arguing that on methodological and philosophical grounds one ought not to presume the falsity of the traditions one is studying before the analysis has even begun.
5. For an attempt to 'think outside' the confines of the Kantian epistemological paradigm by engagement with classical South Asian philosophies on this issue see Sallie B. King, 1988, and King, 1999: 175–86.

References

Barnard, G. William, *Exploring Unseen Worlds: William James and the Philosophy of Mysticism,* Albany, NY: State University of New York Press, 1997.

Beer, Frances, *Women and Mystical Experience in the Middle Ages,* Rochester, NY and Woodbridge: Boydell, 1992.

Bouyer, Louis, *The Christian Mystery: From Pagan Myth to Christian Mysticism,* Edinburgh: T and T Clark, 1990.

Bynum, Caroline Walker, *Jesus as Mother: Studies in the Spirituality of the High Middle Ages*, Berkeley: University of California Press, 1982.

Carrette, Jeremy and King, Richard, *Selling Spirituality: The Silent Takeover of Religion*, London and New York: Routledge, 2005.

Certeau, Michel de, ' "Mystique" au XVIIe siècle: Le problème du langage "mystique," ' in *L'Homme devant Dieu: Mélanges offerts au Pere Henri du Lubac Vol. 2*, Paris: Aubier, 1964, pp. 267–291.

Certeau, Michel de, *La Fable Mystique, XVIe–XVIIe Siècle*, Gallimard, 1982. (English translation: *The Mystic Fable Volume 1: The Sixteenth and Seventeenth Centuries*, trans. Michael B. Smith, Chicago: University of Chicago Press, 1992.)

Dilworth, David, 'The Initial Formations of Pure Experience in Nishida Kitarō and William James', in *Monumenta Nipponica* Vol. 24: 93–111, 1969.

Forman, Robert (ed.), *The Problem of Pure Consciousness: Mysticism and Philosophy*, New York: Oxford University Press, 1990.

Heelas, Paul, *The New Age Movement*, Oxford, UK and Cambridge MA: Blackwells, 1996.

Huxley, Aldous, *The Doors of Perception and Heaven and Hell* (London: Grafton Books (Collins), 1977), originally published London: Chatto & Windus, 1954 and 1956.

James, William, *The Varieties of Religious Experience: A Study in Human Nature*, the Centenary Edition of The Gifford Lectures 1901–2, with a foreword by Micky James and new introductions by Eugene Taylor and Jeremy Carrette, London and New York: Routledge, 2002.

Jantzen, Grace, *Power, Gender and Christian Mysticism*, Cambridge: Cambridge University Press, 1995.

Katz, Steven, 'Language, Epistemology and Mysticism', in Steven Katz (ed.), *Mysticism and Philosophical Analysis*, New York: Oxford University Press, 1978.

King, Richard, *Orientalism and Religion: Postcolonial Theory, India and 'the Mystic East'*, London and New York: Routledge, 1999.

King, Richard, *Indian Philosophy: An Introduction to Hindu and Buddhist Thought*, Edinburgh University Press (UK); Georgetown University Press (USA), 2000.

King, Sallie B., 'Two Epistemological Models for the Interpretation of Mysticism', in *Journal of American Academy of Religion* Vol. LVI No. 2, 1988.

Lau, Kimberley J., *New Age Capitalism: Making Money East of Eden*, Philadelphia: University of Pennsylvania Press, 2000.

Leuba, James H., *The Psychology of Religious Mysticism*, London and Boston: Routledge & Kegan Paul, revised edn, 1929.

Petroff, Elizabeth A., *Medieval Women's Visionary Literature*, Oxford: Oxford University Press, 1986.

Pinch, William R. *Peasants and Monks in British India*, Berkeley: University of California Press, 1996.

Proudfoot, Wayne, *Religious Experience*, Berkeley: University of California Press, 1985.

Rose, Nikolas, *Inventing Our Selves: Psychology, Power and Personhood*, Cambridge: Cambridge University Press, 1998.

Schmidt , Leigh Eric, 'The Making of Modern "Mysticism" ' in *Journal of American Academy of Religion* Vol. 71, No. 2, June 2003: 273–302.

Scott, David, 'William James and Buddhism: American Pragmatism and the Orient' in *Religion* Vol. 30: 333–52, 2000.

Seneviratne, H.L., *The Work of Kings: The New Buddhism of Sri Lanka*, Chicago: University of Chicago Press, 2000.

Sharf, Robert, 'Buddhist Modernism and the Rhetoric of Meditative Experience', in *Numen* Vol. 42 No. 3: 228–83, 1995.

Shaw, Miranda, 'William James and Yogācāra Philosophy: A comparative enquiry' in *Philosophy East and West* Vol. 37 No. 3: 223–44, 1987.

Smith, John E., 'William James's Account of Mysticism: A Critical Appraisal' in Steven Katz (ed.), *Mysticism and Religious Traditions*, New York: Oxford University Press, 1983.

Stace, Walter, *Mysticism and Philosophy*, London: Jeremy P. Tarcher Inc., 1960.

Taylor, Eugene, 'Psychology of Religion and Asian Studies: The William James Legacy' in *Journal of Transpersonal Psychology* Vol. 10 No. 1, 1978.

Taylor, Eugene, 'Swami Vivekānanda and William James: Asian Psychology at Harvard in the 1890s' in *Prabuddha Bharata* Vol. 91: 374–85, 1986.

Turner, Denys, *The Darkness of God: Negativity in Christian Mysticism*, Cambridge: Cambridge University Press, 1995.

Twiss, Sumner B., 'Revisiting and Revisioning William James's Account of Mysticism' in *Journal of Psychology of Religion* Vol. 4–5: 123–80, 1995.

van der Veer, Peter, *Gods on Earth: The Management of Religious Experience and Identity in a North Indian Pilgrimage Centre*. Athlone Press, Continuum, 1988.

van der Veer, Peter, *Imperial Encounters: Religion and Modernity in India and Britain*, Princeton: Princeton University Press, 2000.

Wasserstrom, Steven M., *Religion After Religion: Gershom Scholem, Mircea Eliade and Henry Corbin at Eranos*, Princeton: Princeton University Press, 1999.

Zaehner, R.C., *Mysticism Sacred and Profane*, New York: Oxford University Press, 1961.

Zaleski, Carol, 'Speaking of William James to the Cultured Among His Despisers', in *Journal of Psychology of Religion* Vol. 2 No. 3: 127–70, 1993–4.

Chapter 8

James and Freud on mysticism

Robert A. Segal

There is a conspicuous difference between the approach to religion by earlier social scientists – anthropologists, sociologists, and psychologists – and the approach by present-day ones. Where, if one dare generalize, present-day social scientists timidly confine themselves to the issues of the *origin* and *function* of religion, earlier social scientists ventured beyond these issues to the issue of the *truth* of religion. Present-day social scientists shun the issue of truth as beyond their professional ken. Assuming a rigid division of labor, they restrict themselves to determining *why* adherents believe what they do and avoid assessing whether what adherents believe is true. At most, they pronounce religion helpful or harmful, but not true or false. Whatever their own religious convictions, *qua* social scientists they profess to be unable to say anything about the truth of religious claims – an issue they readily leave to philosophers and theologians.[1] They fear that their use of their social scientific findings to evaluate the truth claims of religion would commit either the genetic fallacy or what I call its functional counterpart – basing the truth or, more commonly, the falsity of religion on the effect of religion on adherents.[2]

By contrast, earlier social scientists, despite their eagerness to break free of the philosophical roots of their disciplines, rarely hesitated to use their findings about the origin and function of religion to assess the truth of religion. To be sure, some simply declared religion true or, more typically, false on philosophical grounds and then, as social scientists, sought to account for beliefs so blatantly false – for example, Tylor and Frazer. But others went further, using their accounts to evaluate the truth of religion – for example, Marx. Did these more daring social scientists thereby commit the genetic or the functional fallacy? That is the question I raise in two of the grandest cases: that of James and that of Freud on mysticism, which for both means largely religious mysticism.

James

James writes about mysticism in two combined lectures in *The Varieties of Religious Experience* and again in the conclusion. While he recognizes nonreligious cases of mysticism, he focuses on religious cases. Indeed, he goes as far as to root all religion, or at least all individual, noninstitutionalized religion, in mysticism: 'One may say truly, I think, that personal religious experience has its root and centre in mystical states of consciousness' (1936, 370). For James, mystical experience is at once a feeling and a state of knowledge. So central for James is the feeling that he characterizes mystical states 'as more like states of feeling than like states of intellect' (1936, 371). But he also notes that 'although so similar to states of feeling, mystical states seem to those who experience them to be also states of knowledge' (1936, 371). Presumably, mystical states *must* be states of knowledge for truth claims to be based on them and for James to be able to assess those claims.

James offers at least three ways of evaluating the truth claims of mystics: by the *origin* of their experiences, by the *function* of their experiences, and by the *content* of their experiences. In contrast to present-day approaches, James does not consider sociological or cultural origins of mysticism. For him, as also for Freud, mysticism occurs to individuals, not to communities, and however varied mystical experiences can be, they vary with the individual, not with time and place: 'In mystic states we both become one with the Absolute and we become aware of our oneness. This is the everlasting and triumphant mystical tradition, hardly altered by differences of clime or creed . . . which brings it about that the mystical classics have, as has been said, neither birthday nor native land' (1936, 410). Anyone anywhere can have the same kind of mystical experience as anyone else – a position at odds not only with that of contemporary 'contextualists' but also with that of classical authorities like Gershom Scholem.

But James's inattention to 'contextualism' hardly means inattention to any origin of mysticism. James famously takes on those he disparagingly labels 'medical materialists,' for whom mysticism need only be shown to have a physiological or psychological correlate to be exposed as delusory: 'To the medical mind these [mystical] ecstasies signify nothing but suggested and imitated hypnoid states, on an intellectual basis of superstition, and a corporeal one of degeneration and hysteria' (1936, 404). James's response is in effect to invoke the genetic fallacy: 'Undoubtedly these pathological conditions have existed in many and possibly in all the cases, but that fact tells us nothing about the value for knowledge of the consciousness which they induce' (1936, 404).[3]

James goes further. He is prepared to argue that physiological and psychological conditions are *relevant* to mystical experience and even indispensable – but to inducing it, not to falsifying it. Of drinking, he writes:

> The next step into mystical states carries us into a realm that public opinion and ethical philosophy have long since branded as pathological . . . I refer to the consciousness produced by intoxicants and anaesthetics, especially by alcohol. The sway of alcohol over mankind is unquestionably due to its power to stimulate the mystical faculties of human nature, usually crushed to earth by the cold facts and dry criticisms of the sober hour. Sobriety

diminishes, discriminates, and says no; drunkenness expands, unites, and says yes. (James 1936, 377–78)

Likewise 'nitrous oxide and ether, especially nitrous oxide, when sufficiently diluted with air, stimulate the mystical consciousness in an extraordinary degree' (1936, 378).

James, ever open and flexible, allows for any possible spur to mystical experience – this in contrast, for example, to the far more doctrinaire R.C. Zaehner, for whom the claim, made by Aldous Huxley, that mescaline can yield the same level of mystical experience as lifelong training in meditation is an affront. James even grants unabashedly that insanity can hail from the same psychological source as genuine mysticism but, again, stresses that origin does not dictate truth:

> Open any of these [textbooks on insanity], and you will find abundant cases in which 'mystical ideas' are cited as characteristic symptoms of enfeebled or deluded states of mind. In delusional insanity, paranoia, as they sometimes call it, we may have a *diabolical* mysticism, a sort of religious mysticism turned upside down. . . . It is evident that from the point of view of their psychological mechanism, the classic mysticism and these lower mysticisms spring from the same mental level, from that great subliminal or transmarginal region of which science is beginning to admit the existence, but of which so little is really known. . . . To come from thence is no infallible credential. What comes must be sifted and tested, and run the gauntlet of confrontation with the total context of experience. (James 1936, 417–18)

Of seemingly spontaneous cases of mystical experience, James would doubtless assert that a spur is present but simply unknown.

Most scholars of mysticism understandably evaluate the truth claims of mysticism on the basis of the *content* of the experience. But James, at least in the *Varieties*, focuses on the *function* – or, better, the *effect* – of mystical experience, and his term for the effect is the 'fruit.' Against medical materialists, he declares, 'To pass a spiritual judgment upon these states, we must not content ourselves with superficial medical talk, but inquire into their fruits for life' (1936, 404). James names two main fruits: 'stupefaction' and 'energy.' Not both but either is to be found among the accounts of mystics worldwide. James does acknowledge that these fruits can come from delusion as well as from reality:

> Mystical conditions may, therefore, render the soul more energetic in the lines which their inspiration favors. But this could be reckoned an advantage only in case the inspiration were a true one. If the inspiration were erroneous, the energy would be all the more mistaken and misbegotten. So we stand once more before that problem of truth which confronted us at the end of the lectures on saintliness. You will remember that we turned to mysticism

precisely to get some light on truth. Do mystical states establish the truth of those theological affections in which the saintly life has its root? (James 1936, 406–07)

Yet despite this unflinching caution about relying on effects to determine truth, James proceeds to rely further on effects to help decide the issue.

The effects to which James appeals are the states of 'optimism' and 'monism.' While, strictly, these states are not 'fruits,' they are consequences, and consequences with philosophical ramifications:

> In spite of their repudiation of articulate self-description, mystical states in general assert a pretty distinct theoretic drift. It is possible to give the outcome of the majority of them in terms that point in definite philosophical directions. One of these directions is optimism, and the other is monism. We pass into mystical states from out of ordinary consciousness as from a less into a more, as from a smallness into a vastness, and at the same time as from an unrest to a rest. We feel them as reconciling, unifying states. (James 1936, 407)[4]

That is, mystical experience has these effects on practitioners.

In his conclusion James relies even more on the effects to determine truth. Appealing, though with typical caution, to the numbers – to the large number of mystics worldwide with similar experiences – he cites, as one similarity, the 'feelings of security and joy' (1936, 499). While once again recognizing that these feelings may be merely psychological – 'this [set of feelings] may be nothing but [the mystic's] subjective way of feeling things, a mood of his own fancy, in spite of the effects produced' (1936, 499) – he still uses them. He argues that effects so powerful in so many can likely come only from a real encounter with a deeper reality – a tamer version of the argument by Barry Goldwater's supporters in 1964 that so many millions couldn't be wrong. While James calls this conclusion an 'over-belief,' going as it does beyond the evidence, he *is* proposing it as more likely true than false. And he is *basing* the over-belief on, above all, the effects:

> Yet the unseen region in question is not merely ideal, for it produces effects in this world. When we commune with it, work is actually done upon our finite personality, for we are turned into new men, and consequences in the way of conduct follow in the natural world upon our regenerative change. But that which produces effects within another reality must be termed a reality itself, so I feel as if we had no philosophic excuse for calling the unseen or mystical world unreal. (James 1936, 506–07)

James puts the point bluntly: 'God is real since he produces real effects' (1936, 507). Surely James's focus on effects tallies with his pragmatic philosophy – that is, with the difference that belief makes.

It is hard to accept James's argument from effects. Ordinarily, what I call the functional fallacy would mean *rejecting* the truth of mysticism on the sheer grounds that it produces certain effects, which here would doubtless be negative rather than positive ones. Many mystics, such as St Teresa, tie mystical experience to *positive* effects – for example, to the practice of good deeds in the community. For Teresa, purported mystical experience followed by misdeeds would surely falsify the claim to true mystical experience. With James, the question is the reverse: whether good deeds or other positive effects – namely, feelings of a specific kind – *establish* the claim to true mystical experience. To make his case, James would have to prove, not merely assert, that whatever effects he identified could likely – James would never claim definitely – come *only* from true mystical experience. Otherwise he would stand guilty of the functional fallacy: basing the truth of mysticism on an effect which has no necessary bearing on truth since it is equally compatible with delusion. Whether or not James could so tighten his argument, his argument for the truth of mysticism is distinctive in its appeal to consequences rather than to content. His analysis is akin to a medical diagnosis: he infers the likely cause from the equivalent of the symptoms, or effects. But James's 'diagnosis' is of belief – the claim to have had true mystical experience – and he is using the effects to determine not what belief the effects presuppose but whether that belief is true.[5]

Freud

Freud writes about religion in three whole books – *Totem and Taboo*, *The Future of an Illusion*, and *Moses and Monotheism* – but writes about mysticism in only the first, slim chapter of *Civilization and Its Discontents*. While he, like James, subsumes mysticism under religion, in his books on religion he presupposes division rather than oneness. In *Totem and Taboo* and in *Moses and Monotheism* the main divide is between an individual and the rest of the family. In *The Future of an Illusion* the main divide is between an individual and the physical world. In all three books God is set over against the individual. A father-like figure, God tyrannically demands submission to familial mores in *Totem and Taboo* and in *Moses and Monotheism*, but benevolently shelters the individual from a threatening world in *The Future of an Illusion*. In all three works religion is a matter of the unequal relationship between the individual and a separate God. As a social scientist, Freud is concerned chiefly with accounting for the origin and the function of this relationship.

In *Civilization and Its Discontents* religion and God are conceived of differently. Indeed, Freud is here responding to the argument of Romain Rolland that in *The Future of an Illusion* – and one could add in the other two books as well – Freud has missed the true origin of religion. Rolland, for his part, does not consider the function of religion. The true origin of religion, according to Rolland, is, in Freud's words, a 'feeling as of something limitless, unbounded – as it were "oceanic"' (Freud 1962, 11). The feeling is of oneness with the world.

In deriving all religion, or at least all personal, noninstitutionalized religion, from this mystical experience, Rolland is like James. For Rolland, and presumably also for James, the feeling of separation from the world comes only later, so that *The Future of an Illusion*, which derives religion from the most intense feeling of separation from the world – the feeling of helplessness before the world – cannot account for the origin of religion. How the feeling of oneness with the world can lead to its seeming opposite yet still be the origin of religion *per se*, Rolland never explains. Somehow religion not only begins with mysticism but also continues with mysticism even in its subsequent, nonmystical stages: the feeling 'is the source of the religious energy which is seized upon by the various Churches and religious systems' (Freud 1962, 11). The brand of mysticism that Rolland describes is what W.T. Stace calls 'extrovertive' rather than 'introvertive': oneness is with the external world, not with something removed from the external world. In religious mysticism oneness is thereby with God, however God is additionally conceived.[6]

What is Freud's rejoinder to Rolland? Freud does not try to match Rolland feeling for feeling, or helplessness for oneness. Despairing of treating the oceanic feeling as a mere feeling, Freud 'fall[s] back on the ideational content which is most readily associated with the feeling' (1962, 12). Even though Rolland himself differentiates the *feeling* from any *belief* – 'One may . . . rightly call oneself religious on the ground of this oceanic feeling alone, even if one rejects every belief and every illusion' (1962, 11) – Freud, like James, links the two. For both, mysticism is at once beliefs and feelings. Where James stresses feeling over belief, Freud stresses belief over feeling. He asserts that the feeling of oneness with the world 'seems something rather in the nature of an intellectual perception, which is not, it is true, without an accompanying feeling-tone, but only such as would be present with any other act of thought of equal range' (1962, 12). On Freud's behalf it might be argued not just that the feeling of oneness with the world seems inextricably tied to a belief in the oneness of the world but that, contrary to Rolland, the feeling qualifies as religious only when it does.

Freud's tactic is to take Rolland to be offering the feeling as not simply the *accompaniment* of a belief but the *justification* for the belief: the *feeling* of oneness with the world can for Rolland come from only the *fact* of oneness with the world. Nothing else can account for this feeling, for anything else presupposes separation between oneself and the world. Freud's procedure is not to deny the feeling but to account for it otherwise – and, more, to account for it *within* the camp of separation from the world. Where Rolland is arguing that only the fact of oneness with the world can account for the feeling of oneness, Freud argues that he, Freud, can account for the feeling without having to postulate the fact. To be able to attribute the feeling of oneness to other than the fact of oneness would, for Freud, be to undermine the use of the feeling as justification for the belief in oneness with the world.

Freud offers an account of the feeling that is, I think, superior to Rolland's on several grounds. Where Rolland pits, and eagerly pits, the feeling of oneness with the world against our ordinary feeling toward the world, Freud fits the feeling of oneness with the world snugly within our ordinary feeling toward the world. Rolland's whole point is that the feeling of oneness is unique. Freud's whole point is that it is not. Where Rolland separates the feeling of oneness from all religious belief, Freud connects the feeling to all religious belief. Where Rolland takes the feeling of oneness as given, Freud seeks to account for it: what for Rolland is the stopping point is for Freud the starting point. Where Rolland takes the feeling as a sign or glimpse of our true condition *vis-à-vis* the world, Freud takes the feeling as a symptom of the human personality, which continually wishes things to be other than they truly are.

Freud's argument is that the feeling of oneness, far from independent of the feeling of separation, is a *reaction* to that feeling, which therefore comes first. According to Freud, infants initially experience themselves as one with the world and only gradually learn to differentiate themselves from the world. The infantile feeling of oneness may persist in many persons alongside the mature feeling of separation: 'If we may assume that there are many people in whose mental life this primary [i.e., infantile] ego-feeling has persisted to a greater or less degree, it would exist in them side by side with the narrower and more sharply demarcated ego-feeling of maturity, like a kind of counterpart to it' (1962, 15). The beliefs that would correspond to this feeling 'would be precisely those of limitlessness and of a bond with the universe – the same idea with which my friend elucidated the "oceanic" feeling' (1962, 15). Like other memories from infancy and early childhood, the memory of oneness has been 'repressed.'

But if, as Freud claims, 'in mental life nothing which has once been formed can perish,' so that 'everything is somehow preserved' and 'can once more be brought to life' (1962, 16), the feeling should be found among all humans and not just among many. Yet Freud confesses that 'I cannot discover this 'oceanic' feeling in myself' (1962, 12). But even if Freud were to concede that the feeling is preserved in everyone, he could still explain why the feeling is presently felt by only some. Freud's argument is that once infants or children come to differentiate themselves from the world, they feel helpless before it. Most then turn to religion to overcome this feeling. This is the theory of *The Future of an Illusion*, not the very different, more truly 'Freudian' theory of *Totem and Taboo* and *Moses and Monotheism*. In *The Future of an Illusion*, the work that Rolland is seeking to elude, religion is an attempt by adults, not children, to recreate for themselves the security that their idealized, childhood fathers accorded them while they were growing up. God is created to protect adults from a threatening world, just as their father did when they were young.

But Freud must still encompass the feeling of oneness within his theory of religion. He does so by taking the feeling as simply the most extreme form of the restoration of infantile and childhood security. If some adults, not least Freud himself, are strong enough to accept the world as cruel and indifferent, most need religion to cope with the world. But for some a restored father is not sufficient, for even if he is wholly reliable, he serves only to mediate between them and the still mean world 'out there.' The weakest humans are unable to endure even that kind of threat. They yearn not merely for a savior from the mean world but for the dissolution of the world itself. Only oneness with the world eliminates the threat from a separate world. Hence Freud writes that 'I can imagine that the oceanic feeling became connected with religion later on. The "oneness with the universe" which constitutes its ideational content sounds like a first attempt at a religious consolation, as though it were another way of disclaiming the danger which the ego recognizes as threatening it from the external world' (1962, 19).

Like James, Freud typifies the bold, earlier social scientific approach to mysticism and, in general, to religion exactly because he does not confine himself to the origin and function of mysticism. Certainly he employs his non-religious account to refute the religious account offered by Rolland, but he does more. Because he takes Rolland to be using Rolland's account of the origin of mysticism to offer a justification for mysticism – that is, to justify the belief that humans are really one with the world – he takes his refutation of Rolland's account of the *origin* of mysticism to be as well a refutation of Rolland's *justification* for mysticism. Freud enlists his social scientific theorizing about the origin (and, for Freud, function) of mysticism to evaluate the truth of mysticism. Does he mean to conclude that mysticism is false? No. He is not precluding other justifications, which he would then have to consider. Rather, he is taking on the justification based on origin. He is arguing not that mysticism is necessarily false because it originates in an infant's delusions – that contention would commit the genetic fallacy – but that because mysticism likely originates in infantile delusion, the argument that it is true *because* it originates in an adult's feeling of oneness with the world is undone. Because he is working to falsity *through* the account of origin proposed by Rolland, he is not jumping from origin to falsity and so is not committing the genetic fallacy.

I am not claiming that Freud's argument is convincing. After all, his argument rests on many assumptions, not least the assumption that what is infantile is delusory and that what is adult is real. I am claiming only that Freud's argument does not commit the genetic fallacy, where, by contrast, James commits the functional fallacy.

Undeniably, there is a difference between James's use of social scientific findings and Freud's. James does not utilize his own psychological findings to assess the truth of mysticism. He simply utilizes standard descrptions of mystical experience. By contrast, Freud uses his own psychoanalytic findings to assess the truth of mysticism. Still, both assess truth not on the basis of content but on the basis of effect or of origin. In so doing, both link the social sciences to philosophy in a way that is no longer found today. Obviously, many philosophers today employ the findings of the social and of the natural sciences, but how many present-day social scientists dare to enlist their own findings to decide the truth of mysticism?

Notes

For many helpful comments on this chapter I want to thank Paul Marshall.

1. Typical – one might say 'archetypical' – here is Jung, who, as in a litany, seems to begin his every writing on religion with the disclaimer that he, a mere psychologist, can never say anything about the truth of religion – a matter properly left to philosophers. For example: 'Notwithstanding the fact that I have often been called a philosopher, I am an empiricist and adhere to the phenomenological standpoint. ... I approach psychological matters from a scientific and not from a philosophical standpoint. In as much as religion has a very important psychological aspect, I am dealing with it from a purely empirical point of view, that is, I restrict myself to the observation of phenomena and I refrain from any application of metaphysical or philosophical considerations. I do not deny the validity of other considerations, but I cannot claim to be competent to apply them correctly' (Jung 1938, pp. 1–2). That Jung, in an interview, once confessed that he knew that God is real misses the point: he was not basing his conviction on his psychological expertise. For me, Jung, while perhaps a mite too old to qualify, epitomizes the present-day approach.

2. There are exceptions to this characterization of present-day social scientists – most notably, Peter Berger, from *A Rumor of Angels* (1970) on.

3. Against medical materialist dismissals of religion in general, not just of mysticism in particular, see James 1936, 11–21.

4. Later, James acknowledges that optimism and monism are by no means characteristic of all brands of mysticism: see James 1936, 416–17.

5. In her provocative paper Grace Jantzen, too, focuses on effects. But she focuses on the effects *of* James's account of mysticism, not, like me, on the effects *in* James's account.

6. Where Freud unquestioningly accepts Rolland's equation of mysticism with extrovertive mysticism, James, who is far more knowledgeable about mysticism, considers both introvertive and extrovertive forms, though oddly he sometimes limits himself to one variety or the other.

References

Berger, Peter, *A Rumor of Angels.* Garden City, NY: Doubleday Anchor Books, 1970.

Freud, Sigmund, *Civilization and Its Discontents*, tr. James Strachey. New York: Norton, 1962.

James, William, *The Varieties of Religious Experience.* New York: Modern Library, 1936 [1902].

Jung, C. G., *Psychology and Religion.* Terry Lectures. New Haven: Yale University Press, 1938.

Chapter 9

Mystical assessments

Jamesian reflections on spiritual judgments

G. William Barnard

William James insightfully points out how every moment of experience takes shape, in part, as a result of the activity of what he calls our 'selective interest'; that is, out of the confused, dynamic, ever-changing flux of sensations that comes our way moment by moment, we pay attention only to those that 'fit' our expectations, our predilections, our interests at the time. My task, in attempting to write an essay in honor of the centennial of *The Varieties of Religious Experience*, is somewhat analogous. Out of the rather daunting torrent of lucid philosophical and psychological analyses of religious and mystical narratives that come together in the pages of the *Varieties*, I have to choose a highly circumscribed cluster of ideas as the focus for this essay – a choice that may well say as much about my own interests as it does about the *Varieties* as a text.[1] None the less, this task of selection is made substantially less difficult by the fact that the *Varieties* contains such a wealth of insightful ideas that almost any direction that one might choose to explore in the text is almost inevitably bound to be fruitful.

Therefore, this chapter, rather arbitrarily, focuses on a cluster of issues pertaining to James's attempt to articulate three criteria that he claims can be used to assess religious and mystical states of mind: (1) *immediate luminosity* (my up-to-date revision of James's Victorian 'luminousness'); (2) *philosophical reasonableness*; and (3) *moral helpfulness*. What I hope to do is to look carefully at how James uses these three criteria, not only to provide a normative assessment of mystical experience, but also to offer a rough-hewn pragmatic warrant for the existence of a spiritual 'unseen reality.' In essence, therefore, this essay focuses on the possibilities and problems of James's attempt to offer a normative assessment of religious life in the *Varieties*.

In the pages of the *Varieties*, James gathers together a wide-ranging mass of data on religious life. He discusses religious conversion experiences, the mind-cure movement, prayer, and saintliness – not simply to examine these phenomena for their own sake, but rather to use this wealth of phenomenological descriptions as cumulative evidence that belief in an unseen spiritual world can catalyze positive changes in the lives of individuals, especially when that belief is accompanied by dramatic religious experiences. However, as James realizes, to say that strong religious beliefs and intense mystical experiences frequently initiate positive changes in the lives of men and women is not the same as saying that those beliefs and experiences are true. Therefore, in the *Varieties*, James also seeks to formulate criteria that can be used to assess the truth of religious beliefs and experiences, as well as their value – an assessment that James terms 'the spiritual judgment.' I will now examine each of the three criteria of James's spiritual judgement in detail.

'Immediate luminosity' is that aspect of the spiritual judgment that prompts an investigator to take seriously the experiential component of a religious or mystical state of consciousness – its immediate force, its raw voltage, its direct, tangible feeling. 'Philosophical reasonableness' is the criterion that assesses whether these alternate states of awareness can be shown to be reasonable and logical by virtue of its place within an articulate and defensible philosophical system of beliefs. Finally, 'moral helpfulness,' is demonstrated when and if a religious or mystical state of mind can be shown to initiate, on the whole and over the long run, positive consequences for the individual and the community.

These criteria are not mutually exclusive, but rather interact with, and depend upon, each other. James can and does analytically distinguish between the three criteria, but when he actually attempts the concrete process of making a spiritual judgment, it is clear that these three criteria work together as a unit. Attempting to make a spiritual judgment, therefore, is not a matter of precisely weighing the percentage of each criterion's importance, but instead, is a holistic, cumulative process. As James emphasizes, the final test for assessing a state of mind is not the individual 'score' of each of these criteria, but rather, it is their cumulative weight, the way they work as a whole and on the whole.[2]

James recognized that if he was to succeed in his avowed attempt to demonstrate in the *Varieties* that religious life 'as a whole' is 'mankind's most important function,' then he had to draw upon all three of these criteria.[3] In many ways, the criteria of 'immediate luminosity,' 'philosophical reasonableness,' and 'moral helpfulness' can be said to act as the pillars upon which the argumentative structure of the *Varieties* itself is based. In order to prove his thesis, James realized that he not only had to gather empirical data showing that powerful mystico-religious experiences are the basis for a genuine religious life, but he also had to demonstrate clearly that these experiences both make sense and are personally and communally transformative. Therefore, after having given his non-mystically inclined readers a repeated and detailed exposure to the most vivid accounts of mystical experiences that he could find (James's own 'second-hand' version of 'immediate luminosity'), he concentrated, in section by section of the *Varieties*, on the task of convincing his readers that these mystico-religious experiences were both philosophically reasonable and morally helpful.

The *Varieties*, seen in this way, can be understood as split into three distinct, if inter-related, argumentative components, each of which mirror James's three criteria: first, the collection of mystical narratives is a vicarious nod to 'immediate luminosity'; second, the vigorous defense of the importance and centrality of personal experience is an attempt to make mystical experiences seem 'philosophically reasonable' to his audience; and third, the depiction of the physical healings performed by the mind-cure movement, as well as the descriptions of the mystically inspired character transformations undergone by saintly converts, can be seen as a way for James to persuade those who are not mystics themselves that mystico-religious experiences are indeed worthwhile – that is, 'morally helpful'.

James's prolonged and detailed analysis and assessment of the personal transformations undergone by saints is a particularly important example of his attempt to use the criterion of moral helpfulness to demonstrate the value of religion. The thrust of James's argument is as follows: saints, as embodiments of the fruits of religion, are the exemplars of a deeply religious life; therefore, if these religious 'geniuses' are successes, then so is religion.

After an exhaustive analysis of saintliness, in which James claims he is able to avoid using 'theological criteria,' substituting instead 'practical common sense and the empirical method,' James concludes that even with all of its excesses and possible pathologies, saintliness is, on the whole, extremely positive.[4] This positive assessment of saintliness is what, in turn, allows James to assert that 'in a general way ... and "on the whole,"' religion has been shown to be extremely valuable for mankind.[5]

What are we to make of these provocative conclusions? To begin with, while saintliness might well deserve an overall positive spiritual judgment, it is doubtful that James can support his claim that he has been able to make this normative assessment without utilizing theological criteria. To begin with, James openly admits in several places in the *Varieties* that he draws upon his own theological standards in the process of assessing various saints. Further, if we are true to James's own epistemological perspective, which emphasizes that we always experience and understand whatever we are investigating through the lens of our own, typically hidden, and invariably circumscribed, presuppositions and interests, then we have to concede that all of our attempts to determine whether saintliness is worthwhile will inevitably be affected by whatever theological or philosophical categories we use to make this determination. The seemingly empirical examination of the fruits of saintly living (i.e., its moral helpfulness) will, therefore, always be based upon a cluster of less tangible, but unavoidable, ethical, philosophical, and religious assumptions as to what exactly constitutes the 'good life'; that is, our determination of what is morally helpful will always be intertwined with our notions of what is philosophically reasonable.

Our theological and philosophical presuppositions matter, especially when attempting to assess the worthiness of sainthood. For instance, James's own assessment of saintliness appears to have been crippled by an extremely narrow range of underlying presuppositions as to what qualifies as genuine saintly behavior and what does not. James's depiction of sainthood often tacitly and without question assumes Christian categories of saintliness and relies heavily on a rather sketchy, and often simplistic, portrayal of Catholic saints. James's Christian notions of saintliness are what underlie his claim that saints are meek and nonassertive, that they are like gentle 'herbivorous animals, tame and harmless barn-yard poultry' in comparison to the Nietzschean 'beaked and taloned graspers of the world'; and James's lingering Protestant mistrust of Catholic saintliness is at least conceivably what drives James at times to portray saints (especially female saints) as addled by the extremes of their devotion, or as isolated and cut off from the world, or (especially in the case of male saints) as pathologically masochistic.[6]

If James had possessed a broader and more detailed knowledge of saintliness as it is understood in religious traditions other than Christianity, it is possible that his characterization of saintliness would have been more nuanced and appreciative. Given the Euro-centric nature of his time, James was unable to draw readily upon the knowledge of, for instance, the warrior saints of the Sikh tradition, or the highly skilled artisans who frequent the ranks of Sufi saints, or the sturdy, practical, and 'this-worldly' masters of Zen. Because of the narrowness of his sampling, James's depictions of saintliness are, inevitably, rather two-dimensional and imbalanced. Even if many non-Christian saints might well have appeared to be equally, if not even more, bizarre to James than the Catholic saints who populate the pages of the *Varieties*, it would be fascinating to see in what ways James would have altered his assessment of saintliness if his own tacit notions of saintliness had incorporated a wider range of cultural models.

James's evaluation of saintliness is also affected by another, perhaps less obvious, cluster of philosophical and theological presuppositions. James believed in the reality of an unseen spiritual world, and in light of this belief, he was willing to take saintliness seriously. For James (as well as for the majority of the world's religious traditions), saintliness is a character transformation which takes place as the result of a deep, sustained mystical connection to a powerful, deeply beneficial, trans-natural level of reality. Operating out of an interpretative framework that accepts the reality, power, and beneficence of an unseen spiritual level of existence, it makes sense to posit that saintliness might well be the fulfilment of human existence. For others, however, who operate out of a purely naturalistic perspective, the claim that human beings can be transformed by contact with a trans-natural level of reality seems, at best, childish or nonsensical, and at worst, highly deluded. From this point of view, any claims of sainthood or enlightenment are automatically suspect, and the saint, if not understood as socially aberrant or insane, will be forced to demonstrate his or her worthiness based purely upon socially determined criteria.

However, as James himself reluctantly acknowledges, the attempt to evaluate saintliness based purely on social norms inevitably leads to theoretical problems. If sainthood is assessed using only the criteria by which different cultures attempt to measure worldly success, we might well be able to gather enough stories of saintly successes to argue convincingly that saintliness is worth pursuing, but it would be impossible to claim that saints are *more* valuable than, for instance, Nietzschean 'strongmen,' since these 'strongmen' can often easily point to an equal, if not superior, degree of worldly success. As James is well aware, the question of whether the 'strongman' or the saint is the most ideal model for human emulation is relative to whether those doing the assessing believe solely in this world of everyday experience or also take into account the existence of an unseen spiritual world as well. As James aptly notes, in order to conclude that saints are ultimately *more* ideal than 'strongmen,' then 'in some sense and to some degree both worlds must be acknowledged and taken account of.'[7]

None the less, as James also realizes, evaluations of saintliness cannot and should not be based on purely 'otherworldly' criteria. In order to retain its position as a normative ideal, saintliness *must* provide evidence of positive, this-worldly effects. I would add that, from culture to culture, and throughout history, saints are only understood to be saints by their community if they produce 'miracles' – that is, if the community believes that contact with a particular saint, for example, heals the sick, gives jobs to the poor, creates pregnancies in previously barren women, or more subtly, generates a feeling of renewed energy and purpose, an upsurge of devotion and love, or a deep and tangible experience of stillness and peace within those people who spend time in the saint's presence. A saint, therefore, can be understood to be 'morally helpful' only if the saint's community believes that association with the saint produces publicly observable, communally valued, tangible results.[8]

However, as was pointed out earlier, the judgment that something is 'morally helpful' itself only takes place within a specific philosophical and theological context. For instance, from an atheistic or skeptical perspective, the 'miracles' attributed to different saints would likely be understood as simply the result of delusions, mass hysteria, wish fulfillment, or suggestibility, whereas the conquests and political acumen of the 'strongman' might well be deemed highly valuable. However, individuals coming from a theistic, monistic, or 'Buddhistic' perspective would likely reverse this assessment, looking upon the activities of the 'strongmen' with abhorrence, while giving the saintly 'miracles' much more respect (even if that respect is leavened with an underlying alertness to the possibility of saintly fraud and delusion). Those judged to be saints rarely, if ever, will be given the respect and admiration of the community if they do not offer that community a corpus of tangible and valued demonstrations of their intimate connection with a trans-natural reality (i.e., they won't be respected or valued if they do not perform 'miracles'); but these 'miracles' will typically only be interpreted to be signs of the saint's connection with a spiritual level of existence if this spiritual reality is already a theo-philosophical given. Therefore, in order for someone to be considered a saint, the unseen world has to be a reality, not only in the form of a mystically felt unitive experience within the individual, but also as a philosophically reasonable notion within the intellectual framework of those attempting to assess the would-be saint's overall worth.

From a Jamesian perspective, it becomes clear just how interwoven these three criteria are during any attempt to make a spiritual judgment of religious beliefs and experiences. As long as these three criteria are not kept artificially separated, then they would appear to offer a potentially useful framework from which to begin any normative assessment of religious phenomena. However, the question remains: what would be the underlying purpose for making such an assessment? For James, the answer is fairly straightforward: the spiritual judgment of religious phenomena is intended to produce compelling evidence that living a full, rich, and deep religious life is positive and worthwhile.

However, examined more carefully, it becomes apparent that James is not simply attempting to justify his overt contention that religion is one of the most valuable components of human existence. Instead, James is also covertly attempting to prove the *truth* of his own religious belief in the reality of the unseen world via a pragmatic evaluation of the transformative effects of powerful religious experiences. That is, James is not merely saying that religion is *good*, but that it is also *true*.

This hidden attempt to provide empirical grounds for the truth of religious beliefs in the reality of the unseen world is particularly evident during James's lectures on the 'Value of Saintliness.' In this section of the *Varieties*, James performs a philosophical sleight of hand, and shifts his focus from the relatively innocuous attempt 'to use human standards to help us decide how far the religious life commends itself as an ideal kind of human activity,' to the much more controversial and difficult task of demonstrating that, if the religious life *is* demonstrated to be valuable, 'then any theological beliefs that may inspire it' will thereby 'stand accredited.'[9]

James argues that we only come to believe in something's reality if we can observe that our interaction with this level of experience generates tangible results. Operating out of this pragmatic perspective, James is willing to contend that an examination of the personal and social effects of a saint's mystical level of experience not only demonstrates that religion has value, but also serves to warrant the truth of religious beliefs in the unseen world. The assessment of saintliness, therefore, is not only intended to establish whether religion is worth pursuing (a normative task), but it is also intended to establish, via James's nascent pragmatism, whether religious beliefs in the reality of the unseen world are *true*.

In a very real sense, James's hidden agenda in the *Varieties* is to reverse the standard religiously based verification process. James does not attempt to use 'mystical states' to 'establish the truth' of the theology of saints and mystics; instead, he attempts to demonstrate that mystically based beliefs in the reality of an unseen spiritual world are justified via a philosophical assessment of the long-term psychological and cultural ramifications of the saintly life (taken broadly).[10] From this pragmatic perspective, it is 'the uses of religion, its uses to the individual who has it, and the uses of the individual himself to the world' that present 'the best arguments for the truth' of religious beliefs, even if, as James hurriedly adds, 'the qualification "on the whole" may always have to be added.'[11]

This covert attempt to justify his belief in the reality of the unseen world using pragmatic criteria is difficult to perceive, because in the *Varieties* James is in transition between one understanding of truth and another. On the one hand, James at times aligns himself with an understanding of truth in which truth is seen as that knowledge that correctly mirrors an objective reality. On the other hand, James at times also supports a rough-edged, still developing, proto-pragmatic understanding of truth. From the point of James's nascent pragmatism, truth is seen not as something that is eternal, objective, and aloof from the nitty-gritty inter-subjective process of verification, but rather is understood to be something that emerges out of an examination of the way a belief works, on the whole and in the long run. Therefore, there are frequently moments in the *Varieties* when James, aligning himself with the older understanding of truth, makes a clear-cut separation between truth and utility; but there are other, equally compelling, instances when James reverses himself and argues for a pragmatic understanding of truth.

James's utilization of this pragmatic justification of the truth of religious beliefs in the reality of the unseen world is vividly demonstrated in the final pages of the *Varieties*. He writes:

> The unseen region ... is not merely ideal, for it produces effects in this world. When we commune with it, work is actually done upon our finite personality, for we are turned into new men, and consequences in the way of conduct follow in the natural world upon our regenerative change. But that which produces effects within another reality must be termed a reality itself, so I feel as if we had no philosophic excuse for calling the unseen or mystical world unreal.[12]

At this point in the *Varieties*, James is no longer waffling. Instead, he has fully embraced a pragmatic justification of the truth of religious beliefs in the reality of the unseen spiritual world, a perspective that allows him to claim, in his characteristically blunt fashion, that 'God is real since he produces real effects.'[13]

Several years later, James polished and developed this proto-pragmatic perspective. In his work *Pragmatism*, James argues that truth is determined by making a nuanced assessment of the results that follow in the wake of acting upon a certain set of beliefs or undergoing a particular range of experiences. From this point of view, truth can never be separated from an assessment of the long-range value of that 'truth' to an individual or community. Therefore, from this pragmatic perspective, if mystics receive increased vitality by virtue of their contact with the unseen world, if their mystical inspirations produce positive effects on the whole and over the long run, then we have every right to maintain that the mystic's inspiration is true – true at least for that mystic, in that context, and during that period of time.

However, even in his most pragmatic moments, James never clearly discusses the specifics of how we can determine, with any degree of certainty, that the positive transformations observed in the lives of mystics or saints actually *are* the result of their mystical inspirations. James's pragmatic justification of the truth of religious beliefs is based on the argument that positive effects point to true beliefs. But this argument itself depends upon what appears to be an unexamined assumption: that a certain belief is the cause of a corresponding observable effect (e.g., a mystic's belief in the reality of the unseen world causes the mystic to feel increased vitality). But is there ever really such a clear-cut, one-to-one correspondence between a distinct belief and an equally distinct outcome of that belief? Can we really map the repercussions of each of our beliefs in the same way that we can observe the effects of one billiard ball striking another? Cannot odious beliefs at times lead to beneficial results and worthy beliefs to horrific effects?

Few would dispute James's contention that our structures of belief have clearly observable ramifications. But James never explicitly addresses the ways in which the complexity, ambiguity, and internal inconsistencies of every person's belief system make it difficult, if not impossible, to contend that we can trace a certain personally or socially valuable transformation back to the impetus received from one clearly defined belief.

None the less, even with its areas of ambiguity and unclarity, James's perspective is, potentially at least, extremely valuable, in that it offers a philosophically sophisticated means to examine the truth claims of a wide variety of religious traditions.

If we look with Jamesian 'lenses' at the realities posited by different religious traditions (whether fox spirits, thunder beings, ancestral ghosts, the Holy Spirit, and so on), then it might well be possible to assess the truth claims of these religious realities, but this assessment only 'works' if these realities are *experienced*. And, of course, mystico-religious experiences are not publicly available, which means that verification of a mystico-religious experience is much more problematic than sense experience (hence, almost everyone believes that it is true that Japan exists, whereas there is much less consensus about the truth of God's existence).

However, the difference in difficulty between verifying external objects and verifying religious 'objects' may not be quite as extreme as it might first appear. For many, if not most, individuals within different cultures, the existence of a non-material reality is based primarily on *verifiability*, on the premise that either you can experience its reality for yourself if you are willing and able to practice the necessary spiritual disciplines (bracketing for the moment the idea of grace) or that you can trust in its reality based on the testimony of reliable witnesses – i.e., the testimony of the saints, shamans, and mystics of various traditions throughout history. From a pragmatic standpoint, therefore, testimonials should not be dismissed out of hand, but rather, should be recognized as forming an integral part of the process by which a religious idea comes to be accepted as true, in that it is the testimonies of these 'professional' mystics, acting as spiritual proxies or envoys for those of us who are less gifted or inclined, that enable us indirectly to verify these realities for ourselves.

In this way, just as most Americans believe that Japan exists because that belief both 'works' for us and is ultimately verifiable, either by our direct experience or by the experience of our trusted experts, it could also be argued that it is legitimate to believe in different non-material religious realties, if our beliefs in these realities 'work' for us and are reliably verifiable. For instance, let us posit a culture in which the reality of unseen spiritual phenomena is taken for granted. If, in the context of this culture, a sizable percentage of the population could be led, through appropriate rituals and spiritual disciplines, to a vividly felt, 'sensory-like' experience of what their conceptual 'map' predicts, and if similar experiences were to keep recurring on a regular basis, both to them and to others willing to follow a similar pattern of behavior, and if these experiences, over the long term, and on the whole, could consistently produce effects that were interpreted within the context of that culture as psychologically, socially, and physically positive, then by what possible criteria could the culture's beliefs in these spiritual phenomena be termed 'false'?

This hypothetical situation may appear to be riddled with so many qualifiers that its conclusion becomes, at best, suspect, but perhaps a concrete example will give rhetorical flesh to these rickety speculative bones. In an ethnographic study of the Kalahari Kung that took place during the late 1960s, Richard Katz provides a vivid account of the healing dances that are a central focus of the religious and social life of this hunting-gathering people.[14] The goal of these all-night dances is to activate the *num*, a spiritual energy that 'resides in the pit of the stomach and the base of the spine.'[15] During these dances, men circle for hours around an inner ring of women who surround a fire, clapping and singing spiritually potent songs.[16] While dancing, these men experience the num beginning to 'heat up' within them, and then finally, as it begins to 'boil,' sense the num rising up their spines to the back of their heads.[17] As one healer comments: 'You dance, dance, dance, dance. The num lifts you up in your belly and lifts you in your back, and you start to shiver. Num makes you tremble; it's hot.'[18] Another healer adds: 'In your backbone you feel a pointed something and it works its way up. The base of your spine is tingling, tingling, tingling, tingling. Then num makes your thoughts nothing in your head.'[19]

With the boiling of the num, the healers begin to *kia*, that is, they enter into a state of heightened or altered awareness. The kia state is painful, and greatly feared, because it is experienced as a type of death, in which the healer's soul leaves the body and ascends into the sky in order to confront the gods and spirits who are attempting to lure the souls of the living into their realm of death. As one healer says, 'As we enter kia, we fear death. We fear we may die and not come back!'[20]

However, even if they are afraid, the Kung healers also consciously attempt to bring about this state of kia, since this heightened awareness is essential if the healer is going to *twe*, that is, to 'pull out sickness.'[21] Kia gives the healers, those who are 'masters' or 'owners' of the num, the powers needed to diagnose and to heal. During kia, the healers gain clairvoyant powers. This amplified perception enables them to see into the bodies of those who need healing, it allows them to perceive the 'death things' that have been put inside those who are ill, and it gives them the ability to see the spirits attempting to lure their living relatives to the realm of death.[22] Kia also grants the healers the ability to transfer some of their own num into the bodies of those they are attempting to heal, as well as the ability to pull out the sicknesses that lie hidden within the members of the community. Katz vividly describes this interaction between kia and the ability to heal:

> They may shudder or shake violently, their whole body convulsing in apparent pain and anguish. The experience of kia has begun. And then, either on their own or under the guidance of those who are more steady, the healers who are in kia go to each person at the dance and begin to heal. They lay their fluttering hands on a person, one hand usually on the chest, the other on the back, pulling out the sickness, while shrieking earth-shattering screams and howls known as *kowhedili*, an expression for the pain and difficulty of this healing work. Then they shake their hands vigorously toward the empty space beyond the dance, casting the sickness they have taken from the person out into the darkness.[23]

This arduous and painful process of healing proves to be so efficacious that it is repeated quite frequently, at times almost weekly.

Within the community, the ability of the healers is taken for granted. Stories of cures range from the occasionally dramatic (such as when 'someone who has been clawed by a leopard and 'given up for dead' is healed and recovers miraculously)'[24] to the more frequent, and less dramatic examples, such as when a mother who cannot nurse her infant regains her milk or when a person notices that the swelling caused by infection has subsided. In addition, the healing is not simply physical, in that the dance itself is an occasion for community bonding. The dance provides a context in which the spiritual power of the community can successfully challenge and overcome the threatening forces of the spirits and the gods. Further, the dance also offers an opportunity for lighthearted and playful interactions (the dance is punctuated with raucous joking and laughter).

For the Kung, the reality of the gods, the spirits, and the num, is simply assumed, and for good reason. Within their culture, why would anyone question the truth status of these beliefs? Since a large percentage of the culture vividly and regularly experiences the reality of these spiritual phenomena during a heightened state of awareness that is dependably catalyzed by the performance of a certain set of spiritual practices, and furthermore, since the whole community frequently witnesses the positive healing effects that follow in the wake of the performance of the dance, then the culture's belief in these spiritual phenomena that are so vividly experienced seems imminently sound and reasonable. By what possible criteria could an observer outside of that culture argue with their truth claims? Their truths may not easily conform with the scientific understanding of reality that is taken for granted by many, if not most, individuals in contemporary Western culture, but from what Archimedean standpoint do we claim that this Western understanding of reality is innately superior? Is it anything more than simply cultural arrogance that denies truth to anything outside of one's own culturally defined parameters?

It is important to point out that an argument is not being made at this point for the incommensurability of truth. I am not arguing here that truths are hermetically sealed within the parameters of each culture's language games and life-world. While, from a Jamesian perspective, truths will always be assessed within a particular cultural, historical, and linguistic matrix, each matrix will be understood, not as a self-contained monad, but rather, as a dynamic field that overlaps and interpenetrates other permeable matrices. This 'fields within fields within fields' perspective is highly versatile, in that it can offer a theoretical perspective that can recognize both intra-cultural uniqueness and cross-cultural communication. While a Jamesian understanding of truth would emphasize that the religious experiences indigenous to one culture will be more easily verified within that cultural context (since those truths must answer to the needs and assumptions of that culture), a Jamesian perspective would also stress that, to the degree that these needs and assumptions overlap with the needs and assumptions of another culture, the possibility is created for a genuine exchange of cultural truths.

For instance, Richard Katz's culturally prepared and historically situated need to understand holistic healing practices might well intersect with the needs of the Kung to be healed, and Katz's assumptions about the efficacy of altered states of awareness could also connect with the Kung assumptions about the power of kia to catalyze spiritual healing. To the degree that this cultural overlap takes place, the condition is created in which Kung truths could become a viable possibility for Katz as well, perhaps prompting a willingness within Katz to participate in the dances himself. Indubitably, Katz, as a Western observer, would still lack the depth of cultural insight available to the most novice healer in the Kung religious tradition, even if he were to participate in the Kung healing dances on a regular basis. However, if Katz, during several consecutive dances, were to experience an energy beginning to boil within himself and consequently felt himself propelled into a powerful altered state of awareness, and if he were to see continued connections between the dances and occurrences of healing that could not be easily explained using the models available to Western medical practice, then the likelihood is excellent that some of the Kung's truths would become some of Katz's truths, and legitimately so.[25]

A pragmatically oriented 'fields within fields within fields' perspective offers a provocative, and potentially valuable, philosophical orientation to such cross-cultural, experientially grounded exchanges of truths, in that it posits the existence of fields of experience that are wider or deeper than the conceptual fields generated by each particular culture. Transcending the particularities of each culture, and yet capable of manifesting within them all, these wider or deeper fields of experience could be understood to provide the 'raw material' that underlies the religious truth claims of each culture. These wider or deeper fields of experience could be said to provide that quality of the experience that is directly and powerfully felt, and is immediately convincing. Dynamic, multi-formed, open to numerous interpretations and yet capable of initiating startling and often revolutionary shifts in personal and cultural understandings, these fields of experience could be seen as a fecund 'suchness' that underlies and informs the rich variety of mystico-religious experiences. A Jamesian 'fields within fields within fields' perspective on the self and reality would contend that it is these fields of experience that manifest as the immediacy and power of, for example, the satori experience that convinces a Western novice Zen practitioner of the validity of her new beliefs; it would be these fields of experience that would provide the depth and ecstasy of the experience of God's love that persuades a Liberian tribesman to convert to the Christian beliefs he has been exposed to by the local Lutheran missionary; it would be these fields of experience that would take the form of the shimmering sparks, flying rattles, and laughing voices that convinces a skeptical American nurse participating in an Oglala Sioux yuwipi healing ceremony that spiritual levels of reality do indeed exist.

From a pragmatic point of view, the concept of trans-cultural, spiritually potent fields of experience that provide the 'immediate luminosity' or 'voltage' of mystico-religious experiences would not be understood as literally true, but instead, would be seen as a philosophically reasonable attempt to honor both the diversity and the potential unity of mystico-religious experiences. The exact configurations taken by these fields of experience would inevitably remain elusive, not only because of the inherent inability of language to represent this level of awareness adequately and fully, but also because the aim of a pragmatic methodology, as Eugene Fontinell aptly notes, is 'participation in, rather than abstract representation of, reality.'[26]

It may never be possible theoretically to reconcile the visions of reality assumed by the Kalahari Kung, Zen Buddhism, Lutheran Christianity, and the Oglala Sioux, without a certain amount of vagueness and ambiguity, but the process of making such an attempt, if taken seriously, can itself perhaps begin to challenge our own limited, distorted, and embedded notions of who we are and why we are here. A pragmatically based 'fields within fields within fields' understanding of mystico-religious experience would not be measured by its consistency with scripture, by its impeccable logic, or by its correspondence to some allegedly eternal, static Truth, but rather, by its capacity to offer a vision of the self and reality that is vivid and enlivening enough to act as an antidote to nihilism and skepticism, while it simultaneously remains open and flexible enough to combat fanaticism, dogmatism, and intolerance. Such a vision of the self and reality would prove its worth, not by its ability to demonstrate the logical necessity of its argumentation, but instead, by its ability to catalyze transformations in our personal and communal experience and practice; by its ability to prompt us to re-examine our taken-for-granted premises; by its ability to re-unite, to re-new, to re-envision; and by its ability to empower and endorse our ongoing attempts to explore the unseen worlds that lie within and around us.

Notes

1. For a much less circumscribed exploration of the range of James's thought, especially as it pertains to mysticism and religious experience, see G. William Barnard, *Exploring Unseen Worlds: William James and the Philosophy of Mysticism* (Albany: State University of New York Press, 1997).
2. William James, *The Varieties of Religious Experience* (Cambridge: Harvard University Press, 1985), p. 24.
3. Ralph Barton Perry, *The Thought and Character of William James*, 2 vols (Boston: Little, Brown, and Co., 1935), 2: 326–27.
4. *Varieties*, p. 299.
5. *Varieties*, p. 299.
6. *Varieties*, p. 296.
7. *Varieties*, p. 296.
8. Because these tangible effects of contact with an unseen world are such a critical component of any pragmatic assessment of saintliness, the 'magical,' or 'miraculous' aspects of sainthood and mysticism assume a theoretical importance that they are often denied. From a pragmatic perspective, it is crucially important to pay close philosophical attention to the healing and psychic abilities of the saint and mystic, abilities that are so frequently ignored, or even despised, not only by Western philosophers, but also by philosophers within the various traditions themselves.
9. *Varieties*, p. 266.
10. *Varieties*, p. 329. Admittedly, it is difficult at times to see whether James's pragmatic assessment, especially in the rudimentary form it takes in the *Varieties*, is attempting to justify the *reality* of the unseen world, or the truth of religious *beliefs* in the unseen world.
11. *Varieties*, p. 361.
12. *Varieties*, p. 406.
13. *Varieties*, p. 407. In James's more mature pragmatism, in which there is a clear distinction between reality and truth, James perhaps would have said, 'our belief in the reality of God is true since he produces real effects.'
14. Richard Katz, *Boiling Energy* (Cambridge, MA: Harvard University Press, 1982). Although this study took place several decades ago, and many changes have taken place in this culture since then, I none the less prefer, as is traditional in recounting ethnographic details, to use the present tense.
15. Katz, *Boiling Energy*, p. 41.
16. Women also participate in these dances, but much less frequently than men.
17. Katz, *Boiling Energy*, p. 41.
18. Katz, *Boiling Energy*, p. 42.
19. Katz, *Boiling Energy*, p. 42.
20. Katz, *Boiling Energy*, p. 45.
21. Katz, *Boiling Energy*, p. 42.
22. Katz, *Boiling Energy*, p. 42.
23. Katz, *Boiling Energy*, p. 40.
24. Katz, *Boiling Energy*, p. 54.
25. Richard Katz's latest book, *The Straight Path*, gives intriguing details of how, several years later, in the Fiji islands, this type of cross-cultural appropriation of truths actually did take place, as Katz himself became a practitioner of a spiritual mode of Fiji healing. See Richard Katz, *The Straight Path* (New York: Addison-Wesley Publishing Co., 1993).
26. Eugene Fontinell, *Self, God, and Immortality* (Philadelphia: Temple University Press, 1986), p. 29.

Part IV

James and philosophy

Chapter 10

Varieties of experience and pluralities of perspective[*]

Ruth Anna Putnam

The Varieties of Religious Experience is James's most widely read book.[1] Yet I find it to be extraordinarily complex. The phenomenon of religious experience is examined from at least three perspectives: that of the experimental psychologist, that of the pragmatist, that of the theist or, perhaps, polytheist. The psychologist describes and classifies religious experiences, the pragmatist determines their significance or value, the theist/polytheist reveals his over-beliefs. In addition, James speaks to an audience of Protestant Christians, and he speaks often in their language; nevertheless, he states explicitly that he is unable 'to accept either popular Christianity or scholastic theism.' (410). Of course, one must accept this disclaimer; it is amply supported by James's other writings. However, James was a New Englander, and in his time the culture of New Englanders of his class was a Protestant culture. Without sharing the dogmas of Protestantism, James shared the concepts and vocabulary typical of Protestant Christianity. Not surprisingly, that language permeates his descriptive account of religious experience. Indeed, what seems to him to be the religious experience *par excellence* is the conversion experience in the Protestant sense, and conversely, he writes of 'the admirable congruity of Protestant theology with the structure of the mind as shown in such experiences.' (198–9).

While the *Varieties* speaks in four voices, it addresses only three questions. In fact, in lecture 1, James distinguishes only two questions: 'What are the religious propensities?' and 'What is their philosophical significance?' It will be helpful to restate the second as two questions. First, what is the importance, or meaning, or value of our religious propensities? This is the question of the pragmatist, and James answers it in terms of the 'fruits of religion.' But there is a second question, a metaphysical or theological question, and this question again has two parts. First, one asks whether there is any evidence for the existence of the divine, and if so, of what kind. James considers this to be the key issue addressed in the *Varieties*. The answer that he spells out in great detail is that the evidence consists in religious experiences. Second, there are questions concerning the nature of the divine; James refers to his responses to these questions as his 'over-beliefs.' The

* Keynote address at the Centenary Conference, Edinburgh University, 7 July 2003.

latter questions are barely addressed in the *Varieties*; it is not part of James's self-imposed brief to answer them in these lectures. They are addressed in *A Pluralistic Universe*[2] and, more briefly, in *Pragmatism*.[3]

I shall assume, as an interpretive hypothesis, that in the context of James's work as a whole the *Varieties* forms a transition from *The Will to Believe* to the last chapter of *Pragmatism* and above all to *A Pluralistic Universe*. Very briefly, this is the structure. In *The Will to Believe*, not only in the title essay but in several others as well, James argues for our right to believe religious hypotheses although we do so in advance of the evidence. In the *Varieties*, James provides evidence both for the claim that religious hypotheses are fit to be debated by philosophers and for the claim that they have value; he also raises, more briefly, the question of their truth. Finally in *A Pluralistic Universe* James elaborates his own favored religious hypothesis. Because the *Varieties* provides a transition from a mere right to have over-beliefs to an elaboration of James's own over-beliefs, the *Varieties* requires a multiplicity of perspectives, hence a multiplicity of voices.

A right to believe

In the preface to *The Will to Believe* James describes the purpose of the title essay and the three essays that follow as 'defending the legitimacy of religious faith.' They are addressed to young Christian men who have been taught, so he believes, 'that there is something called scientific evidence by waiting upon which they shall escape all danger of shipwreck in regard to truth.' James knew better – no method could protect us from all error. Therefore, he 'preached the right of the individual to indulge his personal faith at his personal risk.'[4]

In his defense of that right James used the expression 'religious hypothesis.' It is an interesting expression. A hypothesis is for James any proposition that one might consider believing. A religious hypothesis is, then, a hypothesis with a certain content. What is that content?

In *The Will to Believe* James wrote:

> What then do we now mean by the religious hypothesis? Science says things are; morality says some things are better than other things; and religion says essentially two things.
>
> First she says that the best things are the more eternal things, the overlapping things, the things in the universe that throw the last stone, so to speak, and say the final word. . . .
>
> The second affirmation of religion is that we are better off even now if we believe her first affirmation to be true.[5]

James says very little about the first hypothesis other than to point out that for most of us 'the universe is represented in our religions as having a personal form'; therefore, any person-to-person relation is possible between it and us. Thus, just as a suspicious nature would keep us from making friends, so 'a snarling logicality' may deprive one of any opportunity to encounter the divine. On the other hand, we may come to feel that we are 'doing the universe the deepest service we can' by believing that there are gods (yes, he uses the plural here).[6] Pragmatists hold that a belief is what one is prepared to act on, hence religious persons will act on their religious beliefs, and James assumes that they will act differently from agnostics or atheists, and will, in fact, act better. In the *Varieties* he will subject this last assumption – that the religious person acts (morally) better – to empirical examination.

William James called himself a radical empiricist as early as 1896 in the preface to *The Will to Believe*. There he defined empiricism as fallibilism, and he made clear that his empiricism was radical, among other things, because it extended to metaphysical doctrines. In other words, he would treat metaphysical claims, and that includes religious claims, as he would treat scientific claims, namely as hypotheses subject to possible falsification.

Having said that, he immediately launched into an argument for pluralism. '*Prima facie* the world is a pluralism,' though we attempt to impose unity on our experiences. 'But absolute unity in spite of brilliant dashes in its direction, still remains undiscovered, still remains a *Grenzbegriff*.' Finally, he concluded, 'He who takes for his hypothesis the notion that it [pluralism] is the permanent form of the world is what I call a radical empiricist.' Here pluralism means that there are '[r]eal possibilities, real indeterminations, real beginnings, real ends, real evil, real crises, real catastrophes and escapes, a real God, and a real moral life, just as common sense conceives these things.'[7]

Because the world is plural in this sense, there is no single point of view from which the whole of the world can be apprehended. And, as he wrote so eloquently in the preface to *Talks to Teachers*, 'The practical consequence of such a philosophy is the well-known democratic respect for the sacredness of individuality – is, at any rate, the outward tolerance of whatever is not itself intolerant.'[8]

Pluralism, in other words, is itself not a single doctrine; it is in fact three doctrines. First, there is the metaphysical doctrine concerning real possibilities, etc. Second, there is what one might call the epistemological doctrine, that there is no single point of view from which the whole plurality can be apprehended. Finally, there is the moral doctrine of tolerance. The majority of the essays in *The Will to Believe* present arguments in favor of a belief in one item or another of the metaphysical doctrine.

In the preface to *The Meaning of Truth*, James gave another, though compatible, account of radical empiricism as consisting of a postulate, a statement of fact, and a generalized conclusion. Here we are concerned only with the postulate. 'The postulate is that the only things that shall be debatable among philosophers shall be things definable in terms drawn from experience.'[9] Since James, the philosopher, discusses the religious hypothesis, he must show that it concerns things definable in terms drawn from experience. In fact, by the time he wrote the preface to *The Meaning of Truth* in 1909 he would have taken himself to have done so in the *Varieties*. Of course, 'definable' is to be understood loosely – the pragmatists were not positivists.

The evidence of experience

Ralph Barton Perry, in his monumental *The Thought and Character of William James*, tells us, 'James once said: "I myself believe that the evidence for God lies primarily in inner personal experience." '[10] We are, therefore, not surprised to find him characterizing his aims in the *Varieties* as follows.

> The problem I have set myself is a hard one: *first* to defend (against all the prejudices of my 'class') 'experience' against 'philosophy' as being the real backbone of the world's religious life – I mean prayer, guidance, and all that sort of thing immediately and privately felt . . . and *second*, to make the hearer or reader believe, what I myself invincibly do believe, that, although all the special manifestations of religion may have been absurd . . . yet the life of it as a whole is mankind's most important function.

And he describes writing the *Varieties* as '*my* religious act.'[11] In other words, James's aim in the *Varieties* is considerably wider than merely showing that the religious hypothesis is discussible by philosophers. Nevertheless, in the context of his life's work, the *Varieties* does play that role as well.

To achieve his aims, as already mentioned, James distinguishes, two questions: the existential question, 'What are the religious propensities of human beings?' and the spiritual question, 'What is the value of these propensities?' David Lamberth has pointed out that the distinction before us is not the familiar fact/value distinction but rather a distinction between a special science on the one hand and metaphysics on the other.[12] James explained the distinction in the preface to *The Principles of Psychology*: 'Every natural science assumes certain data uncritically, and declines to challenge the elements between which its own "laws" obtain, and from which its own deductions are carried on. . . . Of course the data themselves are discussible; but the discussion of them (as of other elements) is called metaphysics . . .'[13] What then are the data, uncritically assumed, by the psychologist of religion?

The evidence for God lies in inner personal experience, but to find that experience writ large enough for us to study it, we must turn to the writings of individuals who found it worthwhile to make their inner experiences public. James thought of such people as religious geniuses. Their religious experiences, and only theirs, are presented in the *Varieties*. The experiences of ordinary religious persons are dismissed; James holds that they have their religion second-hand and that it would profit us little to study their religious lives. It is as if one were to say that research in the psychology of hearing should be confined to subjects who have perfect pitch. The person with perfect pitch can hear what the rest of us fail to hear; the religious genius senses, at any rate at certain intense moments, the presence of the divine. Are we acquainted with the varieties of musical experiences if we study only the experiences of individuals with perfect pitch?

Charles Taylor in his tribute to James's *Varieties* raises a related objection. He points out that James belongs to one dominant strain in modern North Atlantic Christianity, the strain that emphasizes personal commitment and feelings. This causes him, according to Taylor, to misrepresent and undervalue the role of community, of ritual, of living according to divine commandments in enabling people to find a relation to the divine. Taylor summarizes this criticism: 'What James can't seem to accommodate is the phenomenon of collective religious life, which is not just the result of (individual) religious connections, but which in some sense constitutes or *is* that connection.'[14] (Emphasis in the original.) But this is too strong; James does not deny the phenomenon of collective religious life, but he sees it as a secondary phenomenon. He underestimates, perhaps, the role that religious institutions, lives lived in religious communities, play in preparing the ground from which religious experience springs. Nevertheless, and here I differ from Taylor, a connection to or vivid awareness of the divine, whether experienced in solitude or during a communal ritual, is an intensely private, particular, individual experience.

Be that as it may, the data of the psychologist of religion are 'the feelings, acts and experiences of individual men in their solitude, so far as they apprehend themselves to stand in relation to whatever they may consider the divine' (34). Here 'the divine' is broadly understood. 'The divine shall mean for us only such a primal reality as the individual feels impelled to respond to solemnly and gravely, and neither by a curse nor a jest' (39). Here James appears to include among the data not only the intense experiences he cites but also events in the lives of those of us who have our religion second-hand. That impression is reinforced when James, late in the Gifford Lectures, returns to characterizing religious life. Here, prayer, defined as 'every kind of inward communion or conversation with the power recognized as divine,' is said to be 'the very soul and essence of religion' (365). However, conversation with the divine, though an essential component of religion, cannot be, by itself, its 'very soul and essence.' The religious life does not consist solely in 'feelings, acts and experiences of individual men in their solitude;' it consists also in their feelings and acts toward other human beings (and, in some cases, animals). James counts all of that among the 'fruits,' as consequences rather than as parts of religion. This seems to me too anemic a conception of the religious life.

Here one might also mention, as Charles Taylor does, that James excludes theology from the center of religious life.[15] In so far as he takes himself to give us the 'essence' of religion, that complaint is certainly justified. But in the context of James's goal in the *Varieties* it is not. Theology concerns what James calls 'over-beliefs,' what one is prepared to say about the nature of the divine. James never denies that religious persons have over-beliefs. Perhaps because his own over-beliefs are quite unconventional, he does not give sufficient weight to the role that sacred writings play in the lives of many, perhaps a majority of, believers. But the *Varieties* is not concerned with questions concerning the nature of the divine; its subtitle proclaims it to be 'A Study of *Human* Nature.' (my emphasis). Again, James lays claim to expertise only in psychology. He is interested in the religious propensities of human beings, and these, though not their overt manifestations, are quite independent of theology.

While it may appear as if James had prejudged the question of evidence for God's existence when he defined religious experiences by reference to apprehending oneself to stand in a relationship to the divine, this is not so since all these apprehensions may be hallucinatory. However, while still dealing with the existential, i.e. narrowly psychological, investigation of our religious propensities, James must open a door to the possibility of a theistic explanation. James's genius shows itself, in my opinion, in the manner in which he accomplishes this difficult task.

Although James provides accounts of various kinds of religious experiences, two sorts stand out: the conversion experiences of twice-born Protestant Christians and the mystical experiences of members of various faith communities. In both cases James, the psychologist, draws attention to what religious states of consciousness have in common with other, non-religious states. It is a general thesis of James's work that religious love is a kind of love, religious fear a kind of fear, and religious experience a kind of experience. In other words, religious experiences are to be looked at from an empiricist, not a theological perspective.

Considering conversion experiences, James appeals to the then recent discovery that individuals are sometimes responsive in their conscious behavior, emotions, and beliefs to matters of which they have not been even marginally aware. James points out that in the case of post-hypnotic suggestion, we create and hence know the subliminal source of the behavior. In the case of hysteric patients psychoanalytic techniques will bring the disturbing memories to consciousness and thus effect a cure. James suggests then that the explanation of other pathological phenomena may also be found in the subconscious but that much research will be required to verify this hypothesis, in which research 'the religious experiences of man must play their part' (192).

Of course, this is not nor is it meant to be a 'proof' of the existence of God; James has no truck with proofs. But comparing religious experiences to pathological states does not even look like a proof; in fact, at first sight it looks like debunking. But James does not intend to debunk religion. Even concerning the various creeds for which he has little patience, he urges 'tenderness and tolerance as long as they are not intolerant themselves' (405). What then is the point of introducing subconscious influences, of classifying religious experiences with hysteria (in the technical sense) and with post-hypnotic suggestion? (By the way, people who get converted at revivals turn out to be good hypnotic subjects!) The point is *to open the door to the possibility of divine intervention in an individual's ordinary mental life.* James writes, 'But just as our primary wide-awake consciousness throws open our senses to the touch of things material, so it is logically conceivable that *if there be* higher spiritual agencies that can directly touch us, the psychological condition of their doing so *might* be our possession of a subconscious region which alone should yield access to them' (197, James's emphasis).

When, after many lectures on saintliness and its value, James returns to the question of evidence, he examines mystical states. These experiences are ineffable in the sense that states of feeling are ineffable. Yet these ineffable states are experienced as states of knowing; they are, in other words, peculiar states of consciousness. Once again, James notes that these states of consciousness belong to a class to which various pathological states also belong, e.g. states induced by nitrous oxide or moderate use of alcohol. His own experiments with nitrous oxide, James tells us, have convinced him that 'normal waking consciousness, rational consciousness as we call it, is but one special type of consciousness, whilst all about it, parted from it by the filmiest of screens, there lie potential forms of consciousness, entirely different.' (307–8). The subconscious states mentioned in connection with conversion experiences as possible conduits for possible divine influences are, of course, also such 'potential forms of consciousness.'

While mystical states carry utter conviction for those who experience them, they have no claims on the rest of us. 'But,' James notes, 'the higher ones among them point in directions to which the religious sentiments even of non-mystical men incline. They tell of the supremacy of the ideal, of vastness, of union, of safety, and of rest. They offer us *hypotheses*, hypotheses which we may voluntarily ignore, but which as thinkers we cannot possibly upset. The supernaturalism and optimism to which they would persuade us may, interpreted in one way or another, be after all the truest of insights into the meaning of life' (339). More generally, James compares mystics to travelers to distant shores. We would be foolish, he thinks, to reject the travelers' tales out of hand; we would be equally foolish not to take seriously the mystics' testimony concerning 'the actual existence of a higher world with which our world is in relation' (384).

Here I would like to emphasize (as James himself does) the word 'hypotheses.' The upshot of the examination of the psychological data is just this: religious hypotheses are discussible among empiricist philosophers because they concern, indeed, 'things definable in terms drawn from experience.' They are individuals' responses to certain experiences, experiences we call 'religious' because their object is the divine, just as we call other experiences 'musical' because their object is music. Whether these experiences are veridical is a separate question, to which we must now turn.

Reflecting on the evidence

James was, I think, a deeply religious person, although an unconventional one. Throughout the *Varieties* one senses an inner conflict; James wants to contribute to a science of religion that is in every sense a science, and yet, as we noted above, writing the *Varieties* was for him a religious act. Again, one great virtue he finds in religion is that, unlike science, it does not abstract. Religion deals with the most private moments of individuals, hence with the very core of reality. Yet, he looks for the common core in religious experience, and for the common core in religious beliefs; the results turn out to be either parochial or lifeless generalities. Of course, he rejects the very idea of offering proofs for the existence of God – he debunks all known philosophical proofs in a few breath-taking pages. But he wants to say more than that the religious hypothesis is discussible, more than that we have a right to believe it; he wants to present non-coercive reasons, but reasons none the less in its favor.

In the essay 'The Moral Philosopher and the Moral Life' James gives one such reason:

> ... in a merely human world without a God, the appeal to our moral energy falls short of its maximal stimulating power. Life, to be sure, is even in such a world a genuinely ethical symphony; but is played in the compass of a couple of poor octaves ... When, however, we believe that a God is there, and that he is one of the claimants, the infinite perspective opens out. The scale of the symphony is incalculably prolonged.[16]

This is an inspiring metaphor, but what exactly does religion add to the non-religious moral life? James responds in the concluding Gifford Lecture:

> Taking creeds and faith-state together, as forming 'religions' and treating these as purely subjective phenomena, without regard to the question of their 'truth,' we are obliged, on account of their extraordinary influence on action and endurance, to class them amongst the most important biological functions of mankind. (399)

The essence of religion lies, for James, in the interdependence of religious emotions and the conduct they inspire. The emotions provoked by religious experiences and to a lesser extent by prayer are invigorating, they overcome debilitating melancholy, they add a zest to life. At the very least, then, religion is good for the religious individual. Moreover, by way of the conduct it inspires, it is also good for humanity at large for, James concludes his careful investigation into the fruits of saintliness, 'the saintly qualities are indispensable for the world's welfare.' (299).

Today one hesitates to agree with this enthusiastic moral endorsement of religion, that is, of the conduct religious faith inspires. Religiously inspired violence has become part of the daily news, if not of our own lives.[17] Do we have reasons to regard the violence as an aberration, and only the deeds of loving kindness as genuinely religious? Religious strife and religious warfare are not modern inventions; how could James conclude that on the whole religion is good for humanity? Did he forget about the crusades, about the Thirty Years War, etc.? I don't think so. James believed in progress, particularly in moral progress. He was a tireless advocate of tolerance, and he believed, with some justification, that human beings were indeed becoming more and more tolerant, especially concerning theological questions. It was, therefore, not unreasonable to believe that the practical effects of religion would become increasingly exclusively moral effects. In some form or other all the major religions preach compassion or love of one's neighbor or concern for the poor and downtrodden. In so far as they inspire the corresponding conduct, James's positive judgment is surely justified. However, the effects of religious beliefs, good or bad, compassionate or cruel, appear to be quite independent of their truth.

What then can be said about the truth of religion? What, precisely, is the hypothesis we are to investigate? What is the common core of all particular creeds? Here is one fairly brief statement: 'religion, wherever it is an active thing, involves a belief in ideal presences, and a belief that in our prayerful communion with them, real work is done, and something real comes to pass.' (386). A few pages later, James formulates the common core of all religions as 'a sense that there is *something wrong about us* as we naturally stand' and as 'a sense that *we are saved from the wrongness* by making proper connexion with the higher powers' (400). Notice that the second quotation speaks of a sense, i.e. a rather inchoate awareness, rather than a well-articulated belief as does the first. The second speaks of the common core of religious experiences while the first speaks of the common core of the creeds, the various over-beliefs that almost inevitably accompany an individual's religious feelings.

But let us concentrate on the experience. An experience, James tells us, consists of a field of consciousness, an object of attention, an attitude toward that object, and a sense of the self that has the attitude. In ordinary waking life, we are hardly aware of events at the margins of the fields and entirely unaware of what goes on beyond the margins, though what goes on there may exert an influence on our conscious awareness and behavior. In contrast, James writes, 'In persons deep in the religious life, as we have now abundantly seen – and this is my conclusion – the door into this region [the subconscious] seems unusally wide open; at any rate, experiences making their entrance through that door have had emphatic influence in shaping religious history' (381).

Consider then the experience of being aware of one's own 'wrongness' in the religious sense. One's higher self is aware of what's wrong with one's lower self, and one becomes reconciled, or 'saved', when one identifies with one's higher self. According to James, this happens as follows.

> *He becomes conscious that this higher part is conterminous and continuous with a MORE of the same quality, which is operative in the universe outside of him, and which he can keep in working touch with, and in a fashion get on board of and save himself when all his lower being has gone to pieces in the wreck.* (400)

The question of the truth of religion boils down, then, to the question whether the 'more' really exists or is a mere fancy, and if it does exist, how we are in contact with it.

At this point it comes as no surprise to learn that James finds the subconscious self made to order. He seeks an explanation of religious experience that is acceptable to science. Psychologists agree that there is a wider subconscious self, and that what happens in the subconscious can have real effects on the conscious self. James's appeal to the subconscious is therefore scientifically respectable. At the same time, it is at least possible that events in the subconscious can be affected by forces external to it as well as to the conscious self. James's image of the conscious self as surrounded by the subconscious as by a sea enables him to wonder what is on the farther shore, and thus to introduce his own over-beliefs. Just where the over-beliefs enter is, however, less clear than one might wish it to be.

Consider James's own summing up of the findings of psychology.

> Disregarding the over-beliefs, and confining ourselves to what is common and generic, we have in *the fact that the conscious person is continuous with a wider self through which saving experiences come,* a positive content of religious experience which, it seems to me, *is literally and objectively true as far as it goes.* (405, emphasis in the original)

But is it a fact that 'the conscious person is continuous with a wider self through which saving experiences come?' Or is this already an over-belief? Let us grant that the conscious self is embedded in a wider subconscious self; let us grant even that our impulses to be morally better arise in that wider self. Still, we must admit that our impulses to be worse also arise there. That wider self is simply too limited as well as too fragmented to be 'a wider self through which saving experiences come.' Can the moral energy, the zest for living the morally strenuous life, not to mention the sense of being 'saved' come from being in contact merely with one's own subconscious? Or if it can, what is the input into the subconscious that produces these effects? This question provides James the opportunity to elaborate the image of the subconscious as a sea. He now conceives of the subconscious as the near shore of a sea that on the far shore is God, or the Higher Powers. That is a daring hypothesis. James has suggested a way (a mechanism) by which something other and higher than one's self could influence the conscious self *if there is such a being.*

In his final lecture on pragmatism, 'Pragmatism and Religion,' James said, 'I have written a book on men's religious experience, which on the whole has been regarded as making for the reality of God ...'[18] That suggests that he takes himself to have done more – and that others take him to have done more – than merely uncover a possible mechanism for human–divine communication. Rather, suggesting such a mechanism is taken to support the claim that such communication takes place. But to claim that such communication takes place is to accept the reality of the divine. It is to accept the understanding of certain quite common experiences as indeed *religious* experiences, as *not* being hallucinatory. This seems to me to be an over-belief, but when James speaks of over-beliefs, he seems to mean beliefs concerning the nature rather than the mere existence of the divine.

Conclusion

What then are James's own over-beliefs? They are, as is well known, quite unconventional. 'The gods we stand by,' he wrote, 'are the gods we need and can use' (266). He needed gods to provide moral energy, a zest for life. For him that meant not the certainty but the chance of 'salvation' for the world. In the Postscript he maintained, 'Meanwhile the practical needs and experience of religion seem to me to be sufficiently met by the belief that beyond each man and in a fashion continuous with him there exists a larger power which is friendly to him and to his ideals' (413). His characterizations of that larger power vary. In the Postscript he continues, 'Anything larger will do, if only it be large enough to trust for the next step. It need not be infinite, it need not be solitary. It might conceivably even be only a larger and more godlike self ... and the universe might conceivably be a collection of such selves ...' (413). In *Pragmatism* he tells us that religious individuals of the pluralistic type have 'always viewed God as but one helper, *primus inter pares*, in the midst of all the shapers of the great world's fate.'[19] And in *A Pluralistic Universe* he maintains that 'all the evidence we have seems to me to sweep us very strongly towards the belief in some form of superhuman life with which we may, unknown to ourselves, be co-conscious ... The outlines of the superhuman consciousness thus made probable must remain, however, very vague, and the number of functionally distinct "selves" it comports and carries has to be left entirely problematic.' Finally, he holds that the only escape from the problem of evil is to 'assume that the superhuman consciousness, however vast it may be, has itself an external environment, and consequently is finite.'[20]

I find James's conception of a deity quite appealing and inspiring. But we must recognize that it is just that, a conception. The wealth of evidence presented in the *Varieties* does not support one over-belief over another. James, the pluralist, should have been pleased with that.

I began by recalling that *The Varieties of Religious Experience* is James's most widely read work. I added that it is complex. I have tried to place it in the wider context of James's work. I wish to conclude by recalling James's own aim in the Gifford Lectures, namely to show that experience, not philosophy, is 'the real backbone of the world's religious life.' In the wider context of pragmatism's struggle against too narrow a conception of experience, *The Varieties of Religious Experience* plays an indispensable role.

Notes

1. William James, *The Varieties of Religious Experience* (Cambridge, MA and London: 1985). This and all other works by William James cited in these

endnotes are volumes in *The Works of William James*, Frederick H. Burkhardt, General Editor. *Varieties* was first published in 1902. All references to this work will be given in parentheses in the text.

2. William James, *A Pluralistic Universe* (Cambridge, MA and London: Harvard University Press, l977). These lectures were delivered in 1908 and first published in l909.

3. William James, *Pragmatism: A New Name for Some Old Ways of Thinking* (Cambridge, MA and London: Harvard University Press, l975). These lectures were delivered in the winter of l906–7 and first published in l907.

4. William James, *The Will to Believe and Other Essays in Popular Philosophy* (Cambridge, MA and London: Harvard University Press, 1979), pp. 7, 8. *The Will to* Believe was first published in 1897.

5. *Ibid*, p. 30.

6. *Ibid*, p. 31.

7. *Ibid*, pp. 5–6.

8. William James, *Talks to Teachers on Psychology and to Students on Some of Life's Ideals* (Cambridge, MA and London: Harvard University Press, 1983), p. 4. *Talks to Teachers* was first published in 1899.

9. William James, *The Meaning of Truth* (Cambridge, MA and London: Harvard University Press, l975), pp. 6–7. *The Meaning of Truth* was first published in 1909.

10. Ralph Barton Perry, *The Thought and Character of William James* (Boston: Little Brown & Company, l935), p. 323.

11. *The Letters of William James*, edited by his son Henry James (Boston: The Atlantic Monthly Press, 1920), vol. II, p. 127.

12. David C. Lamberth, *William James and the Metaphysics of Experience* (Cambridge: Cambridge University Press, l999), p. 111.

13. William James, *The Principles of Psychology* (Cambridge, MA and London: Harvard University Press. 1983), p. 6. The 'Publishers Notice' to this one-volume edition in soft covers states, 'This edition was first published in hard covers in 1981 as part of THE WORKS OF WILLIAM JAMES … In the hard cover edition the text is bound in two volumes and a third volume provides extensive annotations, appendices and textual information.' *Principles* was first published in 1890.

14. Charles Taylor, *Varieties of Religion Today: William James Revisited* (Cambridge, MA and London: Harvard University Press, 2002), p. 24.

15. *Ibid*, pp. 25–6.

16. William James, 'The Moral Philosopher and the Moral Life' in *The Will to Believe*, p. 160.

17. Concern about fanaticism was raised more than once during the conference.

18. *Pragmatism*, p. 143.

19. *Ibid*.

20. *A Pluralistic Universe*, p. 140.

Chapter 11

The ecumenicalism of William James

Richard M. Gale

It is especially *à propos* that we should commemorate the centennial of that great masterpiece, *The Varieties of Religious Experience*; for what the world desperately needs now, given that it is about to be blown apart by warring exclusivist religious beliefs, is a good shot of just the sort of ecumenicalism that it delivers so effectively.[1] Ecumenicalism is not only the ultimate message of this book but is of the very warp and woof of William James's philosophy as a whole, finding support in its most basic doctrines and tenets. At the bottom of the pyramid of supporting doctrines is that of a moral democracy based on what is revealed when we enter most intimately into the conscious interiors both of ourselves and of others through an I–Thou experience. This, in turn, supports a democratic metaphysics, as well as the sentiment of rationality. The will to believe can be extended in a thoroughly Jamesian manner to show that we are morally forbidden from having non-ecumenical exclusivist religious beliefs. This, in turn, supplies a powerful motive to seek to discover a vital common denominator among the great extant religions, which task is assigned to the science of religions in the *Varieties*, this being the ultimate culmination of James's quest for ecumenicalism. Although James eschewed writing philosophy in a systematic way, these doctrines will be shown to be a highly integrated and effective defense of ecumenicalism.[2]

The quest for intimacy

William James's distinction between the tough- and tender-minded set the stage for the subsequent schism in the twentieth century between respectively analytic and phenomenological–existential philosophers. The former take the stance of an external observer intent on giving an objective account of reality, in contrast to the latter who attempt to achieve intimacy with reality by entering into its interiors through acts of sympathetic intuition. If reality were a delicatessen with a staggering variety of enticing goodies laid out in its glass cases, the externalist will analyze the composition of the various cold cuts, as might an inspector for the department of health – 'This corned beef has a 5% phosphate content' – but the internalist will want to achieve a deep existential appreciation of them by eating them. James, being the ultimate inside man, wanted to eat the universe at large and everything in it. His philosophy is a desperate quest for intimacy that begins with the introspection of his own consciousness and then attempts to achieve a similar sort of intimacy with the conscious interiors of *everything* else, which includes other persons, both natural and supernatural, as well as animals and fishes, even the universe at large. If James were to have placed an ad in the Personals it would have read:

> Harvard University professor. Equally comfortable in a Norfolk jacket or a woodsman's outfit, doing science or leading the morally strenuous life. Desperately seeking to penetrate to the inner consciousness of other beings: animals and fish okay. No kooks please.

Given how threatened James's contemporaries felt by the dehumanized, impersonal world depicted by science, over half of Boston, and all of Cambridge, would have responded to the ad.

> James's quest for intimacy begins with the introspection of his own psyche since the only form of thing we directly encounter ... is our own personal life. The only complete category of our thinking ... is the category of personality, every other category being one of the abstract elements of that. And this systematic denial on Science's part of personality as a condition of events, this rigorous belief that in its own essential and innermost nature our world is a strictly impersonal world, may ... be the very defect that our descendants will be most surprised at in our own boasted Science. (EPR 136)

This passage reveals the most fundamental assumption of James's philosophy – that the true nature of reality is to be ascertained not through the employment of symbols or concepts but rather through personal experience. 'So long as we deal with the cosmic and the general [as does Science], we deal only with the symbols of reality, but as soon as we deal with private and personal phenomena as such, we deal with realities in the completest sense of the term' (VRE 393). 'Individuality is founded in feeling; and the recesses of feeling, the darker, blinder strata of character, are the only places in the world in which we catch real fact in the making, and directly perceive how events happen, and how work is actually done' (VRE 395).

Through introspective analysis James discovers that he is a bundle of different selves competing with each other for actualization.

> I am often confronted by the necessity of standing by one of my empirical selves and relinquishing the rest. Not that I would not, if I could, be both handsome and fat and well dressed, and a great athlete, and make a million a year, be a wit, a *bon-vivant*, and a lady killer, as well as a philosopher; a philanthropist, statesman, warrior, and African explorer, as well as a 'tone-

poet' and saint ... But to make any one of them actual, the rest more or less must be suppressed. (PP 295)

More serious than the lack of time and opportunity to actualize all these selves is that there are serious conflicts between their different perspectives or takes on what the world is like. His scientific self, for example, accepts determinism, epiphenomenalism, and the bifurcation between man and nature, but his moral-agent self believes that there are undetermined acts of spiritual causation in a world that has human meaning. Furthermore, whereas both selves use concepts as teleological instruments for gaining power to control the world, his mystical self eschews concepts altogether so as to penetrate to the inner core of a cotton-candyish reality through an act of sympathetic intuition. How James neutralized these intra-personal conflicts will be considered shortly.

The next challenge to James's quest for intimacy is to penetrate to the conscious interiors of other beings through a type of I–Thou experience, the outcome of which is that the sort of wondrous complexity that he finds within himself characterizes reality at large. Through an act of sympathetic intuition Jack realizes his beloved Jill concretely, to use James's beautiful example from 'What Makes a Life Significant' (TT 151). He comes to realize what it is like to be Jill. Just how this I–Thouing of another person occurs is best left to Tin Pan Alley: 'I Took One Look at You and Zing Went the Strings of My Heart,' 'It's Magic,' 'I've Got You Under My Skin,' 'You're My Everything.' James's romanticism comes to the fore in his ecstatic descriptions of the marvelous wondrousness of the inner life that one grasps through the I–Thou experience of another. He speaks of its 'vital secrets,' 'zest,' excitement, 'mysterious inwards,' and 'mysterious sensorial life' (TT 132, 135, 137, 149), along with its 'acutest internality' and 'violent thrills of life' (ERM 99). To miss the joy of this inner consciousness in another person is to miss all, for it is this that makes her life significant, provided it is coupled with the requisite strength of character to see to it that it gets properly expressed in her overt behavior. James prizes this inner life so highly that he holds that 'in every being that is real there is something external to, and sacred from, the grasp of every other' (WB 111).

A moral democracy

James deduces from this 'sacredness' of an individual's inner life a principle of moral democracy enjoining us to respect other persons, even nations, and adopt a live-and-let-live hands-off policy. This is a deontological moral principle and clashes with the exclusively consequentialist casuistic rule of 'The Moral Philosopher and the Moral Life' which requires us always to act so as to maximize desire satisfaction over desire dissatisfaction (WB 155). He calls this 'respect for the sacredness of individuality ... the outward tolerance of whatever is not itself intolerant.' James did not stop with I–thouing his fellow humans. He even wanted to I–Thou the beasts and fishes, as well as nature. In a letter of 1873 he writes: 'Sight of elephants and tigers at Barnum's menagerie whose existence, so individual and peculiar, yet stands there, so intensely and vividly real, as much as one's own, so that one feels again poignantly the unfathomableness of ontology, supposing ontology to be at all.'[3] Not to slight the fishes, in a letter of 1899 to his wife, he says: 'four cuttle-fish in the Aquarium. I wish we had one of them for a child – such flexible intensity of life in a form so inaccessible to our sympathy.'[4]

James wanted to go all the way and I–Thou the entire universe, as nature mystics have traditionally done. James is personalizing the universe when he writes: 'The Universe is no longer a mere *it* to us, but a *Thou*, if we are religious; and any relation that may be possible from person to person might be possible here' (WB 31). Taking a religious stance to the world 'changes the dead blank *it* of the world into a living *thou*, with whom the whole man may have dealings' (WB 101). Whereas the I–Thouing of other persons leads to a deontological moral democracy, the I–Thouing of the universe supports an ecological doctrine of the reverence for nature or natural piety. Ecumenicalism, therefore, applies across the board, giving equal legitimacy and value to *every* individual's inner life and perspective.

A democratic ontology

James wants to have a democratic ontology that will be supportive of this ecumenicalism by giving equal reality to all of these many different ways of depicting or experiencing reality. Since each of them finds expression in the way in which one of his many selves experiences the world, the problem is how to achieve an ontological ecumenicalism among the world-views of his many selves. This he achieves by his doctrine of ontological relativism. It has the interests of each of his many selves directed to its own world of interrelated objects, among which are the worlds of scientific theoretical entities, the medium-sized dry goods of common sense, platonic heavens of abstracta, and fictional and mythical worlds. '*Every object we think of gets at least referred to one world or another.* . . . It settles into our belief as a common-sense object, a scientific object, an abstract object, a mythological object, an object of someone's mistaken conception, or a madman's object' (PP 922). There is a democratic equality among these worlds, no one of them winning the coveted title of '*the* actual world *simpliciter*' for there is no such title to be won. For what qualifies one of these worlds as the actual world is relative to the passing interests and needs of persons. 'Reality means simply relation to our emotional and active life. This is the only sense the world ever has in the mouths of practical men. In this sense, whatever excites and stimulates our interest is real' (PP 924–5). 'Actuality' is not the one-place predicate that it grammatically appears to be, but rather is the disguised three-place predicate 'World x is actual (real, existent) for person y at time t.' Through this ontological relativism James gives *carte blanche* to each of his selves to see the light of day, provided that they democratically take turns with the other selves thereby providing an ecumenical solution to the apparent clash between these many selves. The result of this taking-turns solution is a kind of temporal schizophrenia: on weekdays from nine to five I am a scientist and in the evenings I lead the morally strenuous life; on weekends I'm a mystic.

> The doctrine of ontological relativism makes a prominent appearance in *Varieties*. The experiences which we have been studying during this hour (and a great many other kinds of religious experiences are like them) plainly show the universe to be a more many-sided affair than any sect, even the scientific sect, allows for. What, in the end, are all our verifications but experiences that agree with more or less isolated systems of ideas (conceptual systems) that our minds have framed? But why in the name of common sense need we assume that only one such system of ideas can be true? The obvious outcome of our total experience is that the world can be handled according to many systems of ideas, and is so handled by different men, and will each time give some characteristic kind of profit, for which he cares, to the handler, while at the same time some other kind of profit has to be omitted or postponed. (VRE 105)

James's 'conceptual systems' are the many 'worlds' which are the objects of the different interests and needs of his many selves.

The sentiment of rationality

The ecumenicalism that is achieved by ontological relativism is reinforced by James's sentiment of rationality doctrine, which explains the ultimate parting of the ways among philosophers in terms of differences in their psychological make-up, their rival predilections as to what constitutes a rationally satisfying explanation. Some philosophers, for example, find an explanation rational when it reduces a subject matter to a collection of externally related atoms, whereas others want a unifying explanation that has these atoms lose their distinct identities by merging or fusing together. Just as no one of James's many selves could claim to have the absolute truth about the nature of reality, no philosophy can make this claim.

Psychological diversity not only makes for an irreducible pluralism in philosophy, it also does for the spiritual life.

> The whole outcome of these lectures will ... be the emphasizing to your mind of the enormous diversities which the spiritual lives of different men exhibit. Their wants, their susceptibilities, and their capacities all vary and must be classed under different heads. The result is that we have really different types of religious experience. (VRE 94)

Given this diversity, James asks rhetorically, 'Ought all men to have the same religion? ... Are they so like in their inner needs that, for hard and soft, for proud and humble, for strenuous and lazy, for healthy-minded and despairing, exactly the same religious incentives are required?' (VRE 267). That these questions are rhetorical becomes manifest later when James answers ' "No" emphatically' to the questions 'Ought it ... to be assumed that the lives of all men should show identical religious elements?' and 'Is the existence of so many religious types and sects and creeds regrettable?' (VRE 384). Underlying James's ecumenical answer is his denial that there is an ideal man. 'According to the empirical philosophy, however, all ideals are matters of relation' to our different interests and purposes (VRE 297).

The sort of psychologically based diversity among the religious lives and experiences of different persons also produces an irreducible diversity among the theologies and philosophies of religion that they develop.

> The logical reason of man operates ... in this field of divinity exactly as it has always operated in love, or in patriotism, or in politics, or in any other of the wider affairs of life, in which our passions or our mystical intuition fix our beliefs beforehand. It finds argument for our conviction, for indeed it *has* to find them. It amplifies and defines our faith, and dignifies it; it cannot now secure it.' (VRE 344–5)

One of the important grounds for the ultimate disagreements among theologies and philosophies of religion, as well as among philosophies in general, is differences in aesthetic predilections. People have a need to intellectualize their religious experiences, and the manner in which they do so will be based on aesthetic considerations. Although the scholastic theology of Cardinal Newman is not James's personal aesthetic cup of tea, he appreciates its aesthetic value for persons of a certain type of mind set.

> The eloquent passage in which Newman enumerates [the attributes of the deity] puts us on the tract of it. Intoning them as he would intone a cathedral service, he shows how high is their aesthetic value. It enriches our bare piety to carry these exalted and mysterious verbal additions just as it enriches a church to have an organ and old brasses, marbles and frescoes and stained windows. (VRE 361)

There is a counterpart in religion to the clash between the sentiments of atomism and monism in philosophy. 'Although some persons aim most at intellectual purity and simplification, for others richness is the supreme imaginative requirement. When one's mind is strongly of this type, an individual religion will hardly serve the purpose' (VRE 362).

The will to believe

There is a more direct and forceful support for James's religious ecumenicalism than the ones that have so far been considered, all of which involved highly speculative considerations. It is based on an extended use of his famed doctrine of the will to believe. Although James did not himself make this extension, he supplied all of the premises that are needed for it. The basic idea of the will to believe is that one is morally permitted to believe (or retain a belief in) an epistemically nonwarranted proposition when doing so will help to produce good consequences overall, be they understood deontologically or in terms of James's casuistic rule.[5] Speaking about believing at will is elliptical for intentionally doing that which will help to self-induce (or retain) a belief (such as acting as if you believe), since one cannot, except in rare cases, believe at will, voluntarily, on purpose. Whereas James's 'will to believe' doctrine concerns only cases in which one is morally *permitted* to believe (or continue believing) without sufficient epistemic warrant, it quite plausibly can be extended to cases in which one is morally *forbidden* to believe (or continue believing) without sufficient epistemic warrant, namely cases in which believing (or continuing to believe) without sufficient epistemic warrant will have bad consequences overall. It will be shown that James firmly believed that the case of an exclusivist religious belief is a suitable target for this extended version of the will to believe, in which an exclusivist religious belief is one that entails that *all* religious creeds other than the one of which it is a creedal part are mistaken in some of their fundamental creedal beliefs. An example of such a belief is that God is triune and that only those who believe this will find salvation. For reasons that will become manifest, I will restrict the discussion to exclusivist religious beliefs that get publicly promulgated, which is not much of a restriction since almost invariably they do.

The following is an extended 'will to believe' type argument for one being morally forbidden to believe (or continue to believe) an exclusivist religious proposition.

A 'will to believe' argument against religious exclusivism

1. For any proposition, p, if one cannot show that p is epistemically warranted and the consequences of believing p are worse than they would have been if one were not to have believed p, then one morally ought not to believe p. premise
2. An exclusivist religious proposition cannot be shown to be epistemically warranted. premise
3. The consequences of believing an exclusivist religious proposition are worse than they would have been if one were not to have believed it. premise
4. One morally ought not to believe an exclusivist religious proposition.

This hardly is a decisive argument. Its premises call for further clarification and support.

The use of 'epistemically warranted' in premises 1 and 2, for the sake of argument, will recognize two species of epistemic warrant. One is the familiar notion of Lockeian *evidential warrant* and the other the reformed epistemology's notion of *basic warrant* according to which a belief is basically warranted if it is not based on or inferred from another belief and results from the proper functioning of one's cognitive faculties in the right kind of epistemic environment according to a design plan successfully aimed at truth. The very same arguments that James gave for our being morally permitted, in certain special circumstances, to believe upon inadequate epistemic warrant apply *mutatis mutandis* to 1 and will not be repeated here.

Premise 2 is highly controversial, since there are those, such as Richard Swinburne, who argue that exclusivist Christian beliefs are evidentially warranted. It is the purpose of the chapter on 'philosophy' in the *Varieties* to show that this isn't so. Although this chapter's attack on natural theology is much too quick and shoddy, I believe that it can be strengthened and extended so as to work. Contemporary reformed epistemologists, such as Alvin Plantinga, argue only that it is possible that we have basic warrant for believing an exclusivist religious proposition, not that we actually have. To prove the latter requires showing that God exists and has instilled in us a *sensus divinitatis* as part of our original cognitive equipment and directly causes beliefs in us about the great things of the *Gospel* through the internal instigation of the Holy Spirit.

Premise 3 does not admit of any straightforward verification. In the first place, it is very difficult, if not impossible, to total up the goods and evils that have actually resulted from exclusivist religious beliefs; however, given that most of the evils in the present world result from religious exclusivism, it intuitively seems that the evils of such beliefs outweigh the goods. I say 'intuitively' because we are unable to quantify good and evil. But even if the evils 'outweigh' the goods, this does not settle the issue in favor of 3; for we might have a Hobson's Choice with respect to having an exclusivist religious belief, the consequences of each alternative being overall bad. Thus, we must consider what would have happened in the counter-factual situation in which there are no exclusivist religious beliefs. Would things have gone better or worse than they did in the actual world? Again, a strain is put on our verificatory capacities.

James would not be phased by these verificatory complications, since he makes it quite clear in the *Varieties* that he fully and passionately accepts premise 3. In fact, James's basic intention in writing the *Varieties*, to show that the essence of religion consists in personal religious experiences rather than in religious institutions and their creeds, is driven by his abhorrence of what results from institutionalized exclusivist religions, as is amply borne out by the following quotations.

> Certainly the unhesitating and unreasoning way in which we feel that we must inflict our Civilization upon 'lower' races, by means of Hotchkiss guns, etc., reminds one of nothing so much as of the early spirit of Islam spreading its religion by the sword. (VRE 69)

> A survey of history shows us that, as a rule, religious geniuses attract disciples, and produce groups of sympathizers. When these groups get strong enough

to 'organize' themselves, they become ecclesiastical institutions with corporate ambitions of their own. The spirit of politics and the lust of dogmatic rule are then apt to enter and to contaminate the originally innocent thing; so that when we hear the word 'religion' nowadays, we think inevitably of some 'church' or other; and to some persons the word 'church' suggests so much hypocrisy and tyranny and meanness and tenacity of superstition that in a wholesale undiscerning way they glory in saying that they are 'down' on religion altogether. (VRE 268–9)

James locates the cause of this institutional exclusivizing and dogmatizing of what were originally vital personal religious experiences in our 'spirit of corporate dominion.' And when this is combined with our 'spirit of dogmatic dominion' it leads to horrible evils, such as

the baiting of Jews, the hunting of Albigenses and Waldenses, the stoning of Quakers and ducking of Methodists, the murdering of Mormons and the massacring of Armenians, [which] express much rather that aboriginal human neophobia, that pugnacity of which we all share the vestiges, and that inborn hatred of the alien and of excentric and non-conforming men as aliens, than they express the positive piety of the various perpetrators. Piety is the mask, the inner force is tribal instinct. (VRE 271)

It should now be clear why my 'will to believe' argument against exclusivist religious beliefs was restricted to those that get publicly promulgated, for it is through their publicity that repressive, exclusivist religions get founded.

The science of religions

The stage is now set for James to develop a viable ecumenical alternative to exclusivist religions. This is accomplished through his science of religions, which is an empirical study of the great extant religions for the purpose of extracting from them a significant common denominator. James is not interested in off-beat cults or merely possible religions, for they have not passed the pragmatic test of time. All too often ecumenical efforts suffer shipwreck on either the Charybdis of being contentfully too thin or the Scylla of being contentfully too thick and thereby giving pride of place to some pet religion. It will be shown that James manages to steer a viable course between these undesirable extremes.

Initially, it appears as if he passes too close to the contentless Charybdis. There are some unsettling, careless remarks that make it appear as if James's ecumenicalism is to suffer the same disastrous fate as does John Hicks's, which is based on an unknowable and indescribable *ding an sich* as the common denominator among religions. This is disastrous because it strips religious belief of all content and winds up being indistinguishable from atheism. James expounds Kant's doctrine that religious ideas, although devoid of any significance, are pragmatically meaningful in our moral life. He concludes this exposition by saying that 'we have the strange phenomenon, as Kant assures us, of a mind believing with all its strength in the real presence of a set of things of no one of which it can form any notion whatsoever' (VRE 53). Two pages later, James characterizes the religious feeling as '*a feeling of objective presence*,' and then goes on to add that 'so far as religious conceptions were able to touch this reality-feeling, they would be believed in in spite of criticism, even though they might be so vague and remote as to be almost unimaginable, even though they might be such non-entities in point of *whatness* as Kant makes the objects of his moral theology to be' (VRE 55). In spite of James's slide from 'can form no notion whatever' to the last quotation's weaker 'almost unimaginable', James seems to give in too much to Kant.

But when James actually gets down to the task of extracting his religious common denominator, he does manage to give a reasonable amount of positive content to religious belief, so much so that he comes close to giving too much content and thus wrecking on the Charybdis of provincialism. He describes himself as engaged in 'a laborious attempt to extract from the privacies of religious experience some general facts which can be defined in formulas upon which everybody may agree' (VRE 342). This will have a desirable ecumenical upshot, since it 'can offer mediation between different believers, and help to bring about consensus of opinion' (VRE 359; see also 402). The contentful, as contrasted with psychological, common denominator that James discovers is summarized as follows:

1. That the visible world is part of a more spiritual universe from which it draws its chief significance;
2. That union of harmonious relation with that higher universe is our true end;
3. That prayer . . . is a process wherein . . . spiritual energy flows in and produces effects . . . within the phenomenal world. (VRE 382)

James then attempts to supply further content to the conception of the 'more spiritual' or 'higher' universe, also called the 'More.' The aim is to find a generic account of the More that will be neutral between rival 'over-beliefs' or philosophical theories about its nature. Among the many contentful things James says about the More is that it is a supernatural spiritual entity that is 'of the same quality with our own higher self' (VRE 401). Furthermore, it has 'exteriority' to us (VRE 400) but we can achieve 'union with it' (VRE 402).

But just how exterior is it and how complete is our union with it? James is well aware that monistic and dualistic mystics give incompatible answers to these questions, the former, unlike the latter, denying that there is any numerical distinction between the subject and object of a mystical experience. 'Religious mysticism . . . is much less unanimous than I have allowed . . . It is dualistic in Sankhya, and monistic in Vedanta philosophy' (VRE 336–7). James attributes these differences to the 'various theologies and various personal temperaments' of the individual mystics (VRE 401), although he personally favors the dualistic over-belief about what mystical experiences reveal.

More can be done to achieve ecumenical harmony between individuals and religions holding apparently incompatible over-beliefs. One way James does this is to assert that you must look to feelings and the conduct as being the very essence of religion and then point out that 'the feelings ... and the conduct ... are almost always that same, for Stoic, Christian, and Buddhist saints are practically indistinguishable in their lives' (VRE 397). This is supposed to show that their over-belief differences are not of much moment and should not be allowed to be divisive. Echoing the very words by which he described his moral democracy – 'the outward tolerance of whatever is not itself intolerant' – we should treat rival over-beliefs 'with tenderness and tolerance so long as they are not intolerant themselves' (VRE 405).

There is another strategy for neutralizing the clash between rival over-beliefs that harks back to that well-known group of blind men simultaneously feeling up the same elephant and making apparently conflicting claims about the nature of the beast, such as would be made by the one who has him by the balls and the one who has him by the trunk, and so on. One and the same More can appear under different guises to differently circumstanced individuals. Each of their descriptions of it can be true as far as it goes, provided that it is not intolerant by denying some modicum of truth to all the other descriptions. Even though the analogy with the elephant limps on all four hoofs, I think something worthwhile can be made of this multiple guises idea.

Notes

1. All James references are to the Harvard University Press editions of The Works of William James and will be included in the body of the paper using the following abbreviations: (VRE) *The Varieties of Religious Experience*; (EPR) *Essays in Psychical Research*; (PP) *The Principles of Psychology*; (TT) *Talks to Teachers on Psychology and to Students on Some of Life's Ideals*; (ERM) *Essays on Religion and Morality*; (WB) *The Will to Believe and Other Popular Essays in Philosophy*.
2. Before I begin I want to stress that this is not the only account that can find textual support, for James is too profound, subtle, and suggestive a philosopher for any interpretation to lay claim to being *the* correct one. Any account that makes this claim thereby shows itself to be a wrong interpretation.
3. *The Letters of William James.* Edited by Henry James. 2 vols. Boston: Atlantic Monthly Press, 1920. Vol. 1, p. 224.
4. Quoted from Gay Wilson Allen, *William James*. New York: Viking Press, 1967, p. 309.
5. This is a radical oversimplification and for all of the gory details I refer the reader to Chapter 4 of my *The Divided Self of William James*. Cambridge: Cambridge University Press, 1999.

Chapter 12

James on truth (again)

Hilary W. Putnam

I begin with a confession. This chapter is hung onto the subject of James's *Varieties* by what may seem the very thinnest of threads, a single sentence in the *Varieties*, but when you hear that sentence, I think that you will agree that it deserves meditating on, indeed meditating at greater length than the space I am allowed here. The sentence in question is the whole of footnote 23 on page 401 of the Harvard edition of James's *Varieties*. It reads as follows:

> The word 'truth' is taken to mean something additional to bare value for life, although the natural propensity of man is to believe that whatever has value for life is thereby certified as true.

The reason that this footnote invites meditation is twofold. First, it is directly connected in the text with the following pair of questions that James introduced a few pages earlier (399):

> First, is there, under all the discrepancies of the creeds, a common nucleus to which they bear their testimony unanimously? And second, ought we to consider the testimony true?

In fact, the paragraph to which this footnote is appended (401) reads as follows:

> So far, however, as this analysis goes [James's analysis of the 'common nucleus' to which the religious experiences that the *Varieties* has examined 'bear their testimony'], the experiences are only psychological phenomena. They possess, it is true, enormous biological worth. Spiritual strength really increases in the subject when he has them, a new life opens for him, and they seem to him a place of conflux where the forces of two universes meet; and yet this may be nothing but his subjective way of feeling things, a mood of his own fancy, in spite of the effects produced. I now turn to my second question: what is the objective 'truth' of their content?

And precisely *here* James tells us that the word 'truth' is taken to mean something additional to 'bare value for life'.

Thus the whole question as how we are to understand the sense in which James believes that there might be some *objective truth* to what he calls the 'common nucleus' to which the various creeds bear testimony depends for its answer on how we ought to interpret this footnote. And second, as you all know, James has been almost universally accused of *identifying* truth with 'value for life'. Of course, careful readers have pointed out that it is not value for life merely in the case of the individual believer, but value for life 'in the long run and on the whole, of course' that James speaks of,[1] but that truth cannot go *beyond* value for life on the whole and in the long run is agreed upon, or better, simply assumed as a given, by the great majority of writers who refer to James's views on the subject. So how, and at this crucial juncture, can he speak of 'something additional' to 'bare' value for life being required for truth?

This is a crucial question. If we think that when James asks whether the 'common nucleus' of the various religious 'creeds' is true, all he means by truth is 'value for life', then we will have taken him to have answered the question of truth when he pointed out the 'enormous biological worth' and the 'spiritual value' of that nucleus. If we go in that direction, then we will see this footnote as something to be explained away, or (and perhaps this is the more usual treatment) simply ignored. If, on the other hand, we take the footnote seriously, and look for an understanding of James's philosophy on which he is *entitled* to say that, in his view, although value for life is *necessary* for truth, it is not *sufficient* for truth, then that will require to see James's view of truth as applied to religious belief as a more 'realist' one. And this is, I want to argue, what we should do and how we should see James's view.

The history of the treatment of the realist strain in James's philosophy overall is somewhat strange. Perry, James's first great biographer and expositor, writes rather late in the second volume of his famous study, 'Another element of James's philosophy *which is largely ignored in this work* is his realism'[2] (emphasis added) and this may have encouraged other readers, less familiar with James's work than Perry, to feel they could safely ignore it as well. Yet when James replied to a number of 'misunderstandings' of pragmatism in *The Meaning of Truth*, he had listed the idea that 'no pragmatist can be a realist in his epistemology' as the fourth misunderstanding, and in explaining why this is a misunderstanding, he wrote:

> The pragmatist calls satisfactions indispensable for truth-building, but I have everywhere called them insufficient unless reality also be incidentally led to ... Ideas are so much flat psychological surface unless some *mirrored matter* gives them cognitive lustre. That is why as a pragmatist I have so carefully postulated 'reality' *ab initio*, and why, throughout my whole discussion, I remain an epistemological realist.[3] (emphasis added)

Moreover, a central point of James's metaphysics of pure experience is to reject root and branch the idea of a 'veil of perception', the idea that we 'directly perceive' only our own sense-data, and are never in immediate perceptual contact with reality.[4] As Lamberth, Sprigge, myself, and others have pointed out, it is precisely because ideas can 'lead to' and 'terminate in' pure experiences that talk of ideas being about reality, 'agreeing with' reality, makes sense, according to James, and it is because pure experience is in principle public and not private that ideas can refer to a public, intersubjective, reality. Indeed, James insists in 'The Moral Philosopher and the Moral Life' that 'truth supposes a standard outside the thinker to which he must conform.'[5]

Our question, then, in brief, is simply 'What entitles James to speak of truth as requiring "something additional to bare value for life", given that he has so often been read in such a way that the very idea of a constituent of truth additional to value for life is supposed to be meaningless to a Jamesian pragmatist?' In answering this question, I shall have to refer at a certain point to my own published interpretation of James's theory of truth,[6] which I know has been contested by David Lamberth (who has the honor of concluding this collection of essays); and there may well be other scholars here who have interpretations of James on truth different from my own; but I shall begin by making some points that I hope will be accepted by all of us who have written on these issues.

I already quoted James's statement in *The Meaning of Truth* that 'The pragmatist calls satisfactions indispensable for truth-building, but I have everywhere called them insufficient unless reality also be incidentally led to'. In the same essay he insists that a truth must put us in 'fruitful' contact with a reality. The most charming explanation that James gives of how he can hold that truth involves not one but two elements, that is satisfaction of human interests and contact with reality, occurs in a letter to Dickinson Miller.[7] I don't claim this letter answers our interpretative questions, but – as James wished it to do – it gives us the *picture* that lies behind his thought.

> I am a natural realist. The world *per se* may be likened to a cast of beans upon a table. By themselves they spell nothing. An onlooker may group them as he likes. He may simply count them all and map them. He may select groups and name these capriciously, or name them to suit certain extrinsic purposes of his. Whatever he does, so long as he *takes account of them*, his account is neither false nor irrelevant. If neither, why not call it true? It *fits* the beans-*minus*-him, and *expresses* the *total* fact, of beans-*plus*-him.

If, with this picture to guide us, we now try to interpret the more technical accounts that James offers in many books and essays, I think the following is a reasonable summary.

First, the 'beans' are bits of pure experience. Everything that exists is a part of pure experience, and outside of pure experience there is nothing. In particular, the 'finite god' (or sometimes 'gods') that James speaks of (and perhaps believes in) is itself (or are themselves), just as we are, constituted of pure experience. (If this is right, then James's rejection of a transcendent deity fits well with his theory of reference. There is no possibility of genuine reference to anything transcendent, on James's account of reference in terms of experiences 'leading to' and 'terminating in' other experiences.)

Second, the mystery as to what it would take for belief in the finite god to be verified is at least partially removed: human religious experiences would have to lead to and put us in fruitful contact with the finite god, conceived of as something that communicates through and perhaps includes my 'subconscious' but is something MORE than my or your or anyone's subconscious (I have found Sprigge's discussions in his *James and Bradley* especially helpful here).[8]

But might we not be mistaken in thinking that experiences *had* put us in touch with (a) god? Of course, for – and this is my third point – we all know that James is a fallibilist. Belief in God, or the finite god, may be wrong, *either* because there is no reality for the belief to put us in touch with other than 'moods of [our] own fancy' (there are no beans) *or* because thinking of the reality the belief puts us in touch with (assuming it does put us in touch with a reality, a MORE, that goes beyond our own subsciouses) as 'god' (or 'gods') does not correspond to our deepest and best interests, is not a way to relate 'fruitfully' to that reality (does not meet the interest that we have in classifying the beans).

But what does this come to in practice? What is the criterion for either putting us in touch with a reality or for correspondence to our deepest and best interests?

To essay an answer, I have to go beyond the points on which I said I expect us to agree. As I interpret James (and this is what David Lamberth disagrees with, but I shall not attempt to rebut his criticisms in this talk, although I address them in the Afterword on pages 177–80):

1. James distinguishes between mere warranted assertibility, which he in one place calls 'relative' truth (and also 'half truth') and tenseless, or in his terminology 'absolute', truth. (Lamberth believes that 'absolute truth' has only 'phenomenological' significance, and no 'metaphysical' or 'epistemological' significance.)

2. James believes there *are* absolute truths (he tells us, for example, that the pragmatist believes that pragmatism itself is absolutely true), 'I expect that the more fully men discuss and test my account, the more they will agree that it *fits*, and the less they will desire a change,' and, as a good fallibilist, he adds that 'I may, of course, be premature, and the glory of being truth final and absolute may fall upon some later revision and correction of my scheme, which will then be judged untrue in just the measure in which it departs from that final satisfactory formulation.'[9]

3. James proposes a quasi-Peircean account of absolute truth: 'Truth absolute [the pragmatist] says, means an ideal set of formulations towards which all opinions may in the long run of experience be expected to converge.'[10]

4.   The criterion for correspondence to our deepest and best interests, as well as for the other component of truth, fruitful contact with the relevant reality, is, then, just what James said it was in *The Will to Believe*, when he wrote: 'It matters not to an empiricist[11] from what quarter an hypothesis may come to him: he may have acquired it by fair means or foul; passion may have whispered or accident suggested it; but if the total drift of thinking continues to confirm it, that is what he means by its being true.'[12]

One further point

Before I conclude, I want to consider one further question, which I did not discuss when I wrote 'James's Theory of Truth'. That is, the question of the status of the pragmatist's 'definition' of absolute truth. We see that James is *not* claiming to be giving a *semantic* analysis when he mocks Russell's style of criticism a few pages later, writing:

> What a word means is expressed by its definition, isn't it? The definition claims to be exact and adequate, doesn't it? Then it can be substituted for the word – since the two are identical – can't it? Then two words with the same definition can be substituted one for another, *n'est-ce-pas?* Likewise two definitions of the same word, *nicht wahr*, etc., till it will be indeed strange if you can't convict someone of self-contradiction and absurdity.[13]

Recently I have come to think that a sentence of James which has long puzzled me suggests not only that he isn't claiming that the pragmatist's definition of truth is analytic, or conceptually true, or anything of that sort, but that in fact it has the status of a *hypothesis*, for 'the pragmatist', that is, for James himself. The sentence in question is the following[14] 'No pragmatist needs to *dogmatize* about the consensus of opinions in the future being right. He need only *postulate* that it will probably contain more of truth than anyone's opinion now.'[15] For a pragmatist a 'postulate' that he is prepared to give up if experience goes against it has the status of a hypothesis. Thus James's twofold requirement on truth: that a truth must 'fit' the appropriate realities and must also fit our interests in connection with the particular idea or 'formulation', seems to me now to have a more fundamental status in his thought than the postulate that the future 'consensus' will be true.

To sum up, I suggest that the question of the objective truth of the 'common nucleus' to which he claims the several creeds give 'testimony' reduces, for James, to a pair of questions: whether there is indeed a reality to which the 'common nucleus' refers beyond the 'moods of [our] own fancy'; and, if so, whether it is *appropriate* to classify that reality as 'god'. If this isn't nearly as surprising or controversial or radical as some of the views that James gets saddled with, that is, no doubt, because James wasn't nearly as *nutty* as some people like to pretend he was.

Afterword

> It matters not to an empiricist from what quarter an hypothesis may come to him: he may have acquired it by fair means or foul; passion may have whispered or accident suggested it; but if the total drift of thinking continues to confirm it, that is what he means by its being true.[16]

In 'James' Theory of Truth', I argued that James did not repudiate the notion of 'absolute' truth, truth not relativized to a particular moment in time or a particular evidential situation, but actually proposed a complex theory of it. The foregoing talk assumes that interpretation off James's notion of truth. However, as I mentioned there, in his (otherwise) fine study of James, *William James and the Metaphysics of Experience*, David Lamberth has taken issue with me, and proposes that when James speaks of 'absolute truth' he means it not as a 'substantive' notion, but *only* as a regulative idea. I discuss our disagreement here, not only because the talk presupposed the correctness of my interpretation, but because Lamberth's arguments are really arguments against the tenseless notion of truth itself, and this is an independently important philosophical matter.

One of James's definitions of 'absolute truth' is the following:

> [Rickert and Münsterberg] accuse relativists – and we pragmatists are typical relativists – of being debarred by their self-adopted principles, not only from the privilege which rationalist philosophers enjoy, of believing that these principles of their own are truth impersonal and absolute, but even of framing the abstract notion of such a truth, *in the pragmatic sense of an ideal opinion in which all men might agree, and which no man should ever wish to change*. Both charges are wide of the mark.[17] I myself, as a pragmatist, believe in my account of the truth as firmly as any rationalist can possibly believe in his. And I believe in it for the very reason that I *have* the account of truth which my learned adversaries contend that no pragmatist can frame. I expect, namely, that the more fully men discuss and test my account, the more they will agree that it *fits*, and the less they will desire a change. I may, of course, be premature in this confidence, and the glory of being truth final and absolute may fall upon some later revision and correction of my scheme, which will then be judged untrue in just the measure in which it departs from that final satisfactory formulation.[18] (emphasis in original)

Against what seems to me the plain sense of this passage, Lamberth offers his interpretation of James's expression 'absolute truth' as *no more than* a 'phenomenological' expression of a 'mandate' to continue inquiry: 'The pragmatic meaning of absolute truth, then, appears to find its distinction for James in the habit or mandate of searching for more truth [by which Lamberth means merely more and better-confirmed successful belief], a habit that critically does (and should) animate and pervade our actual processes of knowing in the present.'[19] In short, on Lamberth's interpretation, 'absolute truth' is *only* an ideal, and it has meaning *only* as inspiring the practice of continuing to search for revisions and improvements of our present opinions. On his interpretation, James does *not* really believe that his account of absolute truth is impersonally and absolutely true in the way a rationalist believes that his is, *nor* does he really believe there such a thing as 'the shape of that truth'.

The reason for Lamberth's reluctance to concede that James could have meant it when he insisted that he *has* 'the abstract notion of such a truth' and believes that his account of what it is to be an absolute truth is itself 'truth impersonal and absolute' as firmly as any rationalist can possibly believe in his, appears to be that he believes that an absolute notion of truth is a notion of truth as unrevisable, 'guaranteed', and for James to have such a notion would be incompatible with his fallibilism, indeed with pragmatism itself. Thus he writes:

> A crucial question remains from Putnam's analysis, since Putnam rejects this pragmatic interpretation of absolute truth [i.e., Lamberth's analysis of absolute truth as 'ever only a *putative* object' of the drive to test knowledge and 'organize it into systems of knowing'].[20] Does James's notion of absolute truth do any epistemological work beyond articulating this (nonetheless crucial) habitual animation of inquiry? And if so, work of what sort? To put the question another way, does James's notion of truth as a 'regulative ideal' function metaphysically or epistemologically to regulate, or partially yet objectively determine, the truth of particular opinions or statements? Does 'truth absolute' function for James to explain the conditions of the possibility of absolute truths being made (outside of its representation of our psychological drive for truth) beyond what we already know of the functional account of knowledge about?
>
> Based on my interpretation of James in this text, the general answer with respect to absolute truth must be no. For James truth, or perhaps more aptly 'trueness' or 'truthfulness,' applies to particular ideas or statements advanced and tested in concrete, finite processes of knowing. Many of these truths become stable and unquestioned parts of our knowledge, and thus components of our habits of action. But none do so *by virtue* of their connection to something we might refer to as absolute truth. Truth for James is fundamentally piecemeal and plural, always relative to its situated 'trowers' and subject to revision, regardless of how direct or repeated their verifications might be, or how reliable their ideas may prove with respect to other truths and other knowers. ... Truth absolute, then, is a necessary conceptual commitment, expressive of our phenomenological awareness of our philosophical desire for systematic and thorough knowledge, and thus instructive of habit. But truth absolute provides no guarantees, and itself is not guaranteed.'[21]

But this is a confusion. Of course, 'tenseless' truth, truth not relativized to evidence, to the borders of experience at a particular time and place is, once what it concerns has taken place, unalterable (as James himself says).[22] 'Caesar crossed the Rubicon' is unalterable. But 'unalterability' is an ontological notion, while 'subject to revision' is an epistemic one. The fact that Caesar's crossing of the Rubicon is unalterable (if he did) does not mean that the judgment that he crossed the Rubicon is not subject to revision.[23]

Before I answer Lamberth's 'crucial question', I need to make a couple of preliminary observations:

1. In one place,[24] Lamberth reads me (incorrectly)[25] as charging James with violating the disquotational principle of logic (the principle that p is equivalent to 'p' is true). He also claims that on his reading, according to which what James means by 'truth' when it occurs without a qualifier is what *pragmatism* calls 'relative' truth, or truth within the borders of experience at the time a judgment is made, James does not violate the disquotation principle.[26] But this is simply a mistake. To see this, notice that the statement that the earth is 'flat', not a sphere, was warrantedly assertible for thousands of years. Today it is warrantedly assertible that the earth is round. If truth were identical with warranted assertibility ('trueness'), it would follow that the statement that the earth is flat was true for thousands of years while the statement that the earth is round is true today. But, by the disquotational principle, this would mean that the earth was flat for thousands of years and is round today – i.e., that the earth changed its shape, which is not the case.

    Moreover, William James clearly distanced himself from the idea that truth *sans phrase* is tensed in the way that 'relative' truth is when he wrote, 'Ptolmaic astronomy, euclidean space, aristotelian logic, scholastic metaphysics, were expedient for centuries, but human experience has now boiled over those limits, and we call those things only relatively true, or true within those borders of experience. "Absolutely" they are false; for we know that those limits were casual, and might have been transcended by past theorists just as they are by present thinkers.'[27]

2. Lamberth and I are arguing about whether I am right to attribute a 'Peircean strain' to James. So it is important to understand what Peirce's own notion of truth does and does not entail. Famously, Peirce identified what is true with 'the opinion which is fated to be ultimately agreed to by all who investigate'.[28] But that does not mean that truth is not 'piecemeal and plural', in the sense of consisting of individual true statements.[29] What Peirce posits is that for each meaningful question there is a time at which a stable consensus as to which is the right answer to that question will be achieved; this does not mean that at that time (or at any time) we shall have a *guarantee* that we have reached the stable answer, and it does not mean that there is any time at which *all* questions will have reached a stable answer. On my reading, the same is true on James's account. So when Lamberth

attributes to James the view that 'truth absolute is not guaranteed' he is, of course, right, but that is no argument at all against the idea that individual statements can be absolutely (i.e. tenselessly) true on James's account.

What, now, of Lamberth's 'crucial question', the question 'Does "truth absolute" function for James to explain the conditions of the possibility of absolute truths being made (outside of its representation of our psychological drive for truth)?' My answer is that the fact that it is (tenselessly) true that Franklin Roosevelt was President of the United States in 1940 is not a *different* fact from the fact that Franklin Roosevelt was President of the United States in 1940. And that fact certainly is the best explanation why our memories (the ones of those of us who were alive then) and our history books and our newspapers from that year all say that he was. In other words, the tenseless truth of a true empirical proposition *is* (usually) the *best explanation* of its warranted assertibility at the present time.

Notes

1. William James, *Pragmatism* (Cambridge, MA: Harvard University Press, 1975, 1978), 106.
2. Ralph Barton Perry (ed.) *The Thought and Character of William James*, vol. 2 (Boston: Little, Brown & Co., 1935), 591.
3. William James, *The Meaning of Truth* (Cambridge, MA: Harvard University Press,1975, 1978), 106.
4. Nor is this a particularly recent or novel interpretation of James. It is often overlooked that Bertrand Russell, although he attacked James's theory of truth, was a great admirer of precisely James's metaphysics of pure experience. In the preface to *The Analysis of Mind,* originally published in 1921, Russell writes, 'The view that seems to me to reconcile the materialistic tendency of psychology with the antimaterialistic tendency of physics is the view of William James and the American new realists, according to which the "stuff" of the world is neither mental nor physical, but "neutral" stuff, out of which the world is constructed' (6). And he describes his book as an attempt to 'develop the view in some detail.'
5. *The Works of William James; The Will to Believe and Other Essays*, F.H. Burkhardt and F. Bowers (eds) (Cambridge, MA.: Harvard University Press, 1979), 146.
6. 'James's Theory of Truth,' in Ruth Anna Putnam (ed.) *A Companion to William James* (Cambridge: Cambridge University Press, 1997), 166–85.
7. James to Dickinson S. Miller, August 5, 1907. *The Letters of William James; edited by his son Henry James*, vol. 2, 295–6 (Boston: Atlantic Monthly Press, 1920).
8. Timothy L.S. Sprigge, *James and Bradley: American Truth and British Reality* (New York: Open Court, 1993).
9. James, *The Meaning of Truth*, 142.
10. James, *The Meaning of Truth*, 143.
11. By 'an empiricist' James means, of course, a 'radical empiricist' in his sense.
12. James, *The Will to Believe*, 24.
13. James, *The Meaning of Truth*, 148.
14. Lamberth also quotes this sentence, but considers it only a commitment to 'trowing truth, as opposed to being content with mere verification.' By this what

Lamberth means is a commitment to further testing of presently accepted 'truths'.

15. James, *The Meaning of Truth*, 145.
16. James, *The Will to Believe*, 24.
17. The other charge to which James refers is that pragmatists are debarred from believing that their own philosophy is absolutely true.
18. James, *The Meaning of Truth*, 142.
19. *William James and the Metaphysics of Experience* (Cambridge: Cambridge University Press, 1999), 219.
20. *William James and the Metaphysics of Experience*, 219.
21. Ibid, 219–20.
22. Cf. Ralph Barton Perry (ed.) *The Thought and Character of William James*, vol. 2 (Boston: Little, Brown & Co., 1935), 478.
23. There is an old bad argument against the idea of 'absolute' truth, to the effect that 'we can never know' whether a statement is absolutely (i.e., tenselessly) true, and hence the statement that, for example, it is absolutely true that snow is white is without empirical meaning. The mistake is that if we can know that 'snow is white' is confirmed, to at least some degree, then we can also know that the statement 'Snow is white' is true' is confirmed to the same degree, by virtue of the logical equivalence of 'Snow is white' and ' "Snow is white" is true'. I do not know if this argument is behind Lamberth's repeated portrayal of absolute truth as unrevisable (if my account of it is correct).
24. *James and the Metaphysics of Experience*, 222.
25. In fact, the question of violating the disquotation principle arose only as *one horn of a dilemma*. The problem that I raised with James's theory of truth in 'James's Theory of Truth', 182–3, is that, if p's being true always depends on the coming-to-be of a consensus that p, then *the truth-value of every statement about the past depends on what will happen in the future* – and that cannot be right. I argued that if the past is indeed 'inalterable', as James says, then *either* that means that it is a reality that Lizzie Borden committed the murders or a reality that she did not, *independently of whether either of those judgments becomes the consensus in the future*, in which case the disquotation principle wouldn't be valid (it could be that Lizzzie Borden committed the murders, but the eventual consensus would be that she didn't, and so 'Lizzie Borden committed the murders' would not be true); *or*, I suggested, James might say that the reality is immutable but what is *true* of the reality is not – but taking this horn of the dilemma would contradict his reply to Lane, in which the inalterability of the past was explained by saying that it is only those truths about the past that refer to *relations* between the past things and future things that are able to 'grow and alter'. Today I would add that yet another possibility would be to say that the consensus about things that have already happened *became* 'fated' when the things finished occurring; but this would be implausible since, for one thing, the consensus does not only depend on what happened in the past but on how we shall try in the future to determine what happened – and whether we try to investigate this at all – and this sort of human decision is not 'fated', on James's metaphysics. It is because of this difficulty, I believe, that Peirce shifted from defining truth in terms of what the ultimate consensus *will* be to defining it in terms of *what it would be if intelligent investigators went on investigating for ever*. But James is not a Peircean realist with respect to counterfactuals. I believe that James simply never thought through the issue.
26. 'On James's view, should we be in the position of knowing more definitively the fact that p (or not p), then *revision of the truthfulness of the judgment would follow*

dynamically (loc. cit. 222). Lamberth is right that (if we are rational) whenever we *revise* the belief '*p* is warrantedly assertible' we also *revise* the belief that *p*, and *vice versa*, but it is nevertheless false that warranted assertibility (Lamberth's 'truth in the making') obeys the disquotation principle.

27. James, *Pragmatism*, 106–7.
28. Charles Hartshorne and Paul Weiss (eds) *Collected Papers of Charles Sanders Peirce*, vol. 5 (Cambridge, MA: Harvard University Press, 1934), 268 [§407]; on Peirce's fallibilism, see my introduction to Lecture Four in C.S. Peirce, *Reasoning and the Logic of Things* (Cambridge, MA: Harvard University Press, 1992), 72–5.
29. Lamberth believes that it is *the whole system* of absolute truths that James means by 'absolute truth', and not individual statements. I agree that James sometimes uses the term this way, referring to 'absolute truth' as a kind of ideal limit, and I further agree that this ideal limit is *only* an ideal. It is concerning absolute truth in the sense of such an 'ideal vanishing point' or 'ideal set of formulations' that James says in *Pragmatism* (106–7) that 'It runs on all fours with the perfectly wise man, and with the absolutely complete experience.' But James also says that 'absolutely' individual scientific theories such as Ptolemaic astronomy are false. And is also not true, as Lamberth claims, that James never says of *individual propositions* (or small groups of propositions) that they are absolutely true; James's 'scheme' (i.e., his theory of truth) is such a group of individual propositions, and it is this that he says he believes to be true absolutely, in the passage from *The Meaning of Truth*.

Chapter 13

Pragmatism and religious belief in William James

Graham Bird

The Varieties of Religious Experience is rightly acknowledged to be outstanding in its originality, scope, and the light it throws on the character of a deeply felt personal religious belief, but it is also generally acknowledged to contain a number of ambiguities and tensions. At their most general they can be put in terms of James's own contrast between a 'tough-minded' empiricist pragmatism and a 'tender-minded' religious belief in the supernatural, but I want to be more specific about some of those tensions. Of course James's pragmatism includes his account of religious belief, and in the *Varieties* (518–19) he claims that his account of the latter is 'thoroughly pragmatic'. He talks also (455–7) of developing a 'science of religions', and of formulating religious hypotheses open to strict empirical testing in the same way as scientific hypotheses. Yet he also qualifies these claims and makes an important distinction between scientific and religious belief. It is not my intention merely to outline these problems, but rather to consider how James's pragmatism, empiricism, and account of religious belief might be adjusted to minimise, or resolve, them. I shall deal with the issues in an exclusively epistemological way, and say nothing of James's theories of meaning or truth. I consider three related tensions under the headings of pragmatic method, empiricism, and the comparison of religious belief with science.

Pragmatic method

One virtue of pragmatic method is that of settling what James regards as otherwise 'interminable disputes' in philosophy and elsewhere (*Pragmatism* 45). That prescription covers several different kinds of case. It covers the cases where the disputants have not yet agreed on some suitable test, where the seeming dispute turns on misunderstandings about the meanings of the relevant terms and so is not a real disagreement, and also where no test could be provided. In that latter case we might, following terminology which both Kant and James deploy, call the issue 'transcendent' rather than 'immanent'.[1] Neither Kant nor James regard such transcendent issues as meaningless, but both accept that they are in some way pointless or 'empty and futile'.[2] To classify a dispute as 'transcendent' is to treat it as a 'pseudo-dispute' with a recommendation to move on to some other issue, or to re-characterise the old issue in some new, 'immanent' and settlable, form. James's account in *Pragmatism* (52–3) of 'solving names', such as 'substance' or 'God', which do not properly designate transcendent items lying behind our experience but stand only for an injunction to carry out further enquiry within that experience, is very close to Kant's position. But the example of 'God' already marks a potential conflict in which a supernatural reference initially questioned in *Pragmatism* is endorsed in the *Varieties*.

James acknowledges the conflict when he talks of such religious beliefs (*Varieties*, 454) as 'referring or purporting to refer' to a world beyond that of our sensory experience, and it is underlined in his claim that we can have access to such a transcendent world through the non-standard modes of subconscious mystical experience. He speaks sometimes as if we could really know about such a transcendent world through these forms of experience (*Varieties*, 73), accepts that we may speak objectively of such beliefs as true, and thinks they are as acceptable and well supported as scientific beliefs. But he also sometimes prefers to talk only of belief rather than knowledge, and qualifies the ascription of truth to, and the authority of (*Varieties*, 422–3), such mystical claims.

On one side, then, pragmatic method enjoins us to locate immanent ways of settling disputes, while on the other transcendent religious belief is, as James himself notes, liable to go beyond those ways (*Varieties*, 510). Even if James's optimism about a common core of transcendent beliefs among religious believers were accepted, there remains a conflict between those who accept such beliefs and others who do not. Even if the supernatural were accepted as monotheistic rather than polytheistic, there would still be disputes about whether we have good reason to believe, or claim to know, that there is such a supernatural realm at all. But at this stage such tensions remain indecisive. Perhaps supernatural belief is not transcendent after all; there is some uncertainty whether such belief merely re-describes our ordinary, immanent, world or whether it identifies a wholly separate world. Perhaps James would settle in this context for a weaker claim to belief rather than to knowledge or objective truth, or qualify his preference for the 'absolute reality' of inner experiences over the abstract world of developed science. Perhaps he would accept that for us there is no decisive way of establishing the character of the supernatural,[3] and agree that subconscious experience offers at best a weak analogy with immanent sense perception. Pragmatic method begins to disclose potential conflicts in James's crass supernaturalism (*Varieties*, Postscript), but perhaps his empiricism and his comparison of religious and scientific belief can resolve them.

Empiricism

James's empiricism may not be identical to his pragmatism, but it is a near neighbour. The central problem within his empiricism has indeed already arisen in the context of pragmatic method through James's account of the supernatural as a separate world of fact to which we sometimes gain access. James recognises that supernatural belief needs adequate support and that it is 'absolutely hopeless' to demonstrate its truth by 'purely intellectual processes' (*Varieties*, 455). His empiricism requires that the 'unseen order' of a 'more spiritual universe' to which we can adjust harmoniously only through religion should rest on those trans-marginal subconscious experiences (*Varieties*, 47–8, 53, 485). The harmony we may feel in adjusting to the supernatural belongs to the immanent world, but the supernatural itself, its higher beings, and the causal influence they exert on the phenomenal world are all transcendent. In the absence of any immediate consciousness of such a realm, however opaque, the empiricist requirement for some reference to personal experience would not be satisfied.[4]

I have suggested, but not argued for, the claim that the analogy between the trans-marginal access to the supernatural and ordinary sense perception is at best weak and contentious. That issue was extensively discussed by William Alston, Richard Gale, and George Pappas in *Philosophy and Phenomenological Research* (Vol. 54, 1994). I shall not pursue it here except to say that the substantial objections to the analogy in that discussion cannot be disregarded or denied. But it would be possible to abandon, or minimise, these transcendent references by regarding supernatural religious belief as merely a re-interpretation of the immanent world. At one point James considers that option, but seems to reject it. He says (*Varieties*, 518): 'the world interpreted religiously is not the material world over again with an altered expression ... it must have a natural constitution different from that which a materialist world would have'. It is this account that presents a 'thoroughly pragmatic' account of religion, and he goes on to say of religious beliefs that 'they claim, as everything real must claim, a characteristic realm of facts as its very own'. James admits (*Varieties*, 519) that he 'doesn't know what these facts are' but insists on his own 'over-belief' that they exist.

Such passages might still be understood as merely underlining the spiritual aspect of ordinary human life and rejecting a bleakly materialist or physicalist view of reality. They might be understood in conformity to James's account in *The Will to Believe* of the immanent way we may bring about new facts, or new responses in others, but it is difficult to accept this in the religious context. James speaks in that context of 'postulating' new facts rather than merely inducing new responses, of a distinctive realm of reality, and of causal transactions between higher supernatural beings and the phenomenal world. He says quite explicitly (*Varieties*, 515–16) that the supernatural region is 'another dimension of existence' than the sensible and merely 'understandable' world. For him religious claims seem quite different from moral claims which concern only the 'ethical republic here below'.[5] In the religious context James is not merely rejecting a deflationary materialism, but positively advocating the strong thesis that the supernatural exists as a separate realm. Such a conclusion, however, serves only to underline rather than to resolve the earlier conflicts.

Science and religion

It would not be surprising in the light of the discussion so far if James exhibited consequential uncertainties about our convictions of the 'objective truth' of supernatural belief. When he considers in detail the question of the truth of such beliefs he says such things as:

> Does God really exist? . . . What is he? are so many irrelevant questions. Not God but life . . . is in the last analysis the end of religion . . . It would seem that she cannot be a mere anachronism and survival but must exert a permanent function, whether she be with or without intellectual content, and whether if she have any, it be true or false. (*Varieties*, 507)

> The fact that the conscious person is continuous with a wider self through which saving experiences come . . . provides a positive content of religious experience which is . . . literally and objectively true as far as it goes. (*Varieties*, 515)

Such passages testify to James's general suspicion of mere 'intellectual' theorising, especially in the religious context, but they underline further potential conflicts in his account. The first passage (*Varieties*, 507) evidently veers towards an immanent, not transcendent, account of religious belief. Although James insists that religious over-beliefs should be treated with tolerance (*Varieties*, 514–15) he also says (*Varieties*, 490) that 'science is as likely to be adverse as favourable' to such truth claims. And although James is unimpressed by intellectual theorising about religion, he is engaged in such an enterprise himself. It is agreeably paradoxical and disarming in an intellectual account of religion to be told that such accounts are not to be trusted, but the position has inherent problems.[6] It must be unclear in such an account how religious over-beliefs can be literally and objectively true and yet that it is a matter of indifference whether they have intellectual content or not, or whether that content is true.

James has an extended argument (*Varieties*, 498–512) to resolve these tensions. It is designed to mark both a parallel between religion and science and a superiority attached to the former, but it leads to still other ambiguities. The argument turns on the claim that while science deals only with abstract 'symbols of reality', religion in its personal and private aspect deals with 'realities in the completest sense of the term'. James insists that these latter 'egotistic elements' cannot be suppressed, and claims that only by acknowledging these 'private destinies' can we avoid the 'shallowness' of the scientific view and become 'profound'. Later he calls these more profound factors the only 'absolute realities' and compares them to a substantial meal while the scientific view is no more nourishing than a menu. But the essence of the argument is to contrast the abstract, general, symbolic character of scientific theory with the personal, private realities of religious belief, and to infer that the former is shallower, less profound, than the latter.

The argument is open to at least the following summary queries. They may individually be remediable, but I shall suggest that they indicate a central ambiguity in James's position between a complex 'strong' view and a 'weak' counterpart.

1. The argument seems structurally faulty, since it opposes the personal basis for religious beliefs not with that basis for scientific beliefs but with its outcome in scientific theories. There seems no good reason to deny that both contexts have both such resources. Religious beliefs are couched in symbols, even if their personal basis is overpoweringly important to the believer. Similarly individuals' experiences form a basis for scientific theories, even if they have less personal importance for the scientist. James suggests that science utterly 'repudiates the personal point of view' (*Varieties*, 491–2), and 'takes no account of anything private at all' (*Varieties*, 500), but this could not be taken to deny the existence of such personal experiences, or their importance for scientific theory.

2. Even if the personal basis for religious belief has a distinctive importance for the believer it is not obvious that we should conclude, as James does, that religious belief is more profound than its scientific counterpart, or that it alone designates an 'absolute' reality. We might instead draw the neutral conclusion, encouraged by James's own rejection of any appeal to 'value judgements' in favour of a 'purely existential, historical, point of view' (*Varieties*, 4–6), that the two contexts are simply quite different and not that one is superior to the other.[7]

3. When James says in conclusion (*Varieties*, 519) that 'the strict science world view is bosh', he objects not just to science, or scientific theory, but to 'scientism', a metaphysical world view which licences only science, and allows only scientific disciplines to designate reality. But to repudiate that 'world view' it is not necessary to deploy arguments that contrast science unfavourably to religion; and if these queries have any force it would be better not to deploy them. James is entirely right to claim that religion and religious beliefs, like a vast range of other non-scientific interests and beliefs, have a perfect right to co-exist with science, but to defend that right it is necessary to attack only scientism and not science itself.

4. James not only distinguishes science from religion but also assimilates them. He is tempted (*Varieties*, 515 and footnote) to treat some religious expressions, the 'Holy Spirit' for example, as parallel to theoretical concepts in science, despite the disanalogies in their use. Analogies of this kind, like those mentioned earlier between trans-marginal (sub)consciousness and ordinary sense perception, are weak at best. It is not only that they are vulnerable to comparable disanalogies, as James notes in his discussion of Fechner in *A Pluralistic Universe* (151f.), but that there are no clear criteria to distinguish when the balance should incline to one side or the other. That latter feature violates the prescriptions of pragmatic method, and would, unresolved, leave such a dispute in the realms of the interminable and pointless.

5.   It is not surprising in the light of these general problems that James's argument canvasses different, weak or strong, conclusions. The strong conclusions would claim that religious beliefs, judged by the standards of science, are at least as well grounded as scientific beliefs. The weak conclusions, which James also expresses (*Varieties*, 452–3, 510–11), claim only that there are no adequate grounds to reject religious beliefs or their transcendent role. James says that his arguments are 'not coercive' but offer only 'to resist plausible pretexts (e.g. from scientism) for vetoing' any appeal to such beliefs. In a similar way James also limits his conclusion by saying 'I feel as if we had no philosophic excuse for calling the unseen or mystical world unreal'. In the strong forms such conclusions assert a positive commitment to religious belief, but in the weak forms they merely resist the arguments against that commitment.

The arguments relating science and religion in 3, like those considered earlier in the context of pragmatic method and empiricism, are evidently both vulnerable and ambiguous. James's discussion points at every stage to different, weak or strong, positions with respect to religious belief, and to weak or strong conflicts with his underlying pragmatism and empiricism. In the strong claims pragmatism and empiricism aim, contentiously, to assimilate supernatural religious belief as an equal partner with science. In the weak claims pragmatism and empiricism conflict with the truth of supernatural religious belief but are not sufficient to deny the latter's meaningfulness, importance or role.

If James's position were evaluated as a set of variations in a chess manual, then the outcome would be a preference throughout for the weaker, modest claims over the stronger, more vulnerable lines. It is too ambitious, too risky, to insist on the objective truth of claims about the supernatural, or on our knowledge of such truths. It would be positionally more correct to talk of belief rather than knowledge, and to stress, as James himself often does, the limited scope and authority of such beliefs. To treat religious beliefs as subject to, and able to satisfy, the same tests as empirical science, to liken supernatural entities to scientific theoretical constructs, or to dwell on analogies between perceptual and trans-marginal consciousness, are variations to be avoided. James should stick to his arguments against scientism rather than science, and to his rejection of a theoretical approach to religious belief in favour of a recognition of its personal importance, its character and its immanent consequences. Those features constitute the primary merits of James's approach, for which the *Varieties* is rightly applauded. For these reasons in the earlier, still unresolved, conflict between a pragmatic method which eschews transcendent claims and a commitment to religion which endorses them, the advice would be quite generally to modify the latter as I have suggested rather than the former. The resulting position would, I believe, be favourable to James and would not lose what is distinctively valuable in either his underlying pragmatism and empiricism or his account of religion. It would serve to emphasise James's own inclination towards the weaker positions, even in the *Varieties*, resolve some of the ambiguity in that work, and focus attention on the significance and consequences of a personal religious commitment.[8]

I add one final note. Just as pragmatic method echoes Kant's contrast between immanent and transcendent claims, so the preferable lines suggested for James conform naturally with the view that Kant takes of transcendent religious belief. Since James explicitly rejects what he takes to be Kant's position, that conclusion may seem unplausible, but James really misunderstands Kant. He takes Kant to be a 'refined supernaturalist' who denies any meaning to religious 'ideals' (*Varieties*, 53–55) or to any causal interaction between transcendent and immanent realms. But Kant plainly did not regard transcendent beliefs as strictly meaningless. He thought they lacked *Bedeutung* for us, that is an 'objective reality' in which we could identify the referents of such religious expressions.[9] Where James talked of religious beliefs which 'refer or purport to refer' to a transcendent, supernatural realm, Kant would naturally write only 'purport to refer'. Since Kant accepted that we can conceive transcendent realms, other possible worlds inaccessible to our cognitive powers, we can similarly conceive causal interactions between the transcendent and the immanent. But our cognitive limitations mean that we can have no right to claim any knowledge of such items, and disputes about them will be pseudo-disputes which we have no rational means of resolving. By the same token, since nobody can claim knowledge that such beliefs are false, there may be rational motives that encourage and entitle us to hold the associated beliefs. In both Kant and James such motives can be tied to the moral consequences of such beliefs and so to immanent effects in the conduct of the believers. In this more general context, as in the account of pragmatic method, the weaker position suggested for James corresponds closely to Kant.

Notes

References to James's work are to the following editions:
The Will To Believe, London, Longmans Green & Co., 1899.
The Varieties of Religious Experience, London, Longmans Green & Co., 1902.
Pragmatism, London, Longmans Green & Co., 1907.
A Pluralistic Universe, London, Longmans Green & Co., 1909.

1. Kant's *Critique of Pure Reason* (trans. Norman Kemp Smith; London, Macmillan, 1929) provides at B 352–353 the standard account of his distinction between what is immanent and what is transcendent. 'We shall entitle the principles whose application is confined entirely within the limits of possible experience immanent; and those, on the other hand, which profess to pass beyond those limits, transcendent.' It is worth noting that Kant then also distinguishes what is 'transcendent' from what is 'transcendental': 'Thus transcendental and transcendent are not interchangeable terms.' James also uses the term 'immanent', for example in *Pragmatism* (70), where he speaks of an 'immanent or pantheistic deity'.
2. Kant's standard terminology is to call transcendent claims 'futile and empty' (*nichtig und leer*) (B 507 note, B 664). James talks of such disputes in *Pragmatism* Lecture III (99) as 'quite idle and insignificant', and adds 'the wise man ... would turn his back on such a supererogatory discussion'.

3. Even in the later *A Pluralistic Universe* (309–310) James makes provisos about the 'entirely problematic' character of a 'superhuman consciousness' although he claims that there is a 'decidedly formidable probability' in favour of its existence.

4. James makes his general strategy clear in *A Pluralistic Universe* (309): 'The intellectualist objections ... fall away when the authority of intellectualist logic is undermined by criticism, and then the positive empirical evidence remains.' But the position defended in that later work, with its emphasis on a pluralistic pantheism, a finite God, and superhuman consciousness rather than on the supernatural, seems weaker than the strong claims made in the *Varieties*.

5. In *The Will to Believe* (198) James says: 'Whether a God exist, or whether no God exist ... we form at any rate an ethical republic here below.' His view in 'The Moral Philosopher and the Moral Life' (*The Will to Believe*, 184) is that it is only a superstition to suppose an abstract moral order existing independently of feelings and desires (193, 197).

6. One of the underlying inherent problems, which I have not considered, is that of the nature of a science of religions. It is not easy to understand how James's requirements for such a science could be satisfied, for its hypotheses must be subject to test 'in all the usual ways' (*Varieties*, 454) and yet it must also 'drop the theoretic attitude' (*Varieties*, 489) in order to focus attention on personal and private religious experiences. It is not always clear in James's discussion when he is talking of such a projected science of religions and when he is talking more generally of religious experience and belief.

7. James himself (*Varieties*, 122) adopts a more neutral attitude towards science and religion which encourages their tolerant co-existence. He says: 'Evidently then the science and the religion are both of them genuine keys for unlocking the world's treasure-house to him who can use either of them practically. Just as evidently neither is exhaustive or exclusive of the other's simultaneous use.' The passage expresses more generally James's pluralism in admitting what he calls 'many interpenetrating spheres of reality'.

8. David Lamberth pointed out that after the *Varieties* James does not use the term 'supernatural', and it is generally evident that his position in *Pragmatism* and *A Pluralistic Universe* is weaker than in some of the more committed passages in the earlier work (see note 4 above). It would be interesting to establish whether this represents a change of view or only a clarification of earlier views. At the conclusion of *Pragmatism* (299–301) James refers cautiously to his earlier work as 'on the whole regarded as making for the reality of God', and commends his own position as 'neither tough nor tender in an extreme and radical sense'.

9. Throughout the Dialectic of Kant's *Critique of Pure Reason* the central fault in 'ideas of pure reason' is that they lack *Bedeutung*, and it is made clear that this means lacking any identifying reference for us. At B 664, for example, Kant confines the proper use of a principle of causality to the 'field of experience' and says that 'outside this field (it) has no application and is meaningless (*ohne Bedeutung*)'. At B 671 he says: 'We are entitled to suppose that transcendental ideas have their own good, proper, and immanent use, although when their meaning (*Bedeutung*) is misunderstood and they are taken for concepts of real things, they become transcendent in their application.' In one passage (B 396–397) Kant even anticipates, and attempts to defuse, the sort of misunderstanding that James demonstrates. He notes that we might say of ideas of reason that we 'have no concept of their object', but then adds: 'But we should be better advised, and less likely to be misunderstood, if we said that although we cannot have any knowledge of the object corresponding to the idea, we yet have a problematic concept of it.'

Chapter 14

William James as a religious realist

T. L. S. Sprigge

In his book *The Divided Self of William James* Richard Gale distinguishes between James the Promethean pragmatist and James the anti-Promethean mystic. Many readers of James have similarly identified two different philosophical personas at work in his philosophy.

Some prefer the one persona, some the other. Richard Rorty, for example, distinguishes between the good James, i.e. the pragmatist, and the bad James, i.e. the mystic. Personally I am inclined to think that these are a matter of shifts of emphasis rather than changes of mind, but they must surely strike any serious reader of James. And they are particularly important in understanding what James has to say about religion.

Another contrast is that between the mental/physical dualism which seems to be the dominant note of *The Principles of Psychology* and the neutral monism and radical empiricism of his later thought. This contrast, however, is partly simply a consequence of the fact that in the *Principles* he deliberately takes up the assumptions on which he believes that psychology as a science must base itself and avoids the deeper metaphysical questions to which his neutral monism was to be part of the answer. But it is doubtful how far this is the whole explanation and how far there was not also a real shift in his opinion as he turned his mind more to philosophy as opposed to psychology, conceived as a natural science. It is certainly rather puzzling how a thinker so intimately concerned in his earlier work, and in his general medical knowledge, with the relation between brain and consciousness could, in his later work, seem to consider the relation between mind and matter in a way that almost entirely abstracts from the question of how brain and consciousness connect, concentrating almost entirely on how perceived and conceived physical objects in the environment relate to our perception and conception of them.

The American philosopher Samuel Johnson asked Bishop Berkeley why there was any need for physical sense organs, for all the complications of the physical basis of sight, granted that seen and otherwise perceived objects are just directly inserted in our minds by God.[1] One is almost inclined to ask a similar question of the radical empiricist for whom perception of an object is simply the overlap of our personal stream of consciousness with the stream of pure experience constituting the object.

The problem is somewhat eased when we associate the radical empiricism with the panpsychism towards which James moved more and more confidently. For then the brain must in itself really be an enormously complex system of interacting pure experiences, just as is every other physical thing. But that still leaves it problematic not so much how the brain, as thus conceived, relates to our personal consciousness as to how it relates to the physical objects which, according to radical empiricism, we perceive in so direct a way.

Part of the problem is what exactly James was up to in his radical empiricist enterprise. Was it intended more as phenomenology than metaphysics, as an account of what seen or otherwise perceived objects are *for us*, rather than of the actual causal basis of our experience? Or should we see the scientific account of our sense experiences as determined by the brain and the radical empiricist view of them as the actual entry of external objects into our stream of experience as differently pragmatically useful ways of looking at the matter for different purposes?

On the whole the answer that seems best to fit James's later metaphysics is the Bergsonian one that the brain's job is to select that of those impersonal images that constitute physical reality shall enter our mind as our sense impressions or images rather than to create them. This is a view that James considers most explicitly in his essay on immortality. However, in that essay he only suggests it as a possibility, not as something that he actually endorses.

Pragmatism at its best

However all that may be, what concerns us more is a certain apparent tension in James's approach to religion, between, on the one hand, that of a pragmatist for whom whatever truth it has is largely a matter of how it helps us to live our lives, and, on the other hand, that of someone seeking a more objective kind of truth about the real source of religious, and in particular mystical, experience.[2]

Soon after I first started reading William James, which was many long years ago and before I went near a university, I became puzzled as to how a man who in much of his work seemed so earnest to discover how things really are, what the true character of the universe and its more significant parts is, could advocate a view of truth that seems to downplay the very idea of there being a way things really are. As a psychologist, and later as a panpsychist, he seemed to have an overriding concern with knowing the objective truth (understood as something other than a merely useful system of thought) concerning the issues with which he was engaged. This division is noticeably present within *The Varieties of Religious Experience* itself.

For sometimes his concern seems to be with what religion can do for us, or what religious experiences can do for us, and to be concerned only with a truth that plays this pragmatic role.[3] 'We return to the empirical philosophy: the true is what works well, even though the qualification "on the whole" may always have to be added' (*Varieties*, p. 458).

But at other times, as indeed in his doctrine of a finite God, and the possible collective mind which is at the base of all our different consciousnesses, he seems to be looking for an explanation of the world that goes beyond the pragmatic.[4] Thus throughout his discussion of mysticism his main concern would seem to be whether or how far the idea of the world that mysticism seems to bring accords with how things really are or are not. And in the last lecture, called 'Conclusions', he speaks first of the effects of religious belief in terms of feeling and conduct, and passes on from that to considering what he himself calls 'the "objective" truth'[5] of its intellectual content insofar as this is something shared between all the main religions.[6]

Such was long my puzzle until I found what I believe to be the solution. Just for now I shall touch on two matters which cast light on it. First, there is the doctrine of 'the will to believe' and then there is his concern with avoiding Josiah Royce's argument for the existence of the Absolute.

As everyone knows, the article 'The Will to Believe' advised that if one is hesitant between two, or perhaps more, opinions on a given subject, and if after careful reasoning and assessment of all relevant empirical evidence, the case for each seems quite evenly balanced, then, and then only, it is legitimate to take up with the answer that most satisfies one's passional nature.[7]

Personally, like many others, I long thought that James's 'will to believe' position collapsed because it is not possible to decide to believe something. What seems to be doing so is at best self-deception. However, I have become more sympathetic to this view. For although genuine belief is not voluntary, the general way in which one inclines to view things is more open to decision. One can live, and to some extent even feel, as though P were true, even though one does not have that absolute sense of certainty that pertains to a belief in the strong sense of belief mostly favoured by philosophers. Thus if one thinks the case for and against a life after death is an issue of this sort, it seems reasonable to respond to bereavement in a manner that suggests that the dead person survives and may even be met again some day.

However that may be, one does suspect some slide on the part of James from letting one's passional nature influence how one encourages oneself to look at things (provided the options are genuinely evenly based intellectually) to treating what satisfies one's passional nature as an element in determining which of one's beliefs is true. And having departed so far from a correspondence theory of truth, it is easy to see how one might go further and hold that a true belief is one that satisfies one's nature as a whole, and this is pretty well the pragmatic theory of truth. Anyway, from this point of view, James may be taken as recommending us to live as though God exists, if we find the case in favour of His existence evenly balanced with that against. Of course, for James, the existence of God will only pass this pragmatic test if He is conceived as finite rather than infinite, so that there are real independent powers of evil resisting His purposes.

None the less, I believe that by far the most important aspect of James's pragmatic view of truth is one that he developed especially in relation to

Royce's argument for the Absolute. According to that, our minds can only target a real external reality as the object of our thought if that reality and our own consciousness are linked together in the overarching divine mind or Absolute.[8]

To escape the Absolute (which, unlike a finite God, he found morally repellent) James argued that an idea is true if and only if it puts one in desirable theoretical and practical relations with a thing or state of affairs that, for that reason, should be counted as that which it is a belief about and which you are characterising as having those properties that make for this success. In contrast, an idea is a false belief if it would have put one in such relations to a certain something, had it existed in possession of those properties as, in fact, it does not.

This I consider the best form of James's somewhat multi-faceted pragmatism. And it should be emphasised that it is essentially a realist view of truth. For when understood in this way, the pragmatic view of truth tells us that the belief that God exists and has a certain character is true if and only if He does. A very satisfactory result.

It may be suggested that when (in the *Varieties*, chapter XVIII, pp. 442–447) he takes a tough pragmatic line with various metaphysical and theological statements about God (and dismisses them as meaningless, because without practical results), he shows himself in a much more logical positivist light than my account suggests. But this is because these conceptions do nothing, and could do nothing, to put us in useful behavioural relations with anything, an objection that fits perfectly with the realism that I have ascribed to him.[9]

It should be added, however, that this is a highly 'externalist' view of thought just as it stands. For it ascribes truth to the experience of mental symbols which need give us no real genuine sense of the nature of the reality with which they help us engage prosperously. Although James was not altogether clear on the matter, I think his position was one that Bergson in fact attributes to him, as that of interpreting the truth of ordinary beliefs in this semi-behaviourist way while holding that in metaphysics, or indeed in personal relations, one can have a kind of intimate grasp of things which is not required for mere truth.

Bergson puts it thus in his introduction to the French translation of *Pragmatism*.

> The definition that James gives of truth is of one flesh with his conception of reality. If reality is not that economical and systematic universe that our logic likes to represent, if it is not sustained within an intellectual framework, truth of an intellectual order is a human invention the function of which is to utilise reality rather than to introduce us to it. And if the reality does not form an ensemble, if it is multiple and mobile, composed of criss-crossing currents, the truth that is born from a direct participation in one of these currents – truth felt before being conceived – is more capable than the truth, which is simply thought, of seizing and storing up reality itself.[10]

This may be supplemented by the remark that in explaining truth by the behaviour in relation to its object which a true belief promotes, the behaviour in question is what phenomenologists call lived behaviour.

Moreover, at its best truth leads to an actual merging of our stream of consciousness with the stream of pure experience constituting the object of our thought. Understood in the light of the metaphysics of radical empiricism, the pragmatic account of thought and truth appears somewhat less externalist in character although externalist elements remain and are even stressed.

What for James was the most objectively true feature of religion?

But what were the theological beliefs that James took to be true in the more objective of the senses allowed for by his pragmatism? I say 'took to be true', for surely he did believe that God, conceived in the way he favours, does indeed exist. Furthermore, why did he hold this belief?

The finite God

For James, God is a being far more powerful and benevolent than ourselves with whom we can co-operate in promoting the development of the world in as desirable a direction as possible. Moreover, conscious of our own inadequacies, we can on occasion relate to Him so that we receive 'saving experiences' from Him. As well as this, God must be finite, in the sense that He has an other, since otherwise He must be evil for allowing or causing so much evil.[11]

God in Conclusions and Postscript of the Varieties

James clearly thought that one reflecting on the question of the existence of God in some religiously valuable sense, should enquire especially as to the causation of mystical experience, even when he only knows about it as second-hand, as is likely to be the case for many such earnest inquirers, himself included. (Late in his life, however, James did, while walking in the mountains, have something like a mystical experience, but neither he nor anyone else would call him a mystic.)

However, he insists that although mystical experience is properly probative for the mystic, it is not so for others. They must study it critically and try to understand its nature in a more intellectual way.

Final Varieties verdict on the objective basis of religious experience

This conception takes on a richer form in the last lecture ('Conclusions') of the *Varieties*. James starts by concluding from his study of religious psychology that the common nucleus of all religions is that religious human beings have a sense that there is something wrong about them which can only be put right if they make a proper connection with a higher power or powers (*Varieties*, p. 508). In the higher types of religious experience this wrongness 'takes a moral character and the salvation takes a mystical tinge'. This comes about because he identifies himself with the higher aspect of his own personality and 'becomes conscious that it is conterminous and continuous with a MORE of the same quality, which is operative in the universe outside him, and which he can keep in working touch with, and in a fashion get on board of and save himself when all his lower being has gone to pieces in the wreck' (*Varieties*, p. 508).

The matter on which James, going beyond empirical psychology, seeks to know the objective truth is what the nature of this MORE is. Is it 'merely our own notion, or does it really exist? If so, in what shape does it exist? Does it act, as well as exist? And in what form should we conceive of that "union" with it of which religious geniuses are so convinced?' (*Varieties*, p. 510).

James offers first a view which he is prepared to back as an objective and literal truth by a scientific psychology independently of any particular religious claim. This is that the MORE is in the first place our own subconscious or subliminal self.[12]

Anything beyond this will be what James calls an 'over-belief'. All the propositions of any particular religion are over-beliefs in this sense, that is, matters that cannot be established beyond doubt for all serious enquirers. It is absolutely right and appropriate that there should be many different and incompatible over-beliefs which should all be granted respect as suiting the mental make-up of particular people.

None the less, James has his own over-belief, and even though he would not claim to prove it, he clearly thinks it a reasonable inference from the facts of religious experience.

It is best to put this over-belief in some of James's own wonderfully expressive prose:

> The further limits of our being plunge, it seems to me, into an altogether other dimension of existence from the sensible and merely 'understandable' world. Name it the mystical region, or the supernatural region, whichever you choose. So far as our ideal impulses originate in this region (and most of them do originate in it, for we find them possessing us in a way for which we cannot articulately account), we belong to it in a more intimate sense than that in which we belong to the visible world, for we belong in the most intimate sense wherever our ideals belong. Yet the unseen region in question is not merely ideal, for it produces effects in this world. When we commune with it, work is actually done upon our finite personality, for we are turned into new men, and consequences in the way of conduct follow in the natural world upon our regenerative change. But that which produces effects within another reality must be termed a reality itself, so I feel as if we had no philosophic excuse for calling the unseen or mystical world unreal. (*Varieties*, pp. 515–16)

He elaborates on this a bit further in his Postscript where he suggests that 'the practical needs and experiences of religion seem to be sufficiently met by the belief that beyond each man and in a fashion continuous with him there exists a larger power which is friendly to him and to his ideals' (*Varieties*, p. 525). This larger power may just possibly be a fuller, so to speak, supernatural self of which the self of this life is only a fragment. More likely it is a single whole underlying us all although not inclusive of all reality as is the Absolute of the absolute idealists.

The mother sea of consciousness

Another way of expressing James's conception of God is as a mother sea of consciousness from which our own consciousness has temporarily flowed away, but into which it will eventually flow back.[13] But the flow back and forth continues to a greater or lesser extent in this life. How far we continue to exist after death as to some extent distinct eddies in the mother sea, James leaves as an open question.

We must repeat that for James, with his finite God, reality is not just one mother sea to which we all, and everything else, permanently belong, as Advaita Vedanta and Absolute Idealism teach. For one thing, when we flowed out of it, on the Jamesian view, we were no longer part of it (for this life, that is) and for another thing there may well be streams of consciousness which always exist only outside it.[14]

Such watery metaphors play quite a part in James's thought, from the stream of consciousness to the mother sea, and in weighing up the cogency of James's thought one must attempt to cash the metaphors and realise that they function rather differently in different cases. I have attempted to clarify the matter in my own book on James and Bradley.[15]

Were James's views purely empirical or to some extent metaphysical?

For James his form of radical empiricism and panpsychism allowed it as possible that this is how it is, and the evidence of a whole range of religious experiences strongly suggest that this is how it actually is.

On this basis James described his theistic claims as essentially empirical. But I would add to this that there was a strong background of metaphysical thinking which established the possibility of this.[16] Such metaphysics may, indeed, in the broadest sense be empirical, but it is not the fruit of the more usual kind of investigation which we typically think of as empirical.

Thus his claim that science deals only with abstract structures and that it is feeling in a broad sense that is what actualises these structures would usually be regarded as a philosophical claim rather than an empirical one.[17]

Certainly James objected to attempts to establish religious belief on the basis of philosophic argument. 'Ratiocination is a relatively superficial and unreal path to the Deity' (*Varieties*, p. 448). But that does not preclude one metaphysic offering a better basis for the clarification of the message of feeling than another; moreover, the metaphysic may itself, as I think James's is, be in a certain sense grounded in feeling, or perhaps rather in the intellectual contemplation of feeling. In any case what James rejected with some gusto in the *Varieties* VIII were traditional philosophical and theological purported proofs of God's existence and his nature. This is quite compatible with the suggestion that his own metaphysical position offers a better home for a satisfactory interpretation of religious experience than do some other metaphysical outlooks.

What James was objecting to was the idea that rational thought, without empirical evidence, could ever establish a religious belief as true as opposed to clarifying its content.[18] Thus James urges that 'feeling is the deeper source of religion, and that philosophic and theological formulas are secondary products, like translations of a text into another tongue'.[19] But philosophy has the task of finding a more rationally lucid interpretation of what religious experience is than the mystic normally supplies.[20] As such it may develop into 'a critical Science of Religions'.[21] And I don't see why James should deny that certain metaphysical preconceptions may prepare enquirers better for this task than do others.[22]

And although my own thought has led me to a more absolute idealist position than that of James, indeed precisely to that of which he was so frequently critical, I think that James makes a tremendously powerful case for his own position, and one much of which is available for a more fully pantheistic position, which, if we use the mother sea as our metaphor, identifies reality as a whole with the mother sea. By the way, those who wish to speak of God at times as 'She' should favour this expression of James's.

As a believer in the MORE and THE MOTHER SEA James shows himself to be a religious realist

As opposed to many currents in religious thinking today James is, then, a realist about the existence of God. For he really believes, even if not with certainty, in the existence of a supernatural MORE or MOTHER SEA with which our own mind is continuous.

Now, to turn to some modern religious thinking, there is a movement within the Anglican communion known as 'the sea of faith'. This expression, taken from Matthew Arnold, might sound as though the outlook it names would countenance the notion of God as a mother sea of consciousness; in fact that movement is decidedly unlike James. For according to Don Cupitt and the 'sea of faith' movement, on which he is the main influence, God is a human construction, and a non-realist interpretation should be given of all statements about Him which can be regarded as respectable candidates for adoption in the light of modern knowledge.

If one main purpose of this conference is to consider what James's approach to religion can say to us today, it is certainly as a challenge to such non-realism, and as a challenge to consider whether God, somewhat as James describes Him, really, in the strongest sense of 'really', exists. To do this I think we need both to do the metaphysical work necessary for making a judgement on panpsychism, the view that reality consists of a multiplicity of flows of interacting experience, some of them flowing as, to some extent, distinct eddies in a larger flow of consciousness. And then we need to consider the empirical evidence from religious experience as to whether there is a master flow or sea which is worthy of being called God.[23]

The criticism of the *Varieties* that it treats only the individual's private experience as religiously important

At this stage, however, note should be taken of a criticism of James's *Varieties* from when it was first published, and very probably in response to the lectures when given, that James's idea that religion had to be understood mainly with reference to the experiences, of a more or less mystical kind, by individuals on their own[24] (so far as other human beings go) and that institutional religion was just a second-hand,[25] and often decayed, result of this.[26]

Josiah Royce was one of the first to make this criticism, and he made it with great force. According to Royce, true religious experience is that which occurs when many human beings are united in a beloved community. This was the essential message of St Paul, when he taught the early Christian Church that it was the body of Christ of which the individuals belonging to it were the members. However, Royce applies this more generally to any beloved community, as he puts it. Thus for Royce, religion is essentially a social phenomenon.[27]

But there is no need to attempt adjudication between these different visions of religion. Surely both the experience of members of a religious community and more mystical experiences of individuals on their own can serve as examples both of the best and the worst in religion. Cults can be terrible and so can the psychotic lone experiences of some persons who feel intimately related to the divine. But also they can represent human life and consciousness at its best.

Both as a psychologist of religious experience and in his general psychology James takes an approach highly different from that of many philosophers and psychologists today

It is here that much of modern thinking about the mind is pursuing a path so far from James's. For many philosophers and psychologists conceive of the human mind on the analogy of a digital computer. This sort of mechanistic view is very remote from the features of mind that led James, and other such thinkers as Bergson, of a century or so ago, to stress its flowing quality and holistic character, and, in fact, to generalise this conception to reality as a whole. James's whole account of the stream of consciousness in *The Principles of Psychology* in effect stresses the unlikeness of lived experience to a sequential collection of mechanical or electronic clicks interacting in such a way as to present an apparently unified result.[28] Somewhat related to this is the tendency in much recent philosophy to regard our states of mind as a matter of the propositions that we can be said to be believing true or attempting to make true. For James, in contrast, assertions about what someone is thinking or desiring at a particular time, as expressed in a proposition (or even more reductively just in the tendency to utter, aloud or privately, certain sentences) are simply abstractions from a flow of thought and feeling, forming a variegated unity at every moment, which is far from any such atomic character as this. Therefore one of the questions that must be raised, if we are considering what lasting importance James's philosophy, and in particular his philosophy of religion, may possess, is how far his watery metaphors, such as streams and drops of consciousness, not to mention the mother sea thereof, are more suggestive of what consciousness is, and in particular religious consciousness, than treating digital computers as the best guide we have to the workings of mind. I suggest that this is a question that should especially concern those still working on something that may be called a science of religion. That is, the science, if James is right, must be empirical, but not in any sense mechanistic.

Notes

1. 'Philosophical Correspondence between Berkeley and Samuel Johnson 1729–1730' at pp. 273–4 in *The Works of George Berkeley: Bishop of Cloyne*, Volume Two, ed. T. E. Jessop, Thomas Nelson & Sons Ltd, 1949.
2. In Chapter XVIII of the *Varieties* James is quite combatively pragmatic in dismissing many traditional propositions about God's nature, as meaningless, on account of their lack of practical implications. James, *Varieties*, Penguin, 1993, pp. 442 ff. But elsewhere he shows himself properly concerned with truth in what seems a more objective sense.
3. At *Varieties*, pp. 122–3 and note to p. 123 James speaks of religious ideas and scientific ideas as different ways of 'handling the world', each of which works better for some purposes and some people. They are different conceptions and it is an open question whether a synthesis of them will ever be reached – for the present it should be recognised that each corresponds 'to some part of the world's truth, each verified in some degree'.
4. See *Varieties*, Lecture XVIII.
5. 'I now turn to the second question: What is the objective "truth" of their content?' (James, *Varieties*, p. 509). Do the quotation marks round 'truth' show a certain uneasiness here?
6. See James, *Varieties*, pp. 506–7.
7. James, *Varieties*, pp. 78–9.
8. In the note to page 454 James excuses himself from then and there dealing with Royce's argument for the existence of God or the Absolute as implied in the possibility of error. But it is clear that his pragmatic doctrine is especially designed to meet this argument of Royce's. The best presentation of Royce's argument is in Chapter XI of *The Religious Aspects of Philosophy* by Josiah Royce, Gloucester, MA: Peter Smith, 1965, first published in 1885.
9. It is for this reason that the moral attributes ascribed to God are said to be meaningful, as what James calls the metaphysical attributes such as his aseity and simplicity are not.
10. Bergson, 1959, 1449 Oeuvres, Paris: Presses Universitaires de France.

11. An individual like this, but not good, would by definition not be God. There may be such individuals, in addition to evil men, but upon the whole it seems more likely that the most powerful such individual is good, and therefore God. James, *Varieties*, p. 508.

12. As James puts it, 'the conscious person is continuous with a wider self through which saving experiences come'.

13. This idea and phrase occur in 'Human Immortality: Two Supposed Objections to the Doctrine' in *Essays in Religion and Morality* by W. James (edited by F.H. Burkhardt, F. Bowes and I.K. Skrupskellis, Harvard University Press, 1982), a lecture given in 1894 and supplemented in its 1895 second edition, roughly two years before the *Varieties*. I should note, however, that James thought that the idea of God was immensely useful to many people quite apart from whether He really exists or not.

14. I should note, however, that James thinks it possible that each of us has their own larger consciousness, so that there is no universal consciousness to which we all belong. (Final Impressions of a Psychical Researcher, John MacDermott (ed.) *The Writings of William James*, University of Chicago Press, 1977, pp. 798–9, and see 'Human Immortality' in *Essays in Religion and Morality*, p. 94.

15. See T. L. S. Sprigge, *James and Bradley: American Truth and British Reality*, Open Court, Chicago, 1993.

16. James is not concerned to deny the role that philosophy can play in the development of religious belief. He insists only that philosophy or metaphysics cannot be the source of religion, but that its role is to bring conceptual order into what first reached us through feeling (James, *Varieties*, pp. 432 ff). The suggestion above is not really different from this since the best metaphysics (I would agree with James) is itself prompted by reflection on actually felt feeling, so that if religious experience may owe something to metaphysics, that is still ultimately to what is based on feeling. In any case I am only saying that metaphysics plays a role in the conceptualisation of religious experience.

17. James actually speaks of them rather as symbols of reality but I think he supposes that they are symbols of the more abstract structural aspects of reality. See James, *Varieties*, pp. 498–500.

18. James, *Varieties*, p. 436.

19. James, *Varieties*, p. 431.

20. And of winnowing out the essential core of religious experience from cultural accretions, thus he thought, promoting intercultural dialogue and perhaps a move towards consensus. See James, *Varieties*, pp. 436 and 455.

21. James, *Varieties*, p. 456.

22. James, *Varieties*, pp. 432–3.

23. James, *Varieties*, p. 364. For a comparison of Jesus and Whitman, see p. 85. He also sees something in common between Jesus, as opposed to Christianity, and the healthy-minded religion of 'mind cure' (see James, *Varieties*, pp. 98–100). Regarding sin the following is striking: 'Oh, help me! cried I, thou Redeemer of souls, and save me, or I am gone forever; thou canst this night, if thou pleasest, with one drop of thy blood atone for my sins, and appease the wrath of an angry God' (James, *Varieties*, p. 218, quoting from Henry Alline, 1775).

24. See definition of religion at James, *Varieties*, p. 31.

25. See James, *Varieties*, pp. 6 and 30. See also James, *Varieties*, p. 335.

26. Though in part the ignoring of religious institutions is just to circumscribe the topic of the lectures (James, *Varieties*, 29). Still, he is making a judgement of importance by this circumscription (see James, *Varieties*, 30). See also p. 337. He

does, however, recognise a certain aesthetic value in Catholic institutional religion, but it is not a very serious recommendation (pp. 458 ff).

27. He thought, moreover, that there was a group experience, when the group was truly united, which was not simply the resultant of the interactions between the members as this might be charted by an individualist psychology. Just as for James, the individual is lost unless he can relate to the mother sea of consciousness lapping deep down within him, so Royce thought that the individual was lost unless his life was lived as one of loyalty to a beloved community. Surely Royce was right that this is to be counted as a form of religious experience neglected by James. See especially Josiah Royce, *The Problem of Christianity* (2 vols), New York: Macmillan Co., 1913 (reprinted as one volume with an introduction by John E. Smith in 1968 by University of Chicago Press).

Santayana objected not altogether dissimilarly when he accused James of religious slumming. What he meant was that religion was really a form of life associated with religious traditions and imagery, and that peculiar persons with strange experiences were not what religion at the best was about. I should note, though, that Santayana had a low opinion of Royce's philosophy and, what is more, thought that beside social religion there was a more mystical kind of religion which he describes in *Platonism and the Spiritual Life* (New York: Charles Scribner's Sons, 1927). Perhaps its worth noting that Santayana, alone among the American philosophers of this period, devoted much attention to the image of Jesus – see his *The Idea of Christ in the Gospels, or God in Man* (New York: Charles Scribner's Sons, 1946).

One might note in passing that there is something rather elitist in James's notion of religious experience, inasmuch as it implies that those of us who are not mystics, or not very far from being so, can relate to it only on the basis of the reported experiences of others, which we are, many of us, unlikely to share.

28. I say 'apparently' since, for James, genuine wholes can only be explicated mentalistically.

Chapter 15

James's non-rationality and its religious extremum in the light of the concept of pure experience

Michel Weber

Right at the beginning of the *Varieties*, James makes it clear that he will address only 'first-hand and original forms of [religious] experience'[1] – or (individual) religiousness[2] – factually putting into brackets (collective) religion *qua* 'second-hand religious life'. This focus could be 'handed according to many sets of ideas';[3] it will be contextualized here with the concept of *non-rationality* exploited in the *Pluralistic Universe*. The argument unfolds in three epochs, each one involving two steps: a definitional one, using James's concepts themselves, and an interpretational one, expanding their horizon.

First, the concept of non-rationality is defined and refined through a contrast with Greek philosophy (with the help mainly of Aristotle). Second, religiousness is defined and it is argued that, ultimately, non-rationality refers to religiousness itself. The epilogue shows how that conceptual equivalence is operationalized by the ontology of pure experience.

Non-rationality

The definition of the concept of non-rationality is the crux of our argument. It spurs from James's own speculations and is gradually put in contact with the concept of religiousness.

Definition

Here is James speaking in 1909:

> I have finally found myself compelled to *give up the logic*, fairly, squarely, and irrevocably. It has an imperishable use in human life, but that use is not to make us theoretically acquainted with the essential nature of reality [...]. Reality, life, experience, concreteness, immediacy, use what word you will, exceeds our logic, overflows and surrounds it. [...] I prefer bluntly to call reality if not irrational then at least non-rational in its constitution, – and by reality here I mean reality where things *happen*, all temporal reality without exception. (PU 212–213)[4]

So, although logic – or rationality – is essential in everyday life, reality itself – or experience – *exceeds* logic; it is non-rational in its *constitution*, not merely in its (sensorial) appearance. If something has always already escaped us, about what can we seriously claim to discuss? The puzzle this section has to make understandable is thus the following: how are rationality, irrationality and non-rationality respectively contrasted by James?

Rationality

As far as we know, James has never tackled directly (systematically) the question of the exact nature of rationality. But he has left us many clues with regard to his understanding of its whereabouts. Let us isolate two key complementary dimensions – evolutionary epistemology and process pluralism – and then contextualize the concept in his philosophy of religion.

James's basic point is that rationality has gradually evolved out of human beings' interaction with their environment;[5] rationality has always been a matter of 'shaping our *reactions* to the outer world' in the most useful way.[6] In other words, that fitness or adjustment is practically – not theoretically – directed. Although reason has only a practical worth, 'tender-minded' rationalists have endowed it with the supreme virtue of knowing absolute (i.e. eternal and universal) truth. James summarises this very simply: 'In ancient times philosophers defined man as the rational animal; and philosophers since then have always found much more to say about the rational than about the animal part of the definition.'[7] Whereas the rationalist is devoted to abstract principles, the radical empiricist is in love with the facts in all their crude variety.[8] His preferred exemplifications are Hegel, Bradley and McTaggart, for whom 'reality is rational and righteous' and vice versa.[9]

Practical (developed) reason is furthermore necessarily pluralistic[10] – and pluralism should not be understood statically but dynamically, processually: we live in a wide open, i.e. unfinished, universe.[11] In a block universe, the many would be given once and for all; in an open universe, the many are in constant becoming.

From the perspective of his philosophy of religion, the debated question can be specified by contrasting rationalism and mystical intuitionism[12] and by introducing the topic of consciousness:

> Rationalism insists that all our beliefs ought ultimately to find for themselves articulate grounds. Such grounds, for rationalism, must consist of four things: (1) definitely statable abstract principles; (2) definite facts of sensation; (3) definite hypotheses based on such facts; and (4) definite inferences logically drawn. Vague impressions of something indefinable have no place in the rationalistic system, which on its positive side is surely a splendid intellectual tendency, for not only are all our philosophies fruits of it, but physical science (amongst other good things) is its result. [...] If you

have intuitions at all, they come from a deeper level of your nature than the loquacious level which rationalism inhabits. Your whole subconscious life, your impulses, your faiths, your needs, your divinations, have prepared the premises, of which your consciousness now feels the weight of the result; and something in you absolutely *knows* that that result must be truer than any logic-chopping rationalistic talk, however clever, that may contradict it. This inferiority of the rationalistic level in founding belief is just as manifest when rationalism argues for religion as when it argues against it. (VRE 73)

The quest for the principle (or 'arche') and sensationalism will return later in our discussion. For the time being, please notice the arrival of *consciousness* on the speculative scene and its relativization: 'normal waking consciousness' (rational consciousness as we call it) is but *one* special type of consciousness.[13]

Irrationality

Here again, the concept is by no means technically specified and is only used, it seems, in a *pragmatic* common-sensical way. More precisely, the *Varieties* makes the following claims: the orthodox Christian scheme is harsh and irrational;[14] evil is *emphatically* irrational;[15] there are irrational impulses;[16] faith itself is an irrational sentiment;[17] psychopaths are somewhat irrational;[18] sacrificial devotion is divinely irrational.[19] When James evokes 'irrational doorways' provided by poetry, maybe we are getting closer to the debated non-rationality.[20] We certainly *are* getting closer when he speaks of 'primordial irrationality'[21] or of 'ultimate irrationality'.[22]

Non-rationality

Now, quite obviously, 'no one is willing to advertise his philosophy as a system of irrationality'.[23] And, indeed, in James's thought, the irrational does not play as important a role as the non-rational does. The term 'non-rational' itself occurs twice in *A Pluralistic Universe*,[24] each time in debate with Hegel and Bradley. Other related passages are as follows:

> The whole process of life is due to life's violation of our logical axioms. (PU 257)

> I am tiring myself and you, I know, by vainly seeking to describe by concepts and words what I say at the same time exceeds either conceptualization or verbalization. (PU 290)[25]

In the *Varieties* we have two further (psychologizing) occurrences:

I do not yet say that it is *better* that the subconscious and non-rational should thus hold primacy in the religious realm. I confine myself to simply pointing out that they do so hold it as a matter of fact. (VRE 74)

Our intuitions, hypotheses, fancies, superstitions, persuasions, convictions, and in general all our non-rational operations, come from it [the subliminal]. (VRE 483)

Non-rationality manifestly aims at something different from simple irrationality: one can conceive how the irrational could become rational, but (by definition) *never* how the non-rational could be rationalized. It will be the purpose of our next section to systematize the meaning of the concepts of rationality, irrationality and non-rationality.

Relevance

The specification of the concepts at stake will proceed in two steps. First, we propose our own definition and exemplify it with Aristotelian logic; second, we globalize it with a dialogue between Greek cosmos and Jamesian chaosmos.

A judgement is *rational* provided that it is congruent with the set of rules of relevance consensually adopted in a given culture; an *irrational* judgement is not congruent, but could become so, once some fixing-up (tuning-in) is provided. For its part, the *non-rational* is definitely incommensurable with reason, whatever the rational system at stake is; it names the intrinsic – or primordial – opacity of concrete reality.[26] Unfortunately, we cannot afford the detailed analysis of the question of the cultural validation of the rules of relevance here. Let us simply point at two constraints: phylogenetic (evolution in the biosphere) and koinogenetic (education in the ethnosphere).

The simplest way of exemplifying this is to give a quick look at Aristotelian logic, because it fits so well our everyday experience (i.e. our normal state of consciousness).[27] It is traditionally defined by three principles intrinsically linked with the substance-attribute ontology granting permanence amid flux: the principle of *identity*,[28] the principle of *contradiction*,[29] and the principle of *excluded middle*.[30] Consequently, any proposition that does belong to the territory marked out by these three principles is, from an Aristotelian perspective, rational; if it does not, it is irrational. A contradiction is not irrational, since it possesses a clear status in the system: it is a statement that is always false – and *everybody agrees* that it is so (because some mistake must have occurred in the chain of reasoning). A paradox, however, is irrational: as its etymology shows, it is a contradiction that has the appearance of truth, with the result that there are numerous *opinions* regarding the way of understanding them; no consensus prevails. The Aristotelian non-rational is *primary matter* (the ultimate substratum which has no definite characteristic of its own, i.e. the complementary of *form* in his hylemorphism);[31] it embodies the ultimate opacity of existence.

The difference between the irrational and the non-rational is striking if we remember that the paradoxicality of a given statement can vanish in a renewed logical atmosphere: the theory of types, for instance, proposes a solution involving no real modification of either of the Aristotelian principles (it 'simply' uses a sharp distinction between levels of language). The appeal to a contradictory logic, or the dismissal of the principle of excluded middle, are other possible paths that have been variously paced as well: Graham Priest promotes a *transconsistent logic* where some contradictions are true; the *quantum logic*, framed by Garrett Birkhoff and John von Neumann to cope with the advances in microphysics, revokes, for its part, the excluded middle.[32]

But, argues James, it would be misleading to claim that 'reality obeys a higher logic, or enjoys a higher rationality'.[33] A rational dysfunction that can be – or even should be – repaired is *not* what non-rationality is. So far, we have claimed that the non-rational was already present in Greek philosophy under the guise of an *ultimate* opacity of existence. It remains to be shown that opacity becomes a *primordial* fact for James. The contrast between ultimacy and primordiality would be the following: for most Greek thinkers (Sceptics excepted), reason can, and should, go as far as possible (i.e. go a long way) before it reaches its limits (i.e. bangs itself against the non-rational remainder); for James, on the contrary, the non-rational has to be taken into account right at the beginning; it immediately limits the pretensions of reason. Let us quickly contextualize why radical empiricism departs from old-fashioned sensationalism.

Greek philosophy emerged in a cultural context that understood the world as a cosmos [κόσμος]. Three main concepts are expedient to picture it: logos [λόγος], arche [ἀρχή] and theoria [θεωρία]. To live in a cosmos (a fundamentally ordered world; where stability is the built-in feature) means three things: (i) there is a set of rational laws that structure the cosmos, and these laws structure as well the human mind (one *matches* the other); (ii) hence, the quest of the principle (or starting point, 'place' of genesis of all phenomena) is a meaningful endeavour; (iii) that quest has furthermore a holistic transformative virtue (it is through theoretical reason that meaning is personally encountered and hence that one's destiny can be bent).

Specularly, pragmatism understands the world as chaosmos. The three main relevant concepts are: non-rationality, anti-foundation and consequentialism. To live in a chaosmos (a partially ordered world; where stability is earned over creative process, where stability never has the last word) means: (i) natural laws are but processual habits, they cannot pretend to exhaust the phenomena, and their *fitness* with human rationality is purely local, indeed pragmatic; (ii) hence the quest of the principle is at best useless and at worst misleading; (iii) and solely consequences are thinkable.

Whereas Plato's cave is a place of darkness surrounded by the reality of eternal light, the exact opposite is true for James: his cave is a place of artificial light surrounded by the reality of darkness and 'emancipation consists in escaping the definiteness of the intellect through a reliance on instinct and feeling'; one has to 'undo selection and to recover the original plenum of experience'.[34] It is not a matter of 'vision' anymore, but of 'touch'. The closed universe of onto-logism is replaced by the open universe of pragmatism; Egypticism by Heraclitism;[35] repetition is now framed by creativity and 'all noble, clean-cut, fixed, eternal, rational, temple-like systems of philosophy'[36] are dismissed. Vagueness has gained some of the virtues formerly belonging only to clear and distinct ideas; spontaneity positively matters:

> Conceptual processes can class facts, define them, interpret them; but they do not produce them, nor can they reproduce their individuality. There is always a *plus*, a *thisness*, which feeling alone can answer for. Philosophy in this sphere is thus a secondary function, unable to warrant faith's veracity, and so I revert to the thesis which I announced at the beginning of this lecture. In all sad sincerity I think we must conclude that the attempt to demonstrate by purely intellectual processes the truth of the deliverances of direct religious experience is absolutely hopeless. (VRE 455)

Interestingly enough, James's very lucid analysis is reminiscent of the Buddhist 'suchness' or 'thusness' (proximity furthermore exploited by Nishida), as we will see in our third section.

We are now fully equipped to exploit the significance of the concept of non-rationality. The non-rational opacity of experience is not only due to the contingent specialization of our senses (even if interoception and proprioception were taken into account, clarity and distinctness would not be achieved), but also to the deficiencies of our language (even the reformed language of ontological speculation *cuts out and fixes*)[37] and the weakness of our insight (finitude condemns intuitions to be versatile and fleeting), it involves the very nature of our historical chaosmos: a multiverse constantly seeking new perfections. Opacity is rooted in the genuine novelty that manifests itself in the world and that gives its meaning to the strong pluralism advocated by James (again: a pluralism featuring a constant renewal of the crude variety of experience). In other words, non-rationality embodies the intrinsic – or primordial – opacity of concrete reality; it is peculiar to process pluralism.

An additional specification is relevant before launching the next section: we have to contrast primordial opacity with the sensorial opacity opportunely designated by the concept of the fringe.[38] Conscious experience is indeed produced by a filtration obliterating the wealth of details. But since in sensorial vagueness and non-transparency dwells relationality – upon which reason still has some grip – we have to claim that sensorial opacity does not belong to the non-rational *per se*. It deserves to be conceptualized because it casts light on a complementary dimension: even if the world was rational through and through 'in itself', sense perception would still allow only a very partial (focal) picture. On the other hand, even if sense perception was clear and distinct through and through, process pluralism would still allow only *some* rationalization. Two complementary poles are thus underlined: on the one hand, the idiosyncrasy of a given event, its independence and spontaneity – individuality in the making violates logic; on the other hand, the relationality of all events, their interdependence and causal determinism. This is essential from the perspective of meaning because both breaks and continuities are necessary. Without breaks, we are stuck in a block universe; without joints, solipsism reigns. The concepts of *environment* and *multiverse* crystallize this tension: connection and disconnection are basic qualities, conjunctions and separations are equally real in an open universe.[39]

In conclusion, non-rationality should be distinguished not only from rationality and irrationality, but from supra-rationality and arationality as well: if the world was supra-rational, it would mean that we may be like dogs in our libraries[40] (cf. the noumenon – or 'intelligible existence' – in Kant); if it was arational, it would mean that reason does not reach (fit) it *at all* (cf. the crucial differences existing between the concept of the *absurd* in Sartre and in Camus). Exactly: neither James nor Bergson are irrationalists; the non-rationality their prose is pointing at is intrinsically a *private* one; there remains a *public* use of reason.

Religion and religiousness

The goal of this section is to show that religiousness both relativizes and enriches the concept of non-rationality. Non-rationality is relativized because of the importance of interconnectedness; it is enriched because the occurrence of total opacity makes its experience *speak*.

Definition

Although the *Varieties* claims that to give a precise (i.e. abstract) definition of what the essence of religious phenomena consists of would be a futile exercise, it offers – 'for the purpose of these lectures' – three main definitions: a broad definition (actually in two versions), a key arbitrary definition, and a conclusive definition.

Broad

James defines religion in the 'broadest and most general terms possible' twice. At the beginning of his inquiry, he proposes an impersonal definition that works for individual as well as collective religious experiences. Religion is characterized by: 'the belief that there is an unseen order, and that our supreme good lies in harmoniously adjusting ourselves thereto'.[41] In his last lecture, he sums up the discussion 'in the broadest possible way', but factually takes into account the partition between individual and collective experiences installed by his arbitrary definition (cf. infra). Religious life is said to include the following beliefs:

1. That the visible world is part of a more spiritual universe from which it draws its chief significance.
2. That union or harmonious relation with that higher universe is our true end.
3. That prayer or inner communion with the spirit thereof – be that spirit 'God' or 'law' – is a process wherein work is really done, and spiritual energy flows in and produces effects, psychological or material, within the phenomenal world.

Religion includes also the following psychological characteristics:

4. A new zest which adds itself like a gift to life, and takes the form either of lyrical enchantment or of appeal to earnestness and heroism.
5. An assurance of safety and a temper of peace, and, in relation to others, a preponderance of loving affections.[42]

Both versions of the broad definition put emphasis on adjustment with the unseen: in the former the possibility of a rational and social harmonization is left open; in the latter, solely living (personal) relationality (communion) matters.

Arbitrary

The very marrow of James's perspective is disclosed in his arbitrary definition that contrasts immediate personal experiences (religiousness) and mediate collective experiences (religion):

> Religion, therefore, as I now ask you arbitrarily to take it, shall mean for us the feelings, acts, and experiences of individual men in their solitude, so far as they apprehend themselves to stand in relation to whatever they may consider the divine. Since the relation may be either moral, physical, or ritual, it is evident that out of religion in the sense in which we take it, theologies, philosophies, and ecclesiastical organizations may secondarily grow. In these lectures, however, as I have already said, the immediate personal experiences will amply fill our time, and we shall hardly consider theology or ecclesiasticism at all.[43]

Religion, as well as the question of the meshing of religion and religiousness, are factually put into parenthesis. Religion is only a rational by-product, a public 'crystallisation' of a nocturnal epiphany.[44] For its part, the definition of religiousness exploits the two main features already adumbrated in the (second version of the) broad definition: idiosyncratic solitude and holistic relationality ('man's total reaction upon life').[45] From the perspective of our argument, it is significant that the collective religious rationality is obliterated by the individual contact with the non-rational *par excellence*: whatever is considered 'the divine'.

Conclusive

This arbitrary definition is narrowed a few times with the help of concepts like solemnity, self-surrender, pure cosmic emotion,[46] and the like. Finally, James provides what could be called his conclusive definition:

> There is a certain uniform deliverance in which religions all appear to meet. It consists of two parts: —
>
> 1.   An uneasiness; and
> 2.   Its solution.
>
> 1. The uneasiness, reduced to its simplest terms, is a sense that there is *something wrong about us* as we naturally stand.
> 2. The solution is a sense that *we are saved from the wrongness* by making proper connection with the higher powers. [...] When stage 2 (the stage of solution or salvation) arrives, the man identifies his real being with the germinal higher part of himself; and does so in the following way. He becomes conscious that this higher part is conterminous and continuous with a MORE of the same quality, which is operative in the universe outside of him, and which he can keep in working touch with, and in a fashion get on board of and save himself when all his lower being has gone to pieces in the wreck.[47]

We find again the same tension between an individual pole and a relational pole. More precisely, one can see the merging of the two previous definitional steps from the standpoint of the solitude of the *homo religiosus*: isn't the case, indeed, that the uneasiness makes sense only because of the silent presence of the unseen? And that this presence itself acts as an urge for reconciliation? Peace arises from the union with the power beyond;[48] to live, in the strong sense of the term, is nothing else than to be religious.[49]

Relevance

To sum up: on the one hand, non-rationality has been shown to be correlated with process pluralism; it is a primordial form of opacity that *seems* to share only by accident some of the phenomenalities of sense perception (i.e. relationality), the common point being, however, that primordial and sensorial opacities both participate in the existential conditions of possibility of meaning. Non-rationality has indeed typically a non-relational ring: the unpredictability of contemporary events matches the spontaneity (sometimes the liberty) they exhibit. And without cosmic spontaneity *and* human liberty no meaning can be allotted to existence. For its part, relationality provides the community of the world: a totally isolated subject would be foreign to meaning. On the other hand, religiousness also champions the exact same themes – opacity, non-obviousness, uneasiness – while relationality receives a crucial role. Somehow, in its solitude, the individual reaches the Whole. At the apex of the growth process, individuation leads to cosmization and cosmization to individuation. One returns 'from the solitude of individuation into the consciousness of unity with all that is'.[50] Let us now exploit the link that exists between non-rationality and religiousness.

We argue that religiousness's Dark Night is properly depicted by the concept of total opacity – where *total opacity* means that the awareness of primordial opacity *and* of sensorial opacity are at their peak. Even the tangential rationality of the fringes of experience is gone. Hence two complementary sub-theses. On the one hand, religiousness experiences the chief form of non-rationality: not only primordial but sensorial opacity are enjoyed. In first-hand religious experiences, rationality finds itself totally overcome by the ineffable – all the more so since relationality is experienced as dissolutive of the 'ego-like' life.[51] We no longer have one individual aware of the wreckage of his/her rationality: the subject/object duality has vanished, there solely remains a chaosmic – so to speak chaosmotic – emotion.[52] But, on the other hand, one can claim as well that non-rationality finds its very resolution (resorption) in religiousness: non-rationality is not a problem any more, it is a solution; relationality is made fully actual, i.e. sensorial opacity topples into transparency and, as a result, existential meaning is reached.

Pure experience

The epilogue shows how this extremization of the concept of non-rationality is completed and operationalized by the ontology of pure experience. Although one could claim that pragmatism's reversal of the Greek onto-logism is basically instrumented by its refusal to cross the gates of metaphysics, James, for one, has been quickly aware of the fact that 'empirical facts without "metaphysics" will always make a confusion and a muddle'.[53]

Definition

The reception of the concept of pure experience has been rather negative and it is not difficult to understand why.[54] On the one hand, James's vision is 'counter-intuitive' – better: non-rational. Its purpose is to draw all the onto-epistemological *consequences* of anti-foundationalism and of non-dualism. On the other hand, James's style is quite surprising and it takes time to organize the intrication of the semantic layers involved.

In the lines that follow, we exploit a tripartite grid to organize the layers of meaning of the concept. By doing so, we take advantage of the very categories that need to be bypassed. Here lies the fatum of process thought: to depict a radical onto-epistemological renewal – and thereby arouse a modification of consciousness – can only be achieved through the use of *specialized* everyday language, i.e. a language that is substantialistic – dualistic at heart (exactly what needs to be reformed – if not destroyed).

Subjective

From the subjective, or 'inner' point of view, pure experience is the 'immediate flux of life' in which feelings inflame the whole experiencing being. It is the prepredicative penumbra of newborn babes (or intoxicated adults) who intuit a '*that* which is not yet any definite what'.[55] It is a bare sense of presence characterized by a state of primordial innocence ignorant of distinctions. Experience is just as it is, *without the least addition of deliberative discrimination*.[56]

Objective

From the objective, or 'outer' point of view, pure experience is the 'primal stuff' or 'materia prima' of the world. It is to be noticed that James uses the concept of 'stuff' in various analogical ways: positively as well as derogatorily. Positive occurrences[57] aim at the full thickness of the concrete, at its overall chaosmic structure; derogative occurrences[58] denounce the understanding of reality's core as a permanent *substance* underlying changes. '*Experience as a whole is self-containing and leans on nothing*.'[59] Basically, the question of the 'primal stuff' is the one of (realistic) pluralism; without some 'objective something' standing out there, we end up *volens nolens* with some form of solipsistic idealism; the 'many' collapses, once and for all, into an all-embracing 'one'. This is definitely not the case in the 'normal' state of consciousness.

Unitive

From the unitive, or 'in-between' point of view, pure experience is the 'ineffable union'[60] that sees the unison of the experiencing and the experienced. The immediate flux of life is intertwined, or even dissolved, in the universal experiencing tissue; one undifferentiated whole reaches meta-consciousness. In a typically Bergsonian fashion, James asks to put ourselves '*in the making* by a stroke of intuitive sympathy with the thing',[61] i.e. to reach an 'ontological intuition, lying beyond the power of words to tell of'.[62] *The Will to Believe* has even more adventurous utterings (besides the fact that it still speaks of a 'mind'):

> The key-note of the experience is the tremendously exciting sense of an intense metaphysical illumination. Truth lies open to the view in depth beneath depth of almost blinding evidence. The mind sees all the logical relations of being with an apparent subtlety and instantaneity to which its normal consciousness offers no parallel [...]. The center and periphery of things seem to come together. The ego and its objects, the *meeum* and the *tuum*, are one.[63]

The world of pure experience is the world in which there occurs an immense emotional sense of reconciliation, it is the world in which every opposition vanishes to the benefit of the law of togetherness of events in a common world. This emotional awareness embodies the fact that 'there are no differences but differences of degree between different degrees of difference and no difference.'[64] The experience aimed at by James is probably the one Nishida and his fellow Zen practitioners enjoy. 'Suchness' or 'thusness' means viewing things as they are; the absolute experience is made of oneness and purposelessness, it makes plain that there was actually nothing to reconcile in the first place, just a seamless eventful tapestry.[65]

Relevance

We can now see why *non-rationality qua* extremized as *total opacity* finds a proper framework with the concept of *pure experience*. Since pure experience attempts to depict the original experiential plenum, it gives us a beautiful tool to make sense out of that 'nocturnal and tactual' experience ('a touching in the night').[66] Whereas the categories congenial with diurnal and visual experience break down, this limit concept still holds because it defines itself as the only asymptotical approach to the state of dissolutive relationality that is so characteristic of religiousness.

It goes without saying that the first thing that should be discussed at this point is the paradox of the philosophical enterprise that, by the very fact that it names what has always already escaped its discursive reasoning (the ineffable), puts some grip on it – and yet lets it go. But this would lead us too far. Suffice it to say that that paradox – anexteriority – which is as old as philosophical speculation, has never discouraged the quest for the holistic transfiguration. Better, it has been thematized as such (remember Plato's *Parmenides* main paradox or the Kantian difference between 'Schranke' and 'Grenze').[67]

Anyway, the concept of pure experience gives us the minimal polysemantic technicalities to deal with impressive suggestions, such as this one:

> Looking back on my own experiences, they all converge towards a kind of insight to which I cannot help ascribing some metaphysical significance. The keynote of it is invariably a reconciliation. It is as if the opposites of the world, whose contradictoriness and conflict make all our difficulties and troubles, were melted into unity. Not only do they, as contrasted species, belong to one and the same genus, but one of the species, the nobler and better one, is itself the genus, and so soaks up and absorbs its opposite into itself. This is a dark saying, I know, when thus expressed in terms of common logic, but I cannot wholly escape from its authority. I feel as if it must mean something, something like what the hegelian philosophy means, if one could only lay hold of it more clearly. Those who have ears to hear, let them hear; to me the living sense of its reality only comes in the artificial mystic state of mind. (VRE 388–9)

'Total opacity' topples into 'clear light' during the rapture because dualism is replaced by relationalism. When it ends, there remain only semantic lineaments with which it is quite difficult to make sense unless one accepts the reformation of our everyday categories.

Let us finally remark that the concept of pure experience reintroduces a form of onto-logism: of course, its ontology shapes only a (non-rational) chaosmos, but it embodies an *archeological* hypothesis that obviously has a *theoretical* (contemplative) dimension: 'The peace of rationality may be sought through ecstasy when logic fails.'[68]

Conclusion

The suggestive continuity that the late James happily exploits between his ontological framework and his religious phenomenology should be clearer now. Three main points have been made in this chapter. (i) The concept of 'non-rationality' names the primordial opacity of our chaosmos. In a truly open universe, there is necessarily a non-rational remainder that is furthermore constantly reactualized by the 'creative activity' (or 'creative advance' – Whitehead's term). In other words, non-rationality is the main consequence of the dismissal of a static plurality of individuals in bare mechanical intercourse (besides the global rejection of the block universe, of course). (ii) Religiousness exactly encounters that non-rational boundary. First-hand religious experience comes to grip with a total opacity: i.e. not only with primordial opacity – the non-rationality of individuality in the making – but with sensorial opacity – the collapse of the dim rationality of relations. (iii) Pure experience specifies the ontological framework for the non-rationality of religiousness (versus rationality of religion) and, thereby, for all possible events. Non-rationality does not mean non-intelligibility: pure experience provides the most economical ontological assumption – experience is all there is – and the most daring consequences – relations are fundamentals, relata are abstractions.[69]

As a result, it is not surprising to see James focusing on first-hand religious experiences: since non-rationality is one of the key-features of his worldview, and since that non-rationality is indeed revealed in the most radical way in religiousness, it was quite relevant to bypass the mere contingent rationality of the collective religiosity. Here also, there is no substitute for direct personal experience; only immediate experiences are *absolutely authoritative*.[70]

By means of conclusion, three focal points need to be underlined. Each deserves a separate inquiry. First of all, the core problem of religiousness and religion alike is the status of consciousness. For the *homo religiosus*, the so-called 'normal state of consciousness', opposing a judge-like subject to its apathetic world, is completely unsatisfying. *There is something wrong about us as we naturally stand.* Religion rationalises this state of affairs with the help of narratives weaving concepts (in the loose sense of the word) of desire, suffering, fall, sin, celestial ladder and the like. Religiousness works towards its concrete bypassing. In one of the *Varieties*' most beautiful passages[71] lie all the key questions and their answers: normal consciousness isolates the subject from itself, from others, and from the world; it does not display the world 'as it is' and leaves us with the feeling – if not the knowledge – that the fullness of life has to be sought *elsewhere*, i.e. in some mode of Fechner's *surrounding mother sea of consciousness*.[72] And one should not forget that the tragedy for James (as for most of the human race) was furthermore to be able to access the verges of these states only through a laborious intoxication.

Directly linked with this first focal point is the following. According to the pragmatic standpoint, consciousness is not an entity, but a function – and that function is *knowing*. With that regard, there is a very useful bipolar that articulates *pistis* [πίστις] (faith) and *gnosis* [γνῶσις] (knowledge/experience). James makes it very clear that the answer to the existential tragedy is *not* to be found in pistis, but in gnosis. Of course, the term 'gnosis' is used here speculatively: a precise historical or even doctrinal definition is not relevant for our purpose, suffice it to say that determinism, acosmism, eschatological pessimism and transmigration are bracketed.[73] The gnostic *attitude* remains, privileging knowledge *qua* experience. Personal experience is what matters; experience alone can find its way through heïmarménê [εἱμαρμένη], the universal frozen destiny. The *homo religiosus* is defined by such a *certitude* that, interestingly enough, Jung as well considered of the order of *knowledge*.[74]

Finally, it is very suggestive to flesh out James's religiousness with the help of the concept of intertrajectoriality. We have seen that *pure experience* – a lived solidarity with the universal interconnectedness – can be analyzed in two strands: a subjective 'prelinguistic' one, and an objective 'presubstantial' one. Let us now define religiousness as an experience of *holistic trajectorial dwelling*. It is first and foremost the experience of cosmic communion in which one human trajectory receives its meaning from its inclusion within all trajectories, actual and potential, mundane and supramundane. More precisely, the *only* reality is then one single cosmic unison of immediacies.

In the very same way we scrutinized pure experience, that holistic intertrajectoriality can be analyzed in two steps: a subjective trajectorial positioning and an objective trajectorial positioning. The former qualifies the idiosyncratic feeling of belonging to one's own trajectory, one's own creative advance. We can furthermore distinguish a *relative* positioning in front of the totality of one's trajectory, from birth to death; and an *absolute* positioning which regards the very horizon of the experience of the subject considered: the beginning and the end of his or her present trajectory – i.e. birth and death themselves – and what is beyond. The latter qualifies the feeling of awe experienced in front of the intertrajectoriality of the 'objective' universe.

Religiousness is thus the intimate and vital experience that binds the human trajectory to all other trajectories, mundane or not, human or not, actual or not, past, present or even future. This blissfull dwelling is *lived* religiousness. In traditional terms, it is of the order of *religio* as 'religare': (emotional) binding. We call *archical* religiousness (or religiosity) the reflexive religious moment that questions the meaning and the conditions of possibility of the bare experiential moment. It acts as intermediate between lived religiousness and religion. In traditional terms, it is *religio* as 'religere': (rational) gathering or collecting. Religiosity concludes that the holistic trajectorial dwelling is possible because there is intertrajectoriality, i.e. cosmic solidarity; and that this intertrajectoriality requires a structure of opening, an intrinsic centrifugal propensity in every being.

The wealth of ideas suggested in – not speaking of the ones operationalized by – the *Varieties* is bottomless. If this paper has shown the interest of an expanded horizon of reading, it has reached its main purpose.

Notes

1. VRE 6–7; 'first–hand and original forms of experience' (VRE 201); 'first–hand individual experience' (VRE 335); 'genuine first–hand religious experience' (VRE 337; cf. 6, 30, 95). The abbreviations used are listed in the References. The author wishes to thank Harald Atmanspacher and Anderson Weekes for their very useful comments on a previous draft of this chapter.
2. P 6.
3. VRE 122; cf. 239 and 408.
4. Cf. PU 363.
5. Cf. PP vol. II 659.
6. Cf. BC xxvii.
7. William James, 'Remarks at the Peace Banquet' [1904], in ERM 120.
8. P 3.
9. MT 257sq, VRE 132 et passim.
10. P 4; cf. as well the question of intellectualism.
11. P 11.
12. VRE 73.
13. Cf. VRE 387–8 quoted in the conclusion.
14. VRE 92; cf. VRE 330.
15. VRE 132–133.
16. VRE 170.
17. VRE 184.
18. VRE 297 and VRE 306.
19. VRE 304.
20. VRE 383.
21. EPR 369.
22. EP 63. It would be very enlightening to question in depth that irrationality/non-rationality contrast from the perspective of the Pythagorean discovery of irrational numbers. Cf. the concepts of alogon [ἄλογον] and arreton [ἄρρητον] in Aristotle's *Prior Analytics*, I, 23 and the analysis of David H. Fowler in his *The Mathematics of Plato's Academy. A New Reconstruction*, Oxford, Clarendon Press, Oxford Science Publications, 1987.
23. PU 319.
24. PU 213 quoted *supra* and PU 363.
25. Cf. PU 329 and VRE 456–457 and 498.
26. The concept of opacity has a pretty old philosophical history; for a recent occurrence in the process field, see Nicholas Rescher, *Process Metaphysics. An Introduction to Process Philosophy*, Albany, N.Y., State University of New York Press, 1996, pp. 129–132 and Michel Weber (ed.), *After Whitehead: Rescher on Process Metaphysics*, Frankfurt/Lancaster, Ontos Verlag, 2004. The general

background of our discussion has been elaborated on the occasion of three complementary contributions: Michel Weber, 'The Polysemiality of the Concept of *Pure Experience*', *Streams of William James*, Volume 1, Issue 2, Fall 1999, pp. 4–6; 'James' Contiguism of *Pure Experience*', *Streams of William James*, Volume 1, Issue 3, Winter 1999, pp. 19–22 and 'Polysemiality, Style, and Arationality', *Streams of William James*, Volume 2, Issue 2, Summer 2000, pp. 1–4. Please notice that the concept of 'arationality' is not used here in the same way.

27. Cf., e.g. the claims of Jean Piaget in his *Introduction à l'épistémologie génétique*. Vol. II, *La pensée physique*, Paris, Presses Universitaires de France, 1949, pp. 70–79.

28. It states simply that we come to know all things in so far as they have some unity and identity (*Metaphysics* Beta, 4).

29. It claims that the same attribute cannot, at the same time and in the same respect, belong and not belong to the same subject (*Metaphysics* Gamma, 3; *Posterior Analytics* I, 77a10–22).

30. There cannot be an intermediate between contradictories: of one subject we must either affirm or deny any one predicate; there is no third possibility (*Metaphysics* Gamma, 7; *Posterior Analytics* I, 77a22–25).

31. πρώτη ὕλη (*Physics* 193a29, Waterfield's translation is 'first matter'; the Scholastics used to speak of 'materia prima').

32. H. Atmanspacher has drawn our attention on two points. First, the similarities existing between our speculations and J. Gebser's (*Ursprung und Gegenwart*, Stuttgart, Deutsche Verlagsanstalt, 1949/1953 [*The Ever-Present Origin*. Translated by N. Barstad, Athens, Ohio University Press, 1985]): Gebser also uses the notion of 'acategoriality' in contrast to categorial representations of knowledge and their processing and the figure of paradox as a key motive in the transition from the rational to the arational. Second, according to Atmanspacher's own research, quantum logic as it stands is not sufficient: in order to account for the generation of meaning and novelty by creative processes, we need the non-algorithmicness which is reflected in unstable and transient behavior. (See Harald Atmanspacher, 'Categoreal and Acategoreal Representation of Knowledge', *Cognitive Systems*, 3–3, 1992, pp. 259–288 and Harald Atmanspacher and Eva Ruhnau (eds), *Time, Temporality, Now. Experiencing Time and Concepts of Time in an Interdisciplinary Perspective*. Berlin, Springer–Verlag, 1997.)

33. PU 213.

34. Ralph Barton Perry, *In the Spirit of William James*, New Haven, Yale University Press, 1938, p. 120 citing Aldous Leonard Huxley, *The Olive Tree and Other Essays*, London, Chatto & Windus, 1937, pp. 210–211.

35. Concepts adapted of course from Nietzsche's *Gotzendammerung*; for his part, James is not less clear: 'when we conceptualize, we cut out and fix, and exclude everything but what we have fixed. A concept means a *that-and-no-other*' (PU 113).

36. MT 77; cf. P 8.

37. See PU 106, 235, 244, 253, 261–263, 326, 347; and VRE 456–457, 498.

38. Curiously enough, the concepts of 'nucleus' and 'fringe', introduced in PP, do not occur anywhere else in the corpus.

39. Cf. VRE 22 and ERE 51.

40. PU 309; cf. note 35.

41. VRE 53.

42. VRE 485.

43. VRE 31; cf. VRE 447.

44. Cf. Henri Bergson's *Les Deux Sources de la Morale et de la Religion*, Paris, Presses Universitaires de France, 1932, p. 252.

45. VRE 35 and 39.

46. Cf. P 40, 46, 106.

47. VRE 508; cf. VRE 128.

48. VRE 525 and 395, 513, 525.

49. VRE 500.

50. VRE 395 quoting the words of Malwida von Meysenbug.

51. See 'absolute self–surrender' (VRE 75, cf. 51, 110, 120, 172, 206–216, 223, 227–228, 266, 273, 285–286, 311, 320, 323, 451–2, 470, 509, 521); 'unison' (VRE 66); 'loss of personality' (VRE 384, 394, cf. 70, 287); 'union of love' (VRE 407).

52. 'Cosmic emotion' (VRE 79); 'cosmic consciousness' (VRE 85, 398).

53. James to Ribot, 1888: from an unpublished letter in the James Collection in the Widener Library, Harvard University, cited by Ralph Barton Perry, *In the Spirit of William James*, op. cit., p. 58.

54. Eugene I. Taylor and Robert H. Wozniak (Eds), *Pure Experience. The Response to William James*, Bristol, Thoemmes Press, 1996.

55. Cf. ERE 92–94; cf. PP I488 and II32. Of course, James's claims are now to be read as primarily metaphorical: developmental psychology has shown more or less convincingly that the new–born is not a *tabula rasa*; and the recent advances in the understanding of the status of hypnosis offer interesting complementary approaches to this question. (Cf., e.g., Daniel N. Stern, *The Interpersonal World of the Infant. A View from Psychoanalysis and Developmental Psychology*, New York, Basic Books, 1985; Léon Chertok, *L'Hypnose. Théorie, pratique et technique*. Paris, Éditions Payot, 1989; François Roustang, *Qu'est–ce que l'hypnose?*, Paris, Éditions de Minuit, 1994.)

56. Nishida Kitaro, *An Inquiry into the Good [Zen no Kenkyu, 1911]*. Translated by Masao Abe, New Haven, Yale University Press, 1990, pp. 3–4.

57. See, e.g., ERE 4, 37, 78, 138.

58. E.g., ERE 3, 26.

59. ERE 193.

60. ERE 121.

61. PU 117; cf. VRE 501.

62. William James, Review of 'The Anaesthetic Revelation and the Gist of Philosophy', *The Atlantic Monthly*, November 1874, Vol. 33, No. 205, pp. 627–628.

63. WB 218.

64. WB 220.

65. Cf., e.g., Ames Van Meter, 'Zen and Pragmatism', *Philosophy East and West*, Vol. 3, No. 1, 1954, pp. 19–33.

66. '[...] in a personal relation of contact with the mysterious power' (VRE 464 quoting Auguste Sabatier); 'contact with the only absolute realities' (VRE 503).

67. See, e.g., the meditation of Eric Weil, in *Logique de la philosophie*. Paris, Librairie Philosophique J. Vrin, 1967.

68. EP 62.

69. Cf. the very suggestive process synopsis provided by Harold H. Oliver, 'Theses on Relational Self and the Genesis of the Western Ego', *Theologische Zeitschrift*, Jahrgang 33, Heft 5, 1977, pp. 326–335.

70. VRE 16, 422, 455.

71. 'Some years ago I myself made some observations on this aspect of nitrous oxide intoxication, and reported them in print. [...] Those who have ears to hear, let them hear; to me the living sense of its reality only comes in the artificial mystic state of mind' (VRE 387–389; cf. VRE 423, 519, 523).

72. PU 299; EPR 374, 98, 195 sq.; ERM 92–4; EP 160.
73. Cf. Hans Jonas, *Gnosis und späntantiker Geist*, Teil I: *Die mythologische Gnosis, mit Einer Einleitung zur Geschichte und Methodologie der Forschung*, Göttingen, Vandenhoeck & Ruprecht, 1934. [Translated as *The Gnostic Religion: The Message of the Alien God and the Beginnings of Christianity*, Boston, Beacon Press, 1963; second revised edition, 1970.] Simone Pétrement, *Le Dieu séparé. Les origines du gnosticisme*, Paris, Les Éditions du Cerf, 1984. [Translated as *A Separate God. The Christian Origins of Gnosticism*, San Francisco, Harper & Row, 1990.]
74. 'All that I have learned has led me step by step to an unshakable conviction of the existence of God. I only believe in what I know. And that eliminates believing. Therefore I do not take His existence on belief – I *know* that He exists' (William McGuire and Richard Francis Carrington Hull (eds), *C. G. Jung Speaking: Interviews and Encounters*, Princeton, N.J., Princeton University Press, 1977, p. 251, see also pp. 427–428). Of course this claim should be closely discussed in order, among other things, to encounter its gnostic dimension. Cf. also, e.g., his *Psychologische Typen* and, of course, his seminal work on Basilides' *Septem Sermones ad Mortuos*.

References

BC: William James, *Psychology. Briefer Course* [1892]. Ed. Gordon Allport, Notre Dame, University of Notre Dame Press, 1961.
EP: William James, *Essays in Philosophy*, Ed. Frederick H. Burkhardt e.a.; Introduction by John J. McDermott, Cambridge, Mass., Harvard University Press, 1978.
EPR: William James, *Essays in Psychical Research*. Fred. H. Burkhardt, gen. ed.; Fredson Bowers, text. ed.; Ignas K. Skrupskelis, ass. ed., Cambridge, Mass., Harvard University Press, 1986.
ERE: William James, *Essays in Radical Empiricism* [Posthumously published by Ralph Barton Perry], New York, Longman Green & Co., 1912.
ERM: William James, *Essays in Religion and Morality*, Cambridge, Mass., Harvard University Press, 1982.
MT: William James, *The Meaning of Truth*, New York, Longman Green & Co., 1911.
P: William James, *Pragmatism. A New Name for Some Old Ways of Thinking*, New York, London, Bombay, and Calcutta, Longman Green & Co., 1907.
PP: William James, *The Principles of Psychology* [1890]. Authorized edition in two volumes, New York, Dover Publications, 1950.
PU: William James, *A Pluralistic Universe*. Hibbert Lectures at Manchester College on the Present Situation in Philosophy, New York, Longman Green & Co., 1909.
TT: William James, *Talks to Teachers on Psychology. And to Students on Some of Life's Ideals* [1899], New York, Henry Holt, 1912.
VRE: William James, *The Varieties of Religious Experience. A Study in Human Nature*. Being the Gifford Lectures on Natural Religion Delivered at Edinburgh in 1901–1902, New York, London, Bombay, and Calcutta, Longman Green & Co., 1902.
WB: William James, *The Will to Believe, And Other Essays in Popular Philosophy*. Ed. Frederick H. Burkhardt e.a.; Introd. by Edward H. Madden, Cambridge, Mass., Harvard University Press, 1979.

Chapter 16

James and the question of truth
A response to Hilary Putnam

David C. Lamberth

In *William James and the Metaphysics of Experience* I took issue with Hilary Putnam's interpretation of James on absolute truth from 'James's Theory of Truth,' and sought to present an alternate, more accurate reading.[1] Putnam responds in the Afterword to his contribution to this volume, indicating that his main essay depends on the correctness of his view versus my divergent reading. With truth a difficult terrain in James's writing and thought, there are significant interpretive issues at stake.

Putnam raises a number of questions for my interpretation, not all of which I can treat here.[2] The most important concern: (1) the 'tenseless' notion of truth, as Putnam calls it; (2) whether 'truth' used without a modifier in James's texts should ordinarily be read as relative truth (my view) or absolute truth (Putnam's view); (3) the extent and manner to which James admits of a 'Peircean strain'; and (4) whether James's absolute truths are made piecemeal. Before turning to these points, I will discuss briefly the place of truth and the accounts thereof in James's overall system.

One insight guiding my interpretation was that one gets a better picture of James's mature philosophical vision by denying convention and subordinating pragmatism in favor of the central components of James's radically empiricist metaphysics of experience. I do this explicitly in my opening systematic treatment of radical empiricism by treating the pragmatic conception of truth last. I only return to the issue in the final chapter because the topic has been so contentious in the revival of pragmatism over the last several decades, to which Putnam has been crucial.

This interpretive strategy became clear to me after reading James's corpus in the historical sequence of its composition. One of my overt aims was to demonstrate the early formation (1896) of the central tenets of radical empiricism, relative to their eventual publication and conventional dating (1904–5), with an eye towards opening a different perspective on James's major ideas and publications that followed, among them *The Varieties of Religious Experience*, *Pragmatism*, *A Pluralistic Universe*, and *The Meaning of Truth*. James was, I demonstrate, intent on developing his metaphysics of radical empiricism for publication from 1896.

Although he eventually published a collection of essays on truth, it was not consistently at the forefront of James's mind from 1896 to 1904 when he was developing radical empiricism and, to a lesser extent, pragmatism. Truth does come up frequently in *The Will to Believe*, including a substantive statement resonant with statements of Charles Sanders Peirce on the topic (see Putnam's epigram on page 177). Truth itself, however, is not the objective of James's defense of what he later called 'the right to believe.' In his 1898 'Philosophical Conceptions and Practical Results,' notable for the first printed use of 'pragmatism,' James treats 'truth' conventionally as philosophy's object, none the less expressing his characteristic impression that 'its fulness is elusive.' He then focuses on Peirce's pragmatic principle of determining the meaning of thoughts by the conduct they inspire, notably interchanging 'truth' at one point for 'meaning.' However, he makes none of the comments about satisfaction and leading that become distinctive of what he thinks truth may be 'known as,' much less distinguishing truth from meaning as he later does.[3]

In a February 1904 letter to F.C.S. Schiller concerning the intensifying debate over pragmatism and humanism involving John Dewey and Schiller, James indicates that he did not intend his own pragmatism to involve an account of truth at all:

> *What do we* mean by 'truth'? What is it *known-as?* – those are questions which if once opened up for discussion, will make each side respect the other a little more. I am amused at the way *my* name has been dragged in as that of the Father of all this way of thinking. I recognize it as the continuation of partial thoughts which I have expressed; but 'pragmatism' never meant for me more than a method of conducting discussion (a sovereign method, it is true) and the tremendous scope which you and Dewey have given to the conception has exceeded my more timid philosophizing. I welcome it, and admire it, but I can't yet think out certain parts of it, although something inside of me feels sure that they can be successfully thought out.[4]

'Truth' here is merely a secondary consideration for James, despite his many prior comments about it.

James does enter the truth mêlée before that year's end, goaded on by Schiller and the editors of *Mind* in response to F.H. Bradley's 'On Truth and Practice.'[5] James's resultant 'Humanism and Truth' is shaped heavily by the terms of the discussion he enters and his longstanding debates with Josiah Royce; none the less, James does address questions along the lines of those posed in the letter quoted above, thinking out a position similar to those of Dewey and Schiller. Immediately after writing this essay, James apparently felt compelled to write what become the two central essays on radical empiricism, 'Does Consciousness Exist?' and 'A World of Pure Experience.'[6] Although he penned these days later than 'Humanism and Truth,' 'Does Consciousness Exist?' actually appeared in print first, providing a metaphysical backdrop for the picture of truth James begins to paint. James continued over the next seven months to publish on both subjects, favoring radical empiricism with six more articles, while publishing two on humanism and truth and republishing an abridged 'Philosophical Conceptions and Practical Results.'

A generous reader will certainly wonder what difference this history makes to the central question of how to interpret James on truth. As I noted, I am persuaded by the texts that radical empiricism is, for better and worse, the core set of ideas to James's mature philosophical world-view. From the vantage of this hypothesis, one can see that, despite some of the things he previously had said about truth, once 'Humanism and Truth' appears, James seeks to render truth in terms basically compatible with radical empiricism. The theory of truth itself (if one wants to call it that – James sometimes does) should be read as dependent in its particulars on the mechanics of relations, leading, and experience explicated in radical empiricism. Indeed, James's general goal in all his truth discussions is to state what truth can be 'known as' in experiential and functional, and specifically radically empiricist, terms.[7]

At issue is just how basic, philosophically and ontologically, the notion of 'truth' (relative or absolute) is to James. Putnam concludes his Afterword with the remarkable claim that 'the tenseless truth of a true empirical proposition *is* (usually) the *best explanation* of its warranted assertibility at the present time,' placing tenseless truth into an explanatory and philosophically more basic role than warranted assertibility (in James's terms, the concrete function of knowledge-about or, at times, truth). To the contrary, I am suggesting that James has more of a second-order view of truth.[8] On this reading, truth is explained in terms of (though not always fully reduced to) the more basic features of radical empiricism (its metaphysics of experience, its postulate about the reality of conjunctive relations, and its twofold account of knowing), rather than serving as a primitive term that could itself stand as an explanation of another function such as warranted assertibility, facticity, or reality.[9] Truth turns out to be a distinctive, important, and perhaps even indispensable function within experience in certain circumstances, but it is not philosophically or ontologically basic to James's explanatory scheme.[10] In fact, fundamental, first-order placements of the conception of truth are precisely what James is seeking to invert in his criticisms of Bradley, Royce, *et al.*, and these debates structure almost all of his discussions of truth from 1904 onward. How one locates truth in James's system is critical for evaluating the questions Putnam raises for my interpretation of absolute truth. With this perspective in view, I now turn to the specific issues noted above.

The 'tenseless' notion of truth

What Putnam calls the 'tenseless' quality of truth lies at the heart of our differences. 'Lamberth's arguments are really arguments against the tenseless notion of truth itself,' he writes, 'and this is an independently important philosophical matter.' Although I agree with his latter statement, in my book and here I am concerned principally with establishing the most accurate interpretation of James. I do not, therefore, consider myself simply to have given my own arguments against the tenseless notion of truth, but rather have offered insight into James's understanding. Discussion of the independent matter will have to await another venue.

Putnam's interpretation is heavily determined by his reading of certain of James's discussions concerning the immutability of the past. Rebutting part of my commentary on the function of absolute truth, Putnam writes:

> But this is a confusion. Of course, 'tenseless' truth, truth not relativized to evidence, to the borders of experience at a particular time and place is, once what it concerns has taken place, unalterable (as James himself says). 'Caesar crossed the Rubicon' is unalterable. But 'unalterability' is an ontological notion, while 'subject to revision' is an epistemic one.

Putnam justifies the attribution of this view to James with a reference to James's 1907 exchange with Alfred Lane. Lane inquired about James's understanding of the mutability of the past, present and future, and offered three alternatives: either (1) all are determined, and in principle knowable by an all-seeing mind; (2) only the past is so determined; or (3) nothing is determined, past, present, or future, even to an all-seeing mind. James responded:

> The second horn of the trilemma is mine, – with the future partly indeterminate while the past is given fully. The third horn ... I absolutely repudiate, for I can frame no notion of the past that does n't leave it inalterable. Truths involving the past's *relations* to *later things* can't come into being till the later things exist ... but the past itself is beyond the reach of modification.[11]

Putnam takes this commitment to the unalterability of the past to be a commitment to the unalterability of (tenseless) truths about the past, writing that ' "tenseless" truth ... is ... unalterable.' But James commits only to the unalterability of past facts (the past, *tout court*), not necessarily truths about it.[12] Several sentences later he writes, 'What I have done to deserve the preposterous misunderstanding [of making the past mutable] which I am accused of on all sides ... I can't imagine. ... Probably it comes from confusing the terms 'reality' and 'truth,' – realities are independent variables, but truths about them are functions also of other variables, and must alter.'[13] There may be a confusion of ontological and epistemic notions regarding truths about past facts in James, but it seems more likely Putnam's than mine.[14]

The issue turns, in part, on whether one is right to attribute 'tenselessness' to any of James's conceptions of truth. Putnam takes the comment to Lane and that in *Pragmatism* about Ptolemaic astronomy to indicate that (at least some species of) truth for James is tenseless.[15] But 'tenseless' implies, as Putnam himself perhaps unintentionally indicates in his contrast, that truth is not meaningfully relative to the circumstances of a knower. That feature pertains to James's notion of reality, not his conception(s) of truth. Even James's notion from *Pragmatism* of the '"absolutely" true, meaning what no farther experience will ever alter, [which] is that ideal vanishing-point towards which we imagine that all our temporary truths will some day converge,' is relativized by James to the situation of a knower: it 'runs on all fours with the perfectly wise man, and with the absolutely complete experience.'[16] Truth for James applies only to ideas, propositions, and beliefs held or engaged by someone or some group in a particular context, however wide or inclusive. Moreover, as Putnam argues in his own essay in this volume, what is distinctive about truth is its substantive engagement with interests, and interests are always relatived to particular knowers.[17] Truth, because of James's realism, requires engagement with fact. But ontological fact does not suffice for the epistemic function of truth, relative or absolute. Fully 'tenseless' truth is a misconception of James's view.

James is aware of the distinctive temporal characteristics of truth; indeed this is partly why he has a separate conception in addition to 'knowledge about'.[18] His notion of the function of truth, even truth absolute, is not, however, strictly 'tenseless.' James repeatedly emphasizes that truth is always something that happens within experience. As an experiential function it has a present-tense, historically specific temporality, since ideas become or are made true by the concrete, functional leadings constitutive of or related to them for a knower or set of knowers. (These leadings are, incidentally, not only among the beliefs or ideas in question and the facts intended, but also among other related ideas or beliefs that make up our stock of truths.) When a new truth is made within such experience that contradicts a prior functional ('expedient') belief, the new function carries the retrospective effect not only of being true in the present, but also of having been true as well for the past. 'When new experiences lead to retrospective judgments, using the past tense, what those judgments utter *was* true, even tho no past thinker had been led there. We live forwards, a Danish thinker has said, but we understand backwards. The present sheds a backward light on the world's previous processes. They may have been truth-processes for the actors in them. They are not so for one who knows later revelations of the story.'[19]

This retrospective effect does not, however, render truth tenseless, but rather means that all attributions of truth are tensed (depending on their objects) to the present and past. Today's truths about the past are not, *qua* truths, strictly tensed for the future (thus tenseless), since they are relative to the current borders of experience. Should our borders be final, such truths would be absolute, but they would not be technically tenseless, remaining tensed to that time and the past. (But the issue would be moot, since truth in James's concrete sense pertains to the active functions of knowing.) Just after the comment about the absolutely true, the perfectly wise man, and the absolutely complete experience, all of which, if realized, will be realized together, James notes that, 'Meanwhile, we have to live to-day by what truth we can get today, and be ready to-morrow to call it falsehood.'[20] Today's truth always may be superseded, provided there is a future with knowers in which to supersede it. Hence it makes sense to call all truth relative to James, albeit 'relative' to varying degrees and effects.[21]

'Truth' *tout court*: relative, or absolute?

If all James's uses of 'truth' are relative in this way, then Putnam's claim that 'truth' without a modifier should be understood as 'tenseless,' in contrast to 'relative truth' only where explicitly indicated, is wrong. James is certainly able to distinguish between what *was* taken for true but since has been superseded. In so doing, James continues to admit the prior functionality of such conceptions within certain borders of experience, borders now known to be limited, however, relative to ours. (Hence his occasional practice of calling them 'half-true' or 'relatively' true given stated boundaries.) But distinguishing thus between mere past warranted assertibility and truth (always implying present warranted assertibility) does not require a distinction between relative and absolute truth. Instead, it necessitates only a distinction between better truth functionality now and what was then functionally true only in so far forth. What we now take to be true, in contrast to what was taken at past time *t*, may itself be superseded in the future, and then be so relativized as well. In no way is a notion of absolute truth necessary to comprehend our present claims.

Part of Putnam's difficulty comes from reading too much into certain statements of James. "Absolutely," they [Ptolemaic astronomy, etc.] are false,' James writes, but he does not correspondingly say that what we have replaced them with is absolutely true, as Putnam appears to conclude.[22] To be able to say for certain that something is absolutely false does not require that one think that what one believes in its stead is absolutely true, much less that it be so. Nor does it require knowing what is absolutely true. Falsification conveys an absoluteness and certainty not paralleled in verification, at least not where facts are involved.[23] Putnam might rejoin that he is referring to the absolute truth of the fact *that* these theories are false. Although this makes logical sense, James clearly remonstrated against this sort of mixture of the discourses of fact and truth. James certainly has a conception of absolute truth.[24] But that conception is best understood as built out (via, among other things, an application of the pragmatic principle of meaning) from his conception of the concrete function of truth, with all of its relativity, instead of undergirding, buttressing, or otherwise replacing that concrete function itself. Absolute truth is not the basic notion, but rather a specialized conception derived from the concrete function of truth.

The Peircean strain (part I)

In preliminary observation (ii), Putnam states that what we are debating is whether he is right to attribute a 'Peircean strain' to James's account. One of the many benefits of 'James's Theory of Truth' is Putnam's attention to the different aspects and influences within James's view; his attention to the Peircean influence is certainly constitutive of that benefit. What we are debating, however, is not whether there is a Peircean strain to James's comments on truth; that is non-controversial. Rather, what is at issue is how to interpret that influence, particularly with reference to James's 'mature view,' once he has developed radical empiricism and pragmatism.

Up to this point I have been arguing implicitly against Putnam's privileging the Peircean strain. Specifically, I have indicated that, in terms of logical priority, we should take James's conceptions of reality and knowing from radical empiricism as first order, and consider his understandings of the function of truth to be dependent on them. Moreover, I have argued that James's conception of truth is, as James himself says, fundamentally a conception of concrete truths in the plural, made up out of a variety of similar functions within and relative to particular moments of concrete experience:

> pragmatism insists that truth in the singular is only a collective name for truths in the plural, these consisting always of series of definite events; and that what intellectualism calls *the* truth, the *inherent* truth, of any one such series is only the abstract name for its truthfulness in act, for the fact that the ideas there do lead to the supposed reality in a way that we consider satisfactory.[25]

Relatedly, I contend that James's conception of absolute truth is derivative by one further degree, built up pragmatically from projecting the possible, indeed desirable, practical outcome of his conception of truths in the plural. Thus instead of understanding James to have a theory of (absolute) truth, from which he is positioned to understand partial or relative truths and their relation to reality, I see James having a theory of reality, inclusive of the relations partially constitutive of knowledge and relative truth functions. From this he formulates a conception of a future-completed, absolute truth, drawing liberally on Peirce's statements. (Peirce, by contrast, at one point renders his conception and explanation of reality interdependent with the final opinion, which James consistently refuses.)[26] James still has, in essence, one basic notion of truth, but it is not absolute truth. Instead, the revisable and fallible truthfulness or trueness that exhibits itself daily funds James's abstract and future-oriented conception.

The Peircean strain (part II): are absolute truths made piecemeal?

Putnam turns his comments about the Peircean strain to the question of whether absolute truth should be thought of in the singular and the future, as I concluded from James's usages, or rather as made piecemeal along the way. James's statements about absolute truth once he begins to publish on truth and radical empiricism (1904 on) fruitfully illuminate this issue.

In *Pragmatism,* just after having stated that 'the true' is only the expedient in our thinking, 'in the long run and on the whole of course,' as quoted above James characterizes 'the "absolutely" true' as 'that ideal vanishing point towards which we imagine that all our temporary truths will some day converge,' mentioning the 'perfectly wise man' and the 'absolutely complete experience.'[27] A few lines later he continues:

> This regulative notion of a potential better truth to be established later, possibly to be established some day absolutely, and having powers of retroactive legislation, turns its face, like all pragmatist notions, towards concreteness of fact, and towards the future. Like the half-truths, the absolute truth will have to be *made,* made as a relation incidental to the growth of a mass of verification-experience, to which the half-true ideas are all along contributing their quota.

There are three things to note in this passage. First, James only refers to absolute truth in the singular: 'the "absolutely" true' and 'the absolute truth,' versus the plural half-truths that will be constitutive of it. Second, his references to the absolute truth are, in both cases, tensed to the future, not the present or past. Third, James treats absolute truth explicitly as an ideal (a regulative one, he later states), along with the not presently realized ideals of the perfectly wise man and the absolutely complete experience, on which it depends. Although a conception of present-tense, piecemeal absolute truths might be logically explicable for a Jamesian pragmatist, these passages do not suggest that James held that view.

Putnam's interpretation, at least the piecemeal part, is not without some support. In 'The Pragmatist Account of Truth and Its Misunderstanders,' James argues that pragmatism (in contrast to scepticism, positivism, agnosticism and rationalism, which he accuses of begging the question of what truth is) asks the question 'What does the notion of truth signify *ideally?*':

> 'What kind of things would true judgments be *in case* they existed?' The answer which pragmatism offers is intended to cover the most complete truth that can be conceived of, 'absolute' truth if you like, as well as truth of the most relative and imperfect description. This question of what truth would be like if it did exist, belongs obviously to a purely speculative field of inquiry. … It is not a theory about any sort of reality, or about what kind of knowledge is possible; it abstracts from particular terms altogether and defines the nature of a possible relation between two of them.[28]

This statement reproduces the singular usage of 'absolute truth,' and refers to a 'complete view.' 'True judgments' in the plural and the notion of a relation between only two terms, however, suggest that it might also be read to involve truths, even absolute truths, taken piecemeal. Indeed, given James's view, there is no reason why one could not think *generally and abstractly* that piecemeal absolute truths are arrived at along the way, once their leadings are concretely fixed, never, it just so happens, to be altered. But one could have no reason to think this about any particular truth, except as abstractly possible.[29] Moreover, James's labeling of the inquiry as 'purely speculative' and his comment about its abstraction from the particulars raise flags about his estimation of the import of this discussion, particularly given what he says about the practical and concrete character of pragmatism and its conception of truth in *Pragmatism* and elsewhere.[30]

James offers one other significant discussion of absolute truth in *The Meaning of Truth*, part of which Putnam quotes. James writes:

> They accuse relativists – and we pragmatists are typical relativists – of being debarred by their self-adopted principles, not only from the privilege which rationalist philosophers enjoy, of believing that these principles of their own are truth impersonal and absolute, but even of framing the abstract notion of such a truth, *in the pragmatic sense, of an ideal opinion in which all men might agree, and which no man should ever wish to change.* Both charges fall wide of their mark. I myself, as a pragmatist, believe in my own account of truth as firmly as any rationalist can possibly believe in his. And I believe in it for the very reason that I *have* the idea of truth which my learned adversaries contend that no pragmatist can frame. I expect, namely, that the more fully men discuss and test my account, the more they will agree that it *fits*, and the less they will desire a change. I may of course be premature in this confidence, and the glory of being truth final and absolute may fall upon some later revision and correction of my scheme, which later will then be judged untrue in just the measure in which it departs from that finally satisfactory formulation.[31]

Putnam contends that I overlook the plain sense of this passage in treating absolute truth only as an ideal. Further, he claims that on my interpretation James does not believe, as he says he does, that his account is impersonally and absolutely true the way the rationalist does.

Regarding the latter, James does not claim that he believes his account is true 'in the way a rationalist believes that his is,' as Putnam has it. What James says is that he believes 'in it as firmly' as any rationalist possibly could believe in his own idea, referring to his state of conviction – his willingness to act on it (according to the right to believe) – rather than to its degree of validity, justification or acceptance.[32] Moreover, James apparently intends to question precisely what it means to believe in such a theoretical account, in that, via radical empiricism and pragmatism, he seeks to supplant the rationalist's account of the nature and function of beliefs, ideas, opinions, and statements in general, as well as those of truth and reality in particular. Arguing that I claim that James does not believe as he says he does is wide of the mark.

The issue of whether absolute truth is principally an ideal, and has concrete meaning only in relation to the practice of searching for more and better truth in the meantime, is important. For the purpose of re-entering Putnam's reading, I stopped quoting above where he did. Up to this point, the passage seems compatible with, if not suggestive in its plain sense of, a piecemeal notion of absolute truth. In the very next sentence, however, James begins a gradual specification, moving towards a singular, future-tensed, unified complex rather than a piecemeal conception: 'To admit, as we pragmatists do, that we are liable to correction (even tho we may not expect it) *involves* the use on our part of an ideal standard.' On the next page he writes:

> No relativist who ever actually walked the earth has denied the regulative character in his own thinking of the notion of absolute truth. What is challenged by relativists is the pretence on anyone's part to have found for certain at any given moment *what the shape of that truth is* [emphasis added]. Since the better absolutists agree in this, admitting that the proposition 'There *is* absolute truth' is the only absolute truth of which we can be sure, further debate is practically unimportant.[33]

More definitively, he continues:

> The anti-pragmatist, in postulating absolute truth, refuses to give any account of what the words may mean. For him, they form a self-explanatory term. The pragmatist, on the contrary, articulately defines their meaning. Truth absolute, he says, means an *ideal set of formulations* toward which all opinions may in the long run of experience be expected to converge.[34] (emphasis added)

In the final note of his Afterword Putnam concedes that James's usage of the terminology of absolute truth often is, as I argued, oriented to this regulative 'ideal set of formulations' in the future. Conjoined with my reading here, this would appear to put the matter to rest. Putnam concludes the note, however, by implying that James does still deploy a piecemeal notion of absolute truth with regard to individual propositions, or groups thereof. He offers two pieces of evidence for this suggestion: James's comments about Ptolemaic astronomy from *Pragmatism*, and the statements concerning his believing his own scheme of truth to be true absolutely. Having discussed both of these, I pass on, noting Putnam's reticence.

It is possible, within the bounds of James's articulated philosophical system, to formulate a coherent conception of absolute truths in the plural, established piecemeal. Indeed there are moments that James sees but does not develop this.[35] I am less sure, however, that such a commitment can be made to serve any necessary practical or theoretical function beyond what James has already built into the system, provided we keep his other major commitments. With the exception of the highly limited cases of abstract concepts that do not relate concretely to non-theoretical experience, it is, on James's system, impossible ever to know that a piecemeal absolute truth has become absolute: ' "There *is* absolute truth" is the only absolute truth of which we can be sure.' As a result any functionality of piecemeal absolute truth beyond that of the regulative ideal of the future-completed set reduces practically in any real circumstance to the functionality of a so-called half-truth that would eventually be altered. Relative truth, then, is what works, and what we live by, according to this philosophy.

Putnam finds this untenable, I suspect, precisely because he seeks to delineate absolute truth as having an ontological significance beyond this important, practical epistemic (and experiential) functioning. In the main, James simply disagrees. Instead, he insists on a significant and irreducible distinction between the discourses of epistemology and ontology, truth and reality, settling practically for treating all truth and knowing, even that which will never be altered, as relative and contingent rather than absolute. This does not, as he argues, restrict him from believing that his own theories themselves might prove true absolutely – a belief that, importantly, motivates his philosophical work. This is what I meant by referring to the 'phenomenological' upshot of absolute truth in my book; in retrospect, I might better have labeled this 'practical.'

One crucial question remains. Why does James bother to bring up absolute truth, if it has such limited functionality and relevance? The best answer I can devise parallels the circumstances leading to James's beginning to discuss truth (though with a different ultimate relevance). James's major interlocutors all articulated conceptions of absolute truth (and/or absolute knowers), conceptions that were not only regulative ideals, but constitutive fundamentally not only of piecemeal truth but of their whole philosophical edifices. James intended both to articulate a radically different philosophy from a different point of departure, and to be taken seriously by these very philosophers. For better or worse, it is probable that he simply developed his discussion in some of the terms of this discursive context. In constructing accounts of James's views, we would do well to attend closely to that context, and to James's divergences, despite what may be our own disagreements.

Notes

1. See Hilary Putnam, 'James's Theory of Truth,' in *The Cambridge Companion to William James,* ed. Ruth Anna Putnam (Cambridge: Cambridge University Press, 1997).
2. I do not say in the book that James's view follows the disquotational principle of truth; rather, I try to shift the import of what I took to be Putnam's invocation of that principle when he illustrated what he takes to be wrong with James's view. Compare Putnam's Afterword with *William James and the Metaphysics of Experience* (Cambridge: Cambridge University Press, 1999), 222, and Putnam, 'James's Theory of Truth,' 182–3.
3. See James, 'Philosophical Conceptions and Practical Results,' in *Pragmatism*

(Harvard: Harvard University Press, 1975), 259.

4. James to Schiller, 1 February 1904, in *The Correspondence of William James,* eds Skrupskelis and Berkeley, vol. 10 (Charlottesville: University of Virginia Press, 2002), 369.

5. James there corroborates the point he made to Schiller about his intentions for pragmatism merely as a method for determining meaning. See 'Humanism and Truth,' *The Meaning of Truth* (Cambridge: Harvard University Press, 1975), 37. Bradley's article appeared in *Mind*, 13:51 (July 1904), 309–35.

6. 'Does Consciousness Exist?' appeared in the *Journal of Philosophy, Psychology and Scientific Methods* on 1 September 1904; 'A World of Pure Experience' appeared in two parts in the same journal on 29 September and 13 October 1904; 'Humanism and Truth' appeared in *Mind* (October 1904). Comments in letters indicate that James finished 'Humanism and Truth' by 15 July 1904; 'Does Consciousness Exist?' was written between 22 and 27 July 1904, and the two parts of 'A World of Pure Experience' were completed by 23 August and 1 September 1904, respectively. For corroborating letters, see James to Schiller, 15 July 1904, *Correspondence,* vol. 10, 432; James to Baldwin, 22 July 1904, *Correspondence,* vol. 10, 436; James to Woodbridge, 27 July 1904, *Correspondence,* vol. 10, 439; James to Alice Howe Gibbens James, 23 August 1904, *Correspondence,* vol. 10, 457; and James to Hunter, 1 September 1904, *Correspondence,* vol. 10, 461.

7. Numerous subsequent texts support this interpretation. See, e.g., 'Humanism and Truth,' *Meaning of Truth*, 46, *Pragmatism*, 98, and 117–18. James stated in *Pragmatism* that radical empiricism was not necessary to understanding or endorsing pragmatism (6), but retracted this in part in *Meaning of Truth* (6). This is consistent with his 8 September 1904 comment to Miller: 'I have written 3 full bodied articles on the "new philosophy", one on "Humanism and truth" for the October *Mind*, one already out in Woodbridge's Journal, called "Does 'Consciousness' exist?" and another about to appear there called "A world of pure experience",' *Correspondence,* vol. 10, 466.

8. My interpretation of James here is loosely analogous, structurally speaking, to Robert Brandom's positioning of his inferentialism in contrast to representationalism. See *Making it Explicit* (Cambridge: Harvard University Press, 1994).

9. James's criticism of J.B. Pratt in 'Professor Pratt on Truth' takes up this issue directly, criticizing the 'superior importance which Dr. Pratt attributes to abstract trueness over concrete verifiability in an idea,' *Meaning of Truth*, 95f. In *Pragmatism*, James writes that 'The reasons why we call things true is the reason why they *are* true, for "to be true" *means* only to perform this marrying function,' referring to the concrete conjoining of previous parts of experience to newer parts (37). Something similar holds for 'meaning' and 'reference,' see 'Controversy About Truth,' *Essays in Radical Empiricism* (Cambridge: Harvard University Press, 1976), 153.

10. In the two lead essays of radical empiricism, penned days after he first tackled truth, James lays out a complex theory of knowledge, comprised of direct acquaintance and his multi-layered conception of knowledge about, including a theory of reference, *without so much as a substantive mention of the category of 'truth.'* Relatedly, James insists consistently that it is mistaken to call facts 'true': 'the facts, meanwhile, are not true, they simply are. Truth is the function of the beliefs that start and terminate among them' (*Pragmatism*, 108, 117; *Meaning of Truth*, 87).

11. James to Lane, 28 October 1907, in Perry, *The Thought and Character of William James*, vol. II (Boston: Little, Brown & Co., 1935), 476–8.

12. Perhaps Putnam is taking James's statement that the future is partly indeterminate to indicate that future truths are (part of) what is determined about the future. To demonstrate that depends on showing that James has a conception of 'truth not relativized to evidence, to the borders of experience at a particular time and place,' something for which I can find no evidence.

13. Since James's notion of truth always involves satisfactoriness, as well as relations among current ideas, beliefs, and statements and the facts to which they refer (technically, only ideas, beliefs, and statements can be true), every truth involves an at least minimal dependence on variables in the present, and hence can alter.

14. Putnam's comment about Roosevelt displays this same transitivity between fact and truth, which James positively disallows in 'Two English Critics': 'The great shifting of universes in this discussion occurs when we carry the word "truth" from the subjective into the objective realm, applying it sometimes to a property of opinions, sometimes to the facts which the opinions assert . . . I do not say that for certain logical purposes it may not be useful to treat propositions as absolute entities, with truth or falsehood inside of them respectively, or to make a complex like "that-Caesar-is-dead" a single term and call it a "truth." But the "that" here has the extremely convenient ambiguity for those who wish to make trouble for us pragmatists, that sometimes it means the *fact* that, and sometimes the *belief* that, Caesar is no longer living. When I then call the belief true, I am told that the truth means the fact; when I claim the fact also, I am told that my definition has excluded the fact, being a definition only of a certain peculiarity in the belief – so that in the end I have no truth to talk about left in my possession. The only remedy for this intolerable ambiguity is, it seems to me, to stick to terms consistently. "Reality," "idea" or "belief," and the "truth of the idea or belief," which are the terms I have consistently held to, seem to be free from all objection' (*Meaning of Truth*, 151).

15. See *Pragmatism*, 107. Putnam mentions this concerning how to read James's usage of truth without a modifier, but it assumes the same position on tenselessness as the Lane reference.

16. *Pragmatism*, 106–7.

17. One might rejoin that humans all share particular interests as a species, but James is loath not to allow for individual variation from such specifications.

18. Depending on the context, James is not always sensitive to the potential difference between warranted assertibility and truth. This is so because he ordinarily locates estimations of truth in the present. As the comment from *Pragmatism* just discussed shows, however, he does understand the distinction.

19. *Pragmatism*, 107. In 'Humanism and Truth' James calls this peculiar temporal aspect of the function of truth a 'quasi-paradox,' attending to its peculiarity in contrast to the working of fact. See *Meaning of Truth*, 56.

20. *Pragmatism*, 107.

21. James embraces the label 'relativist' in 'Abstractionism and "Relativismus," ' *Meaning of Truth*, 142. Putnam's longstanding concern about relativism could be behind his desire to help James out of this 'problem.'

22. *Pragmatism*, 107.

23. James is aware that there are narrow areas of theoretical activity (e.g., mathematics) where logic gives more, and bivalence may be relevant, due to our ability to and convention of holding abstract ideas (i.e., ideas that do not refer to reality via the sensational or perceptual) and their interrelations, once defined, as invariant. See *Meaning of Truth*, 52. But because reality itself on James's view ordinarily exceeds the best of conceptualization, this advantage for logic in the case of the abstract does not appear to him to extend far.

24. See note 14.
25. *Meaning of Truth*, 109.
26. See Peirce, 'How to Make Our Ideas Clear,' *Collected Papers of Charles Sanders Peirce* (Cambridge: Harvard University Press, 1934), vol. 5, §407 (268).
27. *Pragmatism*, 106–7.
28. *Meaning of Truth*, 100–1.
29. This is so because there is no peculiarly 'absolute' feature of an idea that will prove to be absolutely true beyond its ordinary qualifications for truth here and now, relative to these borders of experience.
30. This concern about how much stock to put into this passage goes less to the question of whether absolute truth may be made piecemeal, and more to the issue of whether absolute truth for James is the principal and constitutive, rather than the derivative, conception. James's response 'Professor Hébert on Pragmatism' also appears to admit the piecemeal interpretation, albeit with more ambiguity. Considering how the notion of '*absolute* reality ... as a *grenzbegriff* arises,' James writes that:

    > Cognitively we thus live under a sort of rule of three: as our private concepts represent sense-objects to which they lead us, these being public realities independent of the individual, so these sense-realities may, in turn, represent realities of a hypersensible order, electrons, mind-stuff, God, or what not, existing independently of all human thinkers. The notion of such final realities, knowledge of which would be absolute truth, is an outgrowth of our cognitive experience from which neither pragmatists nor anti-pragmatists escape. They form an inevitable regulative postulate in everyone's thinking. Our notion of them is the most abundantly suggested and satisfied of all our beliefs, the last to suffer doubt. (*Meaning of Truth*, 130–1)

    James is concerned here with how we form purely theoretical ideas that do not themselves come directly from or terminate directly in experience, in particular, the concept of 'reality' itself and theories of truth. In the next sentences, however, James attends to the situated, non-absolute character of such conceptions, chastising his critics for taking any particular view of these purely speculative objects as the 'sole paradigm.' 'Meanwhile, reality-in itself, so far as by them *talked of*,' he writes, 'is only a human object. ... There is no idea which is *the* true idea, of anything. Whose is *the* true idea of the absolute? ... It is the idea that most satisfactorily meets your present interest.' This does not rule out the piecemeal interpretation, but it does call into question treating 'absolute truth' as more than regulative. See *Meaning of Truth*, 131.
31. 'Abstractionism and "Relativismus",' *Meaning of Truth*, 142.
32. See 'The Will to Believe' in his book of that name for James's views on the right to believe, and the concluding pages of *A Pluralistic Universe*. There are important restrictions here, logical consistency being one.
33. On Putnam's side, I must note the non-relative tensing of this phrase. But James's footnote referring it to Rickert's and Münsterberg's views, the uniqueness of the statement's object, and his invocation of the clearly tensed 'will to believe' doctrine there raise difficulties for taking this to be definitive of what Putnam wants. I should also note that James here seems to be ruling out that he knows 'what the shape of [absolute truth] is,' thus troubling the interpretation that his notion of absolute truth founds his account of truth.
34. *Meaning of Truth*, 143.
35. See note 23.

Conclusion

Experience and the value of religion – Overview and Analysis[1]

David C. Lamberth

Centenaries of various events come and go, usually without notice. In the case of the Edinburgh Gifford Lectures, the Edinburgh centenary conference on James in 2002 was the first celebration of a centenary, although five have passed. Gathering an august company of scholars to reflect on William James's *Varieties of Religious Experience* – looking back to its contextual contributions and forward toward its continuing relevance – is thus a peculiar circumstance which, while not unheard of in the annals of modern thought, is exceptional enough to warrant reflection.

This circumstance is due primarily to the enduring and continually rewarding character of the erudite oeuvre of James, to its ability to repay with compounded interest the efforts of those delving in to learn from and in reaction to it. It is fair to say that the conference and this subsequent volume of work were not simply to reflect on and celebrate the *Varieties*, but also, as Eugene Taylor indicates, to attend to the work of James as a whole.

While it should be thus admitted that the *Varieties* may not solely, or perhaps even mainly, be responsible for our interest, the text itself has had a major impact on the world of letters and the broader society. The *Varieties* is James's most widely published, assigned, and, I dare say, *read* text, having been in print continuously since its publication a hundred years ago. In its first twenty-seven years, it went through thirty-seven impressions with Longmans and Green. While three publishers' editions dominated the first half of the twentieth century, at least one newly introduced edition has appeared every decade since 1960. Translated into numerous languages, it is currently offered in nine English editions, as well as on audio tape and electronic formats. In April 1999, the Modern Library listed the *Varieties* number two among the 100 best non-fiction books of the twentieth century. Clearly this is not an under-noticed text.

Two characteristics of *Varieties*

Although the *Varieties* is probably James's most read book, it is not his most comprehensive or closely argued text; those honors go respectively to *Principles of Psychology* and *Essays in Radical Empiricism*. The *Varieties* is interesting for other reasons. Part of its popularity derives from having religion, specifically popular religion, as its subject matter, rather than philosophy or psychology (which, as Jacob Belzen notes, is so often very dry). More importantly, however, there is something about James's manner of approach to his topic that distinguishes the text. To begin to account for our own interest, I want to identify and briefly address two of the salient features of the *Varieties* representative of James's thinking: its expansiveness and its fecundity.[2]

With expansiveness, I mean to highlight just how much James pulls into his study of human nature. As his readers know, James the empirical pluralist was committed to inclusivity both as a methodological principle, in the sense of demanding an inclusive gathering of data, and as a requirement for assessing the truth (or satisfactoriness) of ideas or accounts.[3] Though necessarily limited in scope and method, and thus open to much of the criticism brought against it, the *Varieties* is, none the less, noteworthy for bringing in a wider array of material than most other studies of religion – and certainly natural religion – have done. Here I note not only the polyphony of autobiographical voices James sounds from different personalities, religious traditions, and time periods (a group more varied than most initially think), but also the range of theoretical approaches he takes toward these accounts, including physiological analysis, descriptive psychological classification, psychological theory, and theological and philosophical analysis. The subtitle 'A Study in Human Nature' telegraphs how broad a scope James intends. James's appeals to 'a wider self,'[4] 'larger ranges of truth,'[5] the 'many-sided affair' of the Universe,[6] and the 'more'[7] indicate concretely the extent to which he seeks to be true to this criterion of expansiveness and inclusion in his evaluation of the phenomena of religious experience and methodologically. Interestingly, James's interpretation of the function of religion itself inclines strongly to this criterion, with religion (both the concrete, experiential 'religion,' as in the American expression 'Do you have religion?' and the more refined object of the theory) purporting to interconnect us with wider ranges of truth and reality, allowing us selectively to re-order ourselves in such expansive relation.

In addition to this expansiveness, the text is also remarkable for its fecundity, particularly that demonstrated in the interest the *Varieties* has generated. From the opening days of James's readings of the first course of lectures, audiences surprisingly swelled rather than diminished. Likewise, sales of the initial editions outpaced expectations, continuing down to today. More important than the generation of interest, however, is the prolific character of the *Varieties* as a project. The scope of the papers for this event is telling, providing a glimpse into what the *Varieties* has spawned in thought and academic production. In speaking about 'real hypotheses' in lecture 20, James notes that a good scientific hypothesis must not only account for the phenomena it is invoked to explain, but also must postulate new facts and bring into view wider vistas.[8] From the record of this conference alone, it is clear that the project of the *Varieties* has been prolific indeed.

Let me name a few outcomes. The project has effectively brought into being the academic study of mysticism, for better and worse, as Grace Jantzen and Richard King detail above. It has generated steady interest in and contributed a classic text to the psychology of religion, even if its arguments have not, as Jacob Belzen notes, been heeded. Contrary to James's apparent wishes, it has sparked a host of evidentiary arguments for the existence of God in the philosophy of religion. *Varieties* has provided significant impetus and content to work on emotion in its day and ours (well treated by Jeremy Carrette above). And the book has offered religious studies a classic text and an influential theory and 'definition' of religion, albeit often misunderstood. It is perhaps inaccurate to think of the *Varieties* itself as a single hypothesis, but it is fair to say that it has been productive for yielding academic work, if not always knowledge.

Some reasons for misunderstandings of the text

While the book is widely read and appreciated, it is also frequently misunderstood, something no doubt common to books with such broad circulation. Although James wrote his lectures for a popular audience, he certainly could not have imagined how wide a hearing it would have; surely some of the interpretive difficulties encountered can be credited to this disparity between his imagined and actual audiences. That the book is frequently misinterpreted becomes even more comprehensible once one considers the radical changes over the intervening century within the various disciplines in which James trades in the text. Few readers of the *Varieties* now have a grip on the intellectual and historical contexts required to situate the book well. Some of the best recent James scholarship and some of the most insightful papers in this volume have made such contexts more accessible, but the problem does not easily recede.

The fact that the book is hard to interpret is also due to factors intrinsic to James's oeuvre. As Ruth Anna Putnam notes, the book is transitional among James's arguments about religion, bridging his earlier *The Will to Believe* with the later chapters of *Pragmatism* and *A Pluralistic Universe*. I have contended elsewhere that the book is transitional among his published works, albeit differently, standing between his major psychological writings, which transpire overtly under the assumption of psycho-physical correspondence and dualism, and his explicitly 'radical empiricist' writings, which directly contravene those notions.[9] The important complication to note is that, although James had substantively committed himself to radical empiricism by 1896, well prior to conceptualizing the *Varieties*, he had not publicly articulated that formally monistic view. Thus he could not presume his Edinburgh audience or readers to have any knowledge of the details of his 'new' view and its considerable revisions of what he had previously maintained.[10] As Sonu Shamdasani observes, the text thus not surprisingly performs certain things that it does not overtly theorize.

Compounding these developmental complexities is the well-known fact that the *Varieties* as we have it is not the text James intended. In the preface James notes that he had planned a complementary pair of ten-lecture courses, a descriptive set on 'Man's Religious Appetites' and a metaphysical course exploring 'Their Satisfaction Through Philosophy.'[11] Penning this statement, having already delivered the first ten lectures, James also claims that the 'unexpected growth of the psychological matter as I came to write it out has resulted in the second subject being postponed entirely.'[12] Evidence indicates that James had intended to adumbrate the details of his 'radical empiricism' in the second course.[13] The postponement of this topic thus significantly affects how one should read the treatment of the first topic spread over twenty lectures.

James's objectives for the Gifford Lectures

In a well-known letter of April 1900, James told Frances R. Morse that he had a twofold objective for the lectures:

> *first*, to defend (against all the prejudices of my 'class') 'experience' against 'philosophy' as being the real backbone of the world's religious life – I mean prayer, guidance, and all that sort of thing immediately and privately felt, as against high and noble general views of our destiny and the world's meaning; and *second*, to make the hearer or reader believe, what I myself invincibly do believe, that although all the special manifestations of religion may have been absurd (I mean its creeds and theories), yet the life of it as a whole is mankind's most important function.[14]

In the contributions to this volume, significant differences concerning the core argument of the text are evident, ranging from those who see it centered on mysticism, to those who read it as a contribution to psychology (and Jacob Belzen, who doesn't), to those who see it forwarding an argument for the existence of the unseen, to those who take it to be about none of these subjects. In what follows I hope to shed light on the central problem of understanding the *Varieties* as we have it by: (1) reflecting on how each of these two stated tasks should be comprehended; and (2) assessing the extent to which James fulfills these objectives in the text.

Experience versus philosophy

The first task – to defend 'experience' against 'philosophy' as the real backbone of the world's religious life – appears to be relatively clear, at least as an objective. In this short phrase, however, several issues are worthy of note.

First, although he uses 'experience' frequently, James never in the *Varieties* defines or treats it technically. Moreover, James does not make explicit exactly what he means by 'religious experience' in the title; he offers an admittedly 'arbitrary' definition of religion in his second lecture, for example, but not of 'religious experience.' Noting this fact unveils a deep historical irony. While James went out of his way to treat religion as an aspect of *human* nature, arguing that religious emotions and feelings are normal emotions and feelings with religious objects, historically his fate was to have launched 'religious experience' as an extraordinary and – depending on who treats it – privileged category in academic discourse.[15]

It is peculiar that James does not use 'experience' technically in the *Varieties*, since by this point he had developed much of his thinking on this fundamental term in his radical empiricism.[16] In the comment to Morse he does clarify something of what he means, pointing to 'prayer, guidance, and all that sort of thing immediately and privately felt.' Given the *Varieties* alone, however, one can easily be at a loss to know why James chose 'experience' rather than simply 'religious feeling' or 'religious emotion' for his project.

In the comparison of these options an important distinction emerges. Even in common usage, 'experience' differs from 'feeling,' 'emotion,' 'perception,' or 'state of mind' in that it implies duration of time and a broader scope and degree of complexity than the now-oriented 'state of feeling' or 'perceptual state.' Charles Sanders Peirce observed this, noting that when a train blowing its whistle passes, we experience rather than perceive the change in the whistle's pitch.[17] Experience pertains not merely to individual perceptual moments, therefore, but implies the dynamism of events. This is often exemplified by underscoring the more complex conceptual and inferential setting for experience. In contrast to a religious perception or a religious feeling, then, James's use of 'religious experience' may be more concerned with something happening over time.

Given James's pragmatic attention to effects – looking to fruits, such an enduring event can be described with reference to its outcome. For James that normally includes: (1) the psychological change over time of a person's attitude; (2) a corresponding change in his or her conduct; and (3) a resulting modification to how the person orders his or her world, personally and socially. In the *Varieties* James is far less interested in individual religious emotions and particular religious feelings, I submit, than he is in *religious experience*, where the latter is distinguished not principally by its momentary, phenomenological characteristics but by what is dynamically enacted through it. This explains why the development of James's understanding of emotion that Jeremy Carrette notes is not explicitly thematized in the way that the stages and forms of transformation effected through religious experiences are, whether one takes conversion, mysticism, or prayer as basic. It also further supports Sonu Shamdasani's suggestion that we think of the *Varieties* not so much as about some particular kind of religious experience, whether mysticism, conversion or prayer, but rather as about transformation. (This is helpful, provided one realizes that James, in the book at least, is not equally interested in all transformations.)

Turning from effects to origins, one can note that the dynamics of transformation recounted in the *Varieties* are principally experienced and explicated as relational, involving interaction with powers, forces or ideas external to the individual's normal waking consciousness (and possibly external to the individual him- or herself) at the time before the dynamic in question. The phrase 'religious *experience*,' then, can be seen to have particular and even somewhat technical import, even though James himself does not overtly indicate this. In this light, better sense can be made of James's famous, yet admittedly arbitrary, definition of religion: 'Religion, therefore, as I now ask you arbitrarily to take it, shall mean for us *the feelings, acts, and experiences of individual men in their solitude, so far as they apprehend themselves to stand in relation to whatever they may consider the divine.*' While James's notion of religion begins in religious feeling, which he underlines throughout under the rubric of 'religious experience,' it should not be understood to end there, either with respect to origins or outcomes.

Turning back to the Morse quotation, what should one say about philosophy, against which James seeks to defend 'experience'? First, as many have noted, James does not intend all philosophy, but only certain forms of rationalism dominant in his day, along with several variants of systematic theology. Second, although he dismisses rationalism pointedly, James is explicit that he does not consider such reflection useless; in the *Varieties* he admits that scholasticism's quintessentially rationalist divine attributes, just excoriated from a pragmatic point of view, actually have independent aesthetic value.[18]

Although James himself ordinarily favors doing philosophy, in the Morse quotation and the *Varieties* he presents a negative view of philosophy in general with respect to the 'real backbone of the world's religious life.' Why this is so can be explained by attending to James's commonplace notion of religious experience just clarified. An emotional experience of a change in overall bearing due to a dynamic experience of relationality is the *sine qua non* of religion, James thinks, because, without excitement of such an emotional dynamic, there is no resultant transformation of the individual, no real religious experience. Empirically speaking, James thinks that the religious facts and documents indicate that philosophy alone does not produce such excitement. Some limited number of people may have experienced significant transformations in their centers of personal energy through philosophical argumentation – the sentiment of rationality is, after all, understood by James as an organic feeling.[19] But if they have experienced such transformation, they neither constitute the bulk of those religious, nor prove frequently to be religious originators. James thus concludes that philosophical ideas and argumentation are not, in point of fact, efficacious for the dynamic function denoted by 'religious experience' constitutive of religion as he thinks we commonly understand it.

Reading the contrast between experience and philosophy in this context, we also can observe a parallel between James's take on philosophy and institutional religion. As with philosophy, James does not claim that institutional religion is without value, as many suppose. He is, however, of the view that, without the individual experiences of at least a religious founder (and the experiences of followers as well – see his comments on prayer), there is little likelihood that these institutional elements would ever have appeared or been sustained within human history. From the standpoint of causal origin and efficacious function, then, James finds institutions and systems of ideas and practices to be relatively derivative, irrespective of how essential or productive they may be in other respects. The experiential moment is, then, definitive of religion on James's view, because it is required for the transformation that marks real religion to be forged.

James's defense of religion

James's prioritization of experience over philosophy and social and institutional aspects of religion derives in significant measure from his observations concerning what religion – including religious experience – is. These observations depend to a large extent on his chosen psychological approach in the *Varieties*, which highlights transformations and a particular data set. But this prioritization depends not only on existential (or even spiritual) judgments for which James thinks he has warrants; it also depends on an over-belief of James's. That over-belief is revealed within his specification of his second task in the Morse letter, where he states that he wants to make his readers and hearers believe what he himself invincibly does believe, that the life of religion as a whole is humankind's most important function.

To unpack this, we might attend first to James's choice of verbs. James does not say that he intends rationally to persuade his hearers or readers; instead, he says he wants 'to make the hearer or reader believe what he himself invincibly does believe . . .' As we know from *The Will to Believe*, and before it Peirce's 'The Fixation of Belief,' belief is a peculiar category in American philosophy. Although as human beings we are, in principle, free to believe a significant array of things, belief is fundamentally an organic state of being. By this I do not mean to be reductive, or claim that belief merely depends on physical processes. However, despite James's strong defense of the right to believe and act ahead of the evidence in certain cases (under restrictions of logical consistency and affinity with one's system of beliefs and truth), one cannot simply believe anything one wishes. Beliefs, James and Peirce insist, are things upon which we are willing to act; once fixed, they habitually compel us without any necessary deliberative activity. But the fixation of belief itself is, in important respects, a limited and persistently opaque process.

James notes the limitations of belief fixation in a number of places. In *The Will to Believe* he states that candidates for belief must be 'live' hypotheses.[20] Being live depends in part on being consistent with or amenable to one's other habits of thought and action, one's world-view. As such, it crucially depends on comprehending the best understandings of the facts as we have them (what is so far true). Interestingly, however, 'live-ness' varies among individuals within the same general intellectual and cultural framework, highlighting the opacity of belief formation. With scientific beliefs, for example, given the same facts, everyone is not as a matter of course equally compelled to entertain in advance of evidence a particular hypothesis. In the case of religious beliefs, some highly emotional or neurotic individuals, for example, are temperamentally more disposed to believe, and to believe particular things, according to James. Contrarily, those with strenuous temperaments are unlikely ever to be affected, despite a strongly facilitating context. Thus the possibility of willing or compelling belief depends not only on the facts, and intellectual and cultural context, but also on idiosyncratic temperament. On this theory, belief in a given proposition may as likely be precluded by idiosyncratic factors as it is by the intellectual context or facts.[21]

This conception of belief is important for understanding James's characterization of his second task for the *Varieties*. One might argue that James had in mind simply the compulsion of 'scientific' belief, belief in the hypothesis that is the best account of the facts in question. To a certain extent this is correct, since James seeks to present an empirical case for his hypothesis of the dynamic of religion. But the account of religion that is scientific in this sense is, strictly speaking, the psychological model – the existential argument about the subliminal region and its cerebration, not the value judgment that religion is humankind's most important function.[22] No doubt the relatively compatible, scientific model of religious experience is of assistance to James's intended belief formation, but accepting this view alone does not warrant the 'most important function' claim.

One might argue that James could justify as scientific a claim that religion is *an* important function for human beings and the species. This could succeed if one worked from a normative conception of human flourishing (which James appears to intend), and understood this to be facilitated by the advantageous adjustment to life and the positive qualities of saintliness afforded to individuals via their peculiarly 'religious' transformations and, by example, to other members of the species. But James's superlative language, that the life of religion is humankind's *most* important function – more important than the capacity for respiration or circulation, for example – is surely a stretch beyond the realm of such 'scientific' judgements, narrowly or broadly construed.

James signals his recognition of this in the line after his 'two tasks' comment to Morse, noting that his attempt to make readers believe is *his* 'religious act.'[23] This, combined with James's use of the adjective 'invincible' for his own belief, leads me to class James's own evaluation of religion as, at least in part, an over-belief, rather than simply a spiritual judgment. What is the significance of this? And does it shed light on the project?

Before addressing these questions, I should clarify that James's 'over-belief' about the value of the religious function is not identical to his self-described over-belief in piecemeal supernaturalism, although the two are clearly mutually reinforcing. This is important because, as Ruth Anna Putnam notes, the fact that the *Varieties* itself does not come down in favor of one particular position to the exclusion of all others is significant to James's philosophical pluralism.[24] What I am arguing, however, is: (1) that James's commitment to the paramount value of religion has certain characteristics of an over-belief; and (2) that recognizing this can illuminate the scope and relative importance of the range of arguments the *Varieties* proffers.

It is often concluded that over-beliefs are, for James, fundamentally private matters, not subjects for fruitful discussion, even though they may themselves admit of cultural or social origins. James suggests this, writing that 'we should treat [over-beliefs] with tenderness and tolerance so long as they are not intolerant themselves.'[25] But over-beliefs are also described as 'buildings-out performed by the intellect into directions of which feeling originally supplied the hint.' As such, they look very similar to James's conception of metaphysical views in other writings.[26] While these latter are, like over-beliefs, influenced by temperament and personality, James is definite that discussion of them is not only warranted, but crucial to continued improvement of the collective lot of human beings.

Part of what is at stake is how various orders of reflection, judgment, and argumentation are interrelated for James. Existential judgments are, first and foremost, closer to the facts. Because facts are retrospective, James tends to characterize these judgments as concerned with origins. Like the special sciences of which they are typical, however, existential judgments depend on certain ways of organizing the facts that reflect evaluative judgments already taken and metaphysical views already construed.[27] It is likewise with spiritual judgements, whose criteria are immediate luminousness, philosophical reasonableness and moral helpfulness; implicit in these criteria are a conception of human nature and of the world as the environment for human life. Hence both existential and spiritual judgments inevitably involve metaphysical perspectives.

The line between spiritual judgments and over-beliefs is not a particularly bright one. Both take in a wide perspective and seek to build out from our knowledge of facts according to our interests and estimations of value, individual and collective. What one can say about James's usage is that the degree of probability and verification arrived at in a typical spiritual judgment is somewhat higher than that of an over-belief. (Hilary Putnam noted in the Edinburgh centenary conference discussion that the verification time-frame of over-beliefs is that of history, not the laboratory. This is right, although spiritual judgments lie between existential judgements and over-beliefs on the time continuum for becoming settled.) Despite what is commonly inferred, I do not think James intended to forward the idea that public, reasoned discussion should stop the moment one begins to engage over-beliefs. Over-beliefs are, in any case, always already engaged, given James's conception of thinking and experience, hence any attempt to sequester them is bound to fail. The important question is how to identify them and their peculiar conditions of argument.

I have dwelled upon James's plan for the *Varieties* because, from its perspective, one can see the *Varieties* offering more levels and types of argument than the text overtly admits to. Not only is there a conception of religion, a psychological description, and a classification of humanity's 'religious appetites,' but also there is an argument for the potential contribution of religion to humanity collectively.

While it is true that, *at the very most*, James demonstrates his spiritual judgment that religion in certain cases proves to have both objective and subjective value for human beings, individually and collectively, he also opens the door to further investigations into the truth of its content, as Hilary Putnam notes.[29] At the same time James invites broader questions about the function and place of religion in the human future. (Here Grace Jantzen's central questions and some of David Wulff's concerns should be seen to be joined by James in principle, even though he did not have the ability or tools to take them on effectively.)

I am also arguing that James is seeking an additional outcome through the text, one not merely the result of existential or spiritual arguments, but drawing on the range of transparent and opaque forces involved in over-belief formation. James has both subjective and objective reasons for his own over-belief in the paramount importance of the life of religion. Subjectively speaking, James understands religion to add something otherwise unavailable which has a unique and necessary productive potential for fulfilling human possibility, individual or social. On the objective side, religion's continual estimation of and push towards wider realms of engagement, inclusion and responsibility provide crucial behavioral and substantive norms for our moral, scientific, and philosophical activities. James's notion seems to be that such an understanding of the value of religion is not merely rosy or fanciful, but resonates with both the existential facts from the past and present (selected though they may be) and our concrete human aspirations toward the future. Attempting to fix his readers' and hearers' belief in the value of religion as a human function is, therefore, understood by James as a critical and productive step in the further realization of this vision. The next step would be to clarify and expound on the particular over-beliefs most amenable to these tasks, with the hope of further determining belief and action.[30]

Where does this leave us? Certainly, it suggests a healthy skepticism concerning many of the narrow, conclusive, or dismissive interpretations of the *Varieties*. Given James's broad interest in human flourishing, and his notion that believing in the value of religion (whether or not one is religious) is a step towards such flourishing, one can suppose reasonably that the multifaceted and inter-disciplinary character of the text may be more intentional than haphazard. Seeing this allows one not only to read the individual arguments and treatments of the text in their local contexts better; but also, one can begin to transform these readings (and some of their noted ill effects) by transcending the parochial qualities of the particular text – its examples, its arbitrary and easily 'mis-taken' focus on certain aspects such as mysticism or Protestant conversion narratives, its individualism, its biases of gender and social location. Perhaps more importantly, one can also begin to read James's *Varieties* as deeply conjoined to his philosophical meliorism laid out more explicitly in *Pragmatism* and *A Pluralistic Universe*. Finally, one can begin to imagine a possible discussion about different over-beliefs with regard to their specific potentialities to promote human and religious flourishing, rather than simply seeing such over-beliefs as private, protected from criticism and discussion.

What would be the import of this reading for the varied constituencies of the *Varieties*? To psychologists, scholars of mysticism, mystics and religionists, it suggests that one recognizes that the *Varieties* effects a larger argument than it initially appears, one tied to his pragmatic philosophy (and its social agenda). To philosophers, it implies that James may have less at stake in the question of the existence of the unseen (or God/gods), since he is attending primarily to the normative issues of human flourishing. Traditional interpretive issues of both groups should continue to be relevant where they are overtly addressed in the text. But the pressing necessity seems to be to create broader argumentative contexts for these discussions.

The *Varieties* is an extraordinarily interesting text, not only for the plenitude it offers, but also because James himself had a great deal at stake in it. While the conversation about its meaning and value – like that of all true classics – is unlikely to end anytime soon, this volume offers a beginning for a reinvigorated look at the text, the issues it raises, and its interpretation to date. Although I write at the end, I have no desire to close the discussion, since I too look forward to its new fruits.

Notes

1. In the spirit of its 'occasional' composition, the paper presented here is only slightly amended from the conference version. While I did seek to address the scope of the papers presented, for organizational reasons I was unable to address the papers in detail.
2. These characteristics are overtly lauded by James with respect to the value of theories and ideas. Including the greatest range of phenomena and beliefs is, to James's mind, a mark of something being more likely true than its rivals. See, e.g., the notebook for the philosophical course to *Varieties* reprinted in William James, *The Varieties of Religious Experience* (Cambridge: Harvard University Press, 1985), 492, and comments demanding inclusivity in *Pragmatism* (Cambridge: Harvard University Press, 1975), e.g. 117–119. On fecundity, see *Varieties*, 407 ('prolific' is James's term).
3. See, e.g., James's argument against the theoretical sufficiency of the mind-cure movement, due to ignoring evil, *Varieties*, 137–8.
4. *Varieties*, 405.
5. *Varieties*, 267.
6. *Varieties*, 104.
7. *Varieties*, 400–3.
8. *Varieties*, 407.
9. See David C. Lamberth, *William James and the Metaphysics of Experience* (Cambridge: Cambridge University Press, 1999), particularly chapters 2 and 3.
10. See Schiller's claim to await James's metaphysics, *Humanism*, 2nd edition (London: MacMillan, 1912), xiii.
11. *Varieties*, 5. See also 491 for title variations. In an 1899 letter to Morse, James characterized the title of the first course as 'Varieties of Religious Experience.' See William James, *The Letters of William James*, vol. 2 (Boston: Atlantic Monthly Press, 1920), 112. In a letter to Pringle-Pattison in September 1899, James titled the second course (then not to be delivered) as 'The Tasks of Religious Philosophy' (Papers of William James, bMS Am 1092.1, typed copy, Houghton Library, Harvard University).

12. James's statement about the growth of the material is not exactly correct. See Lamberth, 97–106.
13. A full account can be found in Lamberth, *William James and the Metaphysics of Experience*, chapter 3.
14. James to Morse, 12 April 1900, *Letters of William James*, vol. 2, 127. James reiterates the second task in the *Varieties*, writing ' "How *can* religion on the whole be the most important of all human functions," you may ask, "if every several manifestations of it in turn have to be corrected and sobered down and pruned away?" Such a thesis seems a paradox impossible to sustain reasonably – yet I believe something like it will have to be our final contention' (48–9).
15. Wayne Proudfoot advances this reading with respect to James, *inter alia*, in *Religious Experience* (Berkeley: University of California Press, 1985). Proudfoot is generally accurate with regard to the reception of the *Varieties*, though less so concerning James's position.
16. In James's notes for the philosophical course, he writes 'a propos of my *reine erfahrung*' (pure experience), a key category in his radical empiricism. The notebook is printed in the *Varieties*, 497; see also Lamberth, *William James and the Metaphysics of Experience*, 83–7.
17. Charles Sanders Peirce, *Collected Papers of Charles Sanders Peirce*, eds. Hartshorne and Weiss (Cambridge: Belknap Press of Harvard University Press, 1960–66), vol 1, 335–6.
18. *Varieties*, 361. James's recognition of aesthetic and moral needs in distinction to rational ones occurs throughout his corpus. See 'Remarks on Spencer's Definition of Mind as Correspondence' and 'Reflex Action and Theism.' In *A Pluralistic Universe* (Cambridge: Harvard University Press, 1977), 55, James states that there are at least four kinds of rationality: theoretical, aesthetic, moral, and practical.
19. Because this is an empirical generalization, finding one person converted through philosophical argument would not necessarily be a defeater for James. For specification of the sentiment of rationality, see the essay of that title in *The Will to Believe*.
20. James, *The Will to Believe and Other Essays in Philosophy* (Cambridge: Harvard University Press, 1979), 14.
21. Note that rationality is not simply limited to the intellectual context here. See comments in *Pragmatism*, 13, on temperament, and the mixture of rationality comment in *Pluralistic Universe*, 55.
22. For the psychological model, see *Varieties*, 188–97.
23. Compare this to his 'last will and testament' language used to both Pringle-Pattison (7 February 1897) and Morse (23 December 1899).
24. Not all theological positions fare equally. Versions of refined supernaturalism are more difficult to justify on James's hypothesis.
25. *Varieties*, 405.
26. *Varieties*, 341. For the metaphysical views, see *Pluralistic Universe*, chapter 1.
27. See Lamberth, *William James and the Metaphysics of Experience*, 112, for the parallel between the existential/spiritual and the special science/metaphysics distinctions. See also Barnard in this volume.
28. *Varieties*, 23.
29. For the objective and subjective contents, see *Varieties*, 397–400.
30. As mentioned, James planned to attempt this task in the planned philosophical course. The only sustained articulation is found in the last chapter of *Pragmatism* and *A Pluralistic Universe*.

Index

Also available from Routledge:

The Varieties of Religious Experience: A Study in Human Nature
Centenary Edition
William James
Introduced by Eugene Taylor and Jeremy Carrette
Foreword by Micky James

'*Is life worth living? Yes, a thousand times yes when the world still holds such spirits as Professor James.*'

Gertrude Stein

'*the incomparable style and freshness of Professor James's new book will ensure the position of a classic ... epoch-making*'

The Nation, August 1902

'*A work of genius, admirable alike for the thoughts expressed and the manner of their expression ... one of the great books of our time.*'

The Dial, November 1902

'*One hundred years after its publication* The Varieties of Religious Experience *remains even more vital than before ... it remains a book that empowers individuals, that touches individual lives and that inspires readers to become better persons.*'

Eugene Taylor, Introduction

First published in 1902, *The Varieties of Religious Experience* initiated the psychological study of religion, paving the way for Freud and Jung as well as for clinical and paranormal branches of psychology. The book remains the best introduction to William James's thought, and its theories of conversion, saintliness, ecstasy and mysticism continue to provoke controversy and enquiry. The Routledge Centenary Edition is prefaced with a specially commissioned foreword by the author's grandson, Micky James, and with new introductions from Eugene Taylor and Jeremy Carrette. Entirely reset from the original 1902 edition, it also includes a new expanded index.

Hb: 0-415-27809-0

For ordering and further information please visit:
www.routledge.com